Dostoevsky the Thinker

Fyodor Dostoevsky. Woodcut by Vladimir Favorsky, 1929.

DOSTOEVSKY
THE THINKER

JAMES P. SCANLAN

CORNELL UNIVERSITY PRESS

ITHACA AND LONDON

First published 2002 by Cornell University Press

Printed in the United States of America

Library of Congress Cataloging-in-Publication Data

Scanlan, James P. (James Patrick), 1927–
  Dostoevsky the thinker / James P. Scanlan.
    p. cm.
  Includes bibliographical references and index.
  ISBN 0-8014-3994-9 (cloth : alk. paper)
  1. Dostoevsky, Fyodor, 1821–1881—Philosophy.   I. Title.
PG3328.Z7 P5787 2002
891.73'3—dc21

                            2001006192

Cornell University Press strives to use environmentally responsible suppliers and materials to the fullest extent possible in the publishing of its books. Such materials include vegetable-based, low-VOC inks and acid-free papers that are recycled, totally chlorine-free, or partly composed of nonwood fibers. For further information, visit our website at www.cornellpress.cornell.edu.

Cloth printing   10 9 8 7 6 5 4 3 2 1

Dedicated to the memory of
my mother,
Helen Meyers Scanlan (1902–1942),
and my father,
Gilbert Francis Scanlan (1901–1970)

"That's all philosophy," Adelaida observed. "You are a philosopher and have come to instruct us." "You may be right," smiled the Prince. "Perhaps I really am a philosopher, and—who knows?—I may indeed have instruction in mind."

—Fyodor Dostoevsky,
The Idiot

Dostoevsky is not only a philosopher, he is also a *philosophical problem*.

—George Florovsky,
"On Studying Dostoevsky"

Contents

Preface   ix

Introduction: Dostoevsky as a Philosopher   1

1. Matter and Spirit   14
2. The Case against Rational Egoism   57
3. The Ethics of Altruism   81
4. The Logic of Aesthetics   118
5. A Christian Utopia   158
6. "The Russian Idea"   197

Conclusion: Dostoevsky's Vision of Humanity   231

Index   245

Preface

This book studies Dostoevsky not as a novelist who dealt artfully with philosophical themes but as a philosopher whose fundamental convictions were voiced and rationally defended in both literary and nonliterary works. It seeks, in other words, to take the writer seriously as a philosophical thinker and examine all his writings for evidence not only of his beliefs but of the reasoning by which he supported them.

In recent years, scholars around the world have made significant contributions to Dostoevsky studies, the most notable of which is Joseph Frank's masterly multivolume literary biography, which will be cited often in these pages. Other works as well contain valuable analyses of various aspects of Dostoevsky's thought; they include Stephen Carter's *The Political and Social Thought of F. M. Dostoevsky* (New York: Garland, 1991); A. A. Ivanova's *Filosofskie otkrytiia F. M. Dostoevskogo* (Philosophical Discoveries of F.M. Dostoevsky) (Moscow: n.p., 1995); Robert Louis Jackson's *Dialogues with Dostoevsky: The Overwhelming Questions* (Stanford, Calif.: Stanford University Press, 1993); Liza Knapp's *The Annihilation of Inertia: Dostoevsky and Metaphysics* (Evanston, Ill.: Northwestern University Press, 1996); Marina Kostalevsky's *Dostoevsky and Soloviev: The Art of Integral Vision* (New Haven, Conn.: Yale University Press, 1997); Gary Saul Morson's *Narrative and Freedom: The Shadows of Time* (New Haven, Conn.: Yale University Press, 1994) and other writings; and Bruce K. Ward's *Dostoyevsky's Critique of the West: The Quest for the Earthly Paradise* (Waterloo, Ont.: Wilfrid Laurier University Press, 1986).

Still absent from the Dostoevsky literature, however, is a truly comprehensive analysis and assessment of the writer's work from a specifically philosophical point of view. The older books on his thought by Russian philosophers—

for example, Nikolay Berdyaev's *Mirosozertsanie Dostoevskogo* (Dostoevsky's Worldview) (Prague: YMCA, 1923) and Nikolay Lossky's *Dostoevskii i ego khristianskoe miroponimanie* (Dostoevsky and His Christian Understanding of the World) (New York: Chekhov, 1953)—are limited in scope and are concerned primarily with using Dostoevsky as a vehicle for expounding the philosophies of their authors. The only book in any language that can lay claim to being a broad-based examination of Dostoevsky's philosophy is Reinhard Lauth's *Die Philosophie Dostoewskis in systematischer Darstellung* (The Philosophy of Dostoevsky: A Systematic Exposition) (Munich: R. Piper, 1950); but although it discusses the psychological, ethical, and religious dimensions of Dostoevsky's thinking at some length, even that book almost completely ignores his aesthetic theory, his philosophy of history, and his social and political philosophy. Furthermore, Lauth's book is uniformly laudatory, lacking anything resembling critical distance from its subject. This volume attempts to provide a new perspective on Dostoevsky's thought that is not only more comprehensive but more discriminating in its critical appreciation of his philosophical contributions.

Like most recent work on Dostoevsky, this book has benefited greatly from the publication in Russia, during the last two decades of Soviet rule, of the complete, copiously annotated scholarly edition of his writings entitled *Polnoe sobranie sochinenii v tridtsati tomakh* (Complete Collected Works in Thirty Volumes), compiled by the Institute of Russian Literature of the Academy of Sciences of the USSR (Leningrad: Nauka, 1972–90). With very few exceptions, the references to Dostoevsky's writings in this book are to that publication, cited parenthetically in the text by volume and page and abbreviated elsewhere as *PSS*. Because the last three of the thirty volumes were published in two books each, in referring to those volumes it is necessary to add a book number; hence the citation "28/2:103" signifies volume 28, book 2, page 103. All of the passages quoted are my translations. For quotations from Russian sources other than Dostoevsky's works, I have used existing English translations wherever accurate ones could be found.

Where transliteration of Russian names and words is required, the system employed throughout this book is the Library of Congress system minus its diacritical marks, except that proper names and journal titles (when not occurring in citations of Russian-language works in the notes) are presented in the forms now commonplace in nonscholarly writing—thus 'Dostoevsky' rather than 'Dostoevskii', 'Solovyov' rather than 'Solov'ev', 'Grigoryev' rather than 'Grigor'ev', and '*Vremya*' (the journal) rather than '*Vremia*.'

Although many of Dostoevsky's works exist in English translation (his fiction typically in multiple versions), the decision to translate the quoted passages anew and cite the *PSS* uniformly for all of Dostoevsky's works was dictated by several considerations. First, inaccuracies make many of the existing translations unreliable for scholarly purposes. Second, because different translators sometimes rendered the same Russian terms differently, editorial adjustments and explanations would have been needed to make the reader aware of the connections among the various renderings. Third, even the best of translators may disregard nuances that, while trifling from a literary point of view, are important for the philosophical purposes of this study. Finally, the use of a single primary source that can be cited parenthetically throughout the text greatly reduces the need for separate reference notes.

For readers who wish to consult English versions of Dostoevsky's works, a few comments may be in order concerning editions that stand out as particularly good or bad. The translations of his fiction by Richard Pevear and Larissa Volokhonsky are justly acclaimed for their readability and their faithfulness to the spirit as well as the letter of Dostoevsky's distinctive prose; the team has produced five volumes to date: *The Brothers Karamazov, Crime and Punishment, Demons,* and *Notes from Underground,* all published by Vintage Books, and *"The Eternal Husband" and Other Stories,* published by Bantam Classics. Also worthy of special praise are the editions of Dostoevsky's working notebooks for the major novels edited by Edward Wasiolek and published by the University of Chicago Press; the series, distinguished by fine translations and helpful editorial commentary, includes *The Notebooks for Crime and Punishment* (1967) and *The Notebooks for The Brothers Karamazov* (1971), both translated by Edward Wasiolek; *The Notebooks for The Idiot* (1967), translated by Katharine Strelsky; and *The Notebooks for The Possessed* (1968) and *The Notebooks for A Raw Youth* (1969), both translated by Victor Terras.

With a few notable exceptions, Dostoevsky's nonfiction has not been equally well served. Foremost among the exceptions is *A Writer's Diary* (2 vols. [Evanston, Ill.: Northwestern University Press, 1993–94]), excellently translated and annotated by Kenneth Lantz with an insightful 117-page "Introductory Study" by Gary Saul Morson. The translation of Dostoevsky's *Complete Letters* by David Lowe and Ronald Meyer (5 vols. [Ann Arbor, Mich.: Ardis, 1987–91]) is also generally reliable and is helpfully annotated.

Many of Dostoevsky's journal essays of the 1860s and 1870s have never been translated, including such important statements of his worldview as the 1862 essay "Two Camps of Theoreticians." Aside from an acceptable but poorly annotated translation of *Winter Notes on Summer Impressions* by Richard Lee Renfield (New York: McGraw-Hill, 1965), the only extant collection of the journal writings, comprising mostly articles of the early 1860s from *Epokha* and *Vremya,* is *Dostoevsky's Occasional Writings,* edited and translated by David Magarshack (Evanston, Ill.: Northwestern University Press, 1997). This volume, originally published by Random House in 1963, is flawed not only by unacknowledged ellipses and overly free translations but by the misrepresentation of a series of four short articles written by Dostoevsky for a St. Petersburg newspaper in 1847: it erroneously includes an article not written by him (pp. 3–9), excludes one of the four articles he did write (*PSS* 18:23–29), and misstates the date of another (p. 10). Regrettably, these errors were perpetuated when the book was reissued unchanged in 1997.

Also to be used with caution is *The Unpublished Dostoevsky: Diaries and Notebooks (1860–81) in Three Volumes* (Ann Arbor, Mich.: Ardis, 1973–76), edited by Carl R. Proffer and translated by various hands from the Russian original in *Neizdannyi Dostoevskii. Zapisnye knizhki i tetrady, 1860–1881 gg.* edited by V.R. Shcherbina and others (Moscow: Nauka, 1971). Unfortunately, this 1971 Russian text omitted many words, phrases, and entire sentences that its editors deemed unsuitable, including vulgarities, antisemitic remarks, and some of Dostoevsky's particularly pointed attacks on socialism and communism (all of the omissions were later restored in *PSS*). Moreover, the Ardis translations of this work are uneven and contain inaccuracies, as in the lengthy passage beginning "Masha lies on the table," in which Dostoevsky reflects on the death of his first wife—a section of great importance for his philosophical outlook. A superior translation of that passage was produced under Joseph Frank's supervision by one of his students, Tatyana Kovalenko, and published in 1966 in *Quarterly Review of Literature*, 14:441–45.

I am indebted to many people for pointing out ways in which my text could be improved and for spurring me to complete the project. Maria Carlson and Caryl Emerson read the entire manuscript with meticulous but sympathetic care; they not only saved me from several embarrassments but made me face questions I had shamelessly fudged. George L. Kline's discerning comments on several chapters were similarly corrective and helpful, as were comments on earlier versions of parts of the manuscript by Joseph Frank, Steven Cassedy, and my Ohio State University colleagues Irene Masing-Delic and Frank Silbajoris. Other readers contributed perhaps more than they realize simply by their encouraging responses to parts of the work; they include Tatiana Blagova, Edith Clowes, Philip Grier, Joan Grossman, Richard Gustafson, Malcolm Jones, Deborah Martinsen, and Janet Tucker. The most sustained moral support was provided by my wife, Marilyn Morrison Scanlan, whose interest in Dostoevsky's problems as well as in my problems with Dostoevsky cheered me through five years of writing.

I would like to acknowledge earlier versions of portions of chapter 1, which were published previously in *Archiwum Historii Filozofii i Myli Społecznej* (Warsaw) 44 (1999): 63–71, and in *Russian Review* 59 (2000): 1–20. Also, an earlier version of part of chapter 2 was published in *Journal of the History of Ideas* 60 (1999): 549–67.

Finally, I am indebted to John Ackerman and the staff of Cornell University Press for their enthusiastic and efficient work in turning my manuscript into the present book. To all, I offer sincere thanks.

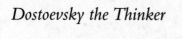

Dostoevsky the Thinker

Introduction

Dostoevsky as a Philosopher

The idea of treating a great writer as a philosopher will be unsettling to both writers and philosophers. The former will complain, justifiably, that to focus on Dostoevsky's thought is to slight his stunning literary productions, which sprang from creative imagination rather than abstract theorizing or conceptual analysis. The latter, with equal justification, will object that the Russian writer produced no philosophical treatises, had no formal training in the subject, spoke scornfully of it at times, and certainly never laid claim to the title 'philosopher'—a word that among Russians, he once jotted in a notebook, "is a term of abuse, meaning 'fool'" (5:329).[1] These facts, together with the largely accurate perception that nineteenth-century Russian thinkers in general were drawn more to personal moral quests than to the cerebrations of the schools, help to explain why there have been few efforts to examine Dostoevsky's writings from a strictly philosophical point of view.

Yet even the sternest critic must concede that Dostoevsky, for all his distance from academic philosophy, was one of the most philosophical of writers. His novels, in the words of Victor Terras, were "about ideas as much as about people."[2] His characters grapple mightily with ultimate questions, and there is abundant evidence that they do so not merely for literary effect but as intellectual surrogates for their creator and his philosophical opponents. "I'm rather weak in philosophy," Dostoevsky wrote his friend (and subsequent detractor)

1. Here and throughout the book, Dostoevsky's works are cited parenthetically by reference to volume and page(s) of his *Polnoe sobranie sochinenii v tridtsati tomakh* (Leningrad: Nauka, 1972–90). All translations are mine.

2. Victor Terras, *Reading Dostoevsky* (Madison: University of Wisconsin Press, 1998), 9.

Nikolay Strakhov, "but not in love for it; in love for it I am strong" (29/1:125). Strakhov, for his part, testified to the writer's intense interest in "the most abstract questions" ("Fyodor Mikhailovich loved these questions about the essence of things and the limits of knowledge"), and he also contested the charge of philosophical weakness. Acknowledging Dostoevsky's lack of training in the history of philosophy, Strakhov nonetheless spoke of the writer's delight in learning it and of his "extraordinary mind, the speed with which he grasped every idea after a single word or allusion."[3]

Indeed, Dostoevsky's countrymen generally, prompted by the richly nuanced expression of his philosophical interests in *The Brothers Karamazov* and other novels, have long since accepted him as a philosopher of supreme importance. To Nikolay Berdyaev, he was "not only a great artist but . . . a great thinker and a great visionary . . . a dialectician of genius, one of Russia's greatest metaphysicians."[4] A present-day Russian scholar, paraphrasing Alfred North Whitehead's famous aphorism about the importance of Plato in the history of Western thought, has described the Russian philosophical tradition of the twentieth century as "a series of footnotes to Dostoevsky."[5]

Still, doubts remain—as the theologian George Florovsky suggested when he remarked that Dostoevsky was both a philosopher and "a philosophical problem."[6] For one thing, there is the question of how to determine what his philosophical convictions really were. The simple fact that he wrote "philosophical" novels does not imply that he himself held the beliefs expressed in the fictional worlds he constructed. It is never legitimate, some will argue, to attribute views enunciated by an author's characters to the author himself. Furthermore, Dostoevsky's characters disagree radically with one another on fundamental questions. The great Russian critic Mikhail Bakhtin has pointed out the distinctive "polyphonic" or dialogical character of Dostoevsky's novels, and Bakhtin's analysis has sometimes been used to suggest (contrary to his intentions) that Dostoevsky equalized the contending voices of his characters

---

3. *Polnoe sobranie sochinenii F. M. Dostoevskago* (St. Petersburg: Izd. A. G. Dostoevskoi, 1882–83), 1:225. After Dostoevsky's death, Strakhov wrote a letter to Tolstoy in which he attacked both his late friend's artistry and his moral character. Tolstoy, for his part, valued Dostoevsky the thinker highly, more highly than Dostoevsky the artist. For a judicious discussion of the letter and the relations among the three figures, see Robert Louis Jackson, *Dialogues with Dostoevsky: The Overwhelming Questions* (Stanford, Calif.: Stanford University Press, 1993), 104–20.

4. R. A. Gal'tseva, ed., *Nikolai Berdiaev: Filosofiia, tvorchestva, kul'tura i iskusstvo* (Moscow: Iskusstvo, 1994), 2:9.

5. Vasilii Vanchugov, *Ocherk istorii filosofii "samobytno-russkoi"* (Moscow: RITS "Piligrim," 1994), 354.

6. Georgii Florovskii, "On Studying Dostoevskii," *Russian Studies in Philosophy* 35, no. 3 (1996–97): 30 (emphasis omitted).

to such an extent that it is impossible to discern an overarching authorial position.[7] If that were so, how could we establish what, if anything, Dostoevsky *himself* believed?

This question might have some force if we were confined to the world of the novels—that is, if we had no independent monological evidence allowing us to identify the author's convictions and helping us to discriminate between authorial and nonauthorial positions as they come forth in the fictional context. But in the case of Dostoevsky we have a mountain of such evidence. In a multitude of texts he incontestably speaks in his own voice and expresses views and arguments concerning many of the basic questions of philosophy. These texts include nearly a thousand personal letters, some of which touch directly on philosophical topics; a great many nonfiction articles on literary, social, and philosophical themes, published for the most part in journals Dostoevsky edited; the voluminous *Writer's Diary*—the misnamed series of journalistic essays in which, in the last decade of his life, he unburdened himself of his most cherished convictions; and finally his capacious notebooks, which cover the years of his most creative work and include philosophical reflections on topics from socialism to immortality. Such texts are not the customary grist for the mill of the historian of philosophy, but what they lack in system and polish they make up in immediacy and absence of artifice, and in Dostoevsky's case they are more than rich enough to form the principal sources for this study.

Dostoevsky's direct expression of his thoughts in these nonfiction writings has been relatively neglected, largely as a result of the quite understandable appropriation of his oeuvre by scholars in the field of literature. These specialists have given us a wealth of provocative and illuminating studies of his fiction, but they often either slight his nonfiction or approach it from the standpoint of its literary qualities; and in looking for philosophy in the fiction they sometimes erect its dynamic interplay of ideas and convictions into a philosophical doctrine of the "unfinalizable" nature of truth, based on a supposed irreducible ambivalence in the writer's thinking.[8] In this they are encouraged by the fact

7. Mikhail Bakhtin, *Problems of Dostoevsky's Poetics*, trans. R. W. Rotsel (Ann Arbor, Mich.: Ardis, 1973), 3–37. On the pros and cons of Bakhtin's interpretation of Dostoevsky, see Caryl Emerson's probing analysis in her study *The First Hundred Years of Mikhail Bakhtin* (Princeton, N.J.: Princeton University Press, 1997), 127–61. For an excellent overall account of Bakhtin's thought, with annotated references to primary and secondary sources, see Gary Saul Morson, "Bakhtin, Mikhail Mikhailovich (1895–1975)," in *Routledge Encyclopedia of Philosophy*, ed. Edward Craig (London: Routledge, 1998), 1:638–45.

8. For a discussion of these tendencies in relation to the ideas of Bakhtin, see Jackson, *Dialogues with Dostoevsky*, 269–92. For a comparison of dialogical and monological approaches to Dostoevsky's thought, see also Aileen Kelly, "Dostoevskii and the Divided Conscience," *Slavic Review* 47 (1988): 239–60; Kelley's argument that Dostoevsky's own moral beliefs were unsettled to the point that there

that Dostoevsky did employ a dialectical or dialogical *method* in philosophy, constantly playing off his own convictions against those of others. But I shall argue that, for all his attention to opposing ideas, Dostoevsky did not spend his life torn between conflicting possibilities. He depicted such tension in his fiction, for dramatic purposes, but his other writings provide unambiguous indications of which side he was on. He was, as Victor Terras has pointed out, an excellent "devil's advocate":[9] he laid out contradictory views so fairly and forcefully that there is a temptation to think he wanted to believe all of them; at the very least one is lured into psychoanalytic speculation about a conflict between levels or types of beliefs (intellectual versus emotional, conscious versus unconscious). But the nonfiction writings are an effective antidote against such temptations. To use Bakhtinian language, I would call Dostoevsky's philosophizing dialogical in style, monological in substance.

Admittedly, seeking a dominant voice amid the polyphony may not be the best way to appreciate Dostoevsky's merits as a literary artist, in which capacity his dialogical gifts are paramount. But it is essential if we are to judge him as a philosophical thinker, and it may enrich to some degree, at least, our understanding of the novels. Fiction allowed Dostoevsky to present provocative incarnations of philosophical concepts and positions and to use forms of argumentation that are not available to the writer of a traditional philosophical treatise. Dostoevsky's fictional creations often serve as the humanistic equivalent of theoretical models in the sciences: they function as intellectual constructs that purport to capture the true nature and significance of a particular set of phenomena in real life, highlighting what is important and stripping away the inessentials. With the nonfiction to guide us, we can establish his own beliefs with considerable confidence and can then treat the fiction selectively as providing elaboration of his views, and sometimes even argumentative support for them, rather than as an opaque polyphonic world in which no views are privileged.

Further doubts are prompted by Dostoevsky's reputation as an enemy of logical thinking. A standard objection to treating him as a philosopher at all is that his thought is "literary" rather than rational or logical. Strakhov began this tradition in 1883 when he commented that Dostoevsky, as an artist, did not elucidate ideas logically but rather "thought in images and was ruled by feelings."[10] Vladimir Solovyov, too, said that in the realm of ideas, "he was more

---

were "unresolvable moral dilemmas in [his] personal moral life" (242) will be taken up in subsequent chapters.

9. Terras, *Reading Dostoevsky*, 6.
10. *Polnoe sobranie sochinenii F. M. Dostoevskago*, 1:195.

a sage and an artist than a strictly logical, consistent thinker."[11] In the present day, Joseph Frank contends that Dostoevsky advanced his views "not by logical persuasion but through sketching character-types, dramatizing attitudes, narrating experiences and observations."[12] Images and sketches are not bound by constraints of rationality; they do not obey logical rules or require evidence of validity. If ideas are reduced to such nonconceptual, nondiscursive entities and their logic is disregarded, is it fruitful or even appropriate to examine them philosophically?

When Dostoevsky *is* accepted as a philosopher, it is typically as an "irrationalist." His harrowing but utterly convincing portrayals of human irrationality in *Notes from the House of the Dead, Notes from Underground, Crime and Punishment,* and *Demons (Besy)* are so powerful that it is difficult to resist ascribing irrationalism as a philosophical position to Dostoevsky himself. On that basis, existentialist philosophers co-opted him in the 1950s, proclaiming him a founding father; such widely read books as William Barrett's *Irrational Man* and Walter Kaufmann's *Existentialism from Dostoevsky to Sartre* took him as a hero.[13] To the existentialists Dostoevsky resembled no one so much as Kierkegaard, and they ascribed something like the Danish philosopher's consummate irrationalism to the Russian thinker. We find echoes of this attitude today when Joseph Frank remarks that on the subject of faith versus reason, Dostoevsky was like Kierkegaard (though less rigorous) in siding with "the irrational of faith against reason" and pushing "the opposition between the two to the point of paradox."[14] But again, if Dostoevsky not only thinks in images but scorns rationality and welcomes paradox, with its disdain for basic laws of logic, can one expect coherent, defensible philosophical positions from him?

It is obvious from Dostoevsky's writings that he did not consider himself a "rationalist," a designation he typically reserved for his philosophical antagonists, the Russian representatives of European Enlightenment thinking. He harbored a healthy skepticism concerning both the power of rationality and the extent of its presence in the human animal. He disputed the claims of reason to serve as the ultimate epistemological authority on all questions: "There is something higher," he told a correspondent in 1877, "than the conclusions

11. *Sobranie sochinenii Vladimira Sergeevicha Solov'eva* (St. Petersburg: Izd. Tovarishchestva "Obshchestvennaia Pol'za," 1901–07), 5:382.

12. Joseph Frank, *Dostoevsky: The Seeds of Revolt, 1821–1849* (Princeton, N.J.: Princeton University Press, 1976), 237.

13. William Barrett, *Irrational Man: A Study in Existential Philosophy* (New York: Doubleday, 1958), 117–24 and passim; Walter Kaufmann, *Existentialism from Dostoevsky to Sartre*, rev. ed. (1956; reprint, New York: New American Library, 1975), 12–14, 52–82.

14. Joseph Frank, *Dostoevsky: The Years of Ordeal, 1850–1859* (Princeton, N.J.: Princeton University Press, 1983), 162.

of reason [*rassudok*]" (29/2:139). As we shall see, he believed that some fundamental philosophical issues are not fully amenable to rational treatment and hence can be resolved with certainty only by faith. He also believed that "life" as a dynamic totality cannot be comprehended fully by the understanding; in a youthful, Schilleresque letter he placed "the heart" above "the mind" as an epistemological authority (28/1:53).[15] He argued later that human beings possess a complex animal-cum-spiritual nature of which "the rational [*rassudochnyi*] capacity" is only a part—a "one-twentieth" part, he once wrote (5:115)—and that nonrational, affective-volitional capacities have immense force in human life.

Such statements are not the end of the story, however. In the foregoing paragraph, I interpolated the Russian terms Dostoevsky uses for 'reason' and 'rational' in those passages in order to flag a problem of translation. Two Russian terms—*razum* and *rassudok*—are typically both translated as 'reason', but, like the comparable German *Vernunft* and *Verstand*, they are not perfect synonyms. *Razum*, like *Vernunft*, signifies an epistemologically higher, freer, more capacious application of the rational faculty, whereas *rassudok*, like *Verstand*, signifies a more limited, narrowly calculating, "rationalistic" application. Hence, in downgrading *rassudok* and its adjectival form *rassudochnyi* in those statements, Dostoevsky is not necessarily scorning reason in the sense of *razum*, as we shall see subsequently.

Furthermore, whatever his philosophical conception of reason, it is evident from his writings that neither that conception, nor his artistic purposes, nor the passions and agonies of his personal life caused him to reject the laws of logic or avoid the effort to provide evidence for conclusions, even conclusions concerning ultimate philosophical and religious questions. No doubt Arseny Gulyga was right in observing that "with Dostoevsky, the image is more powerful than the syllogism";[16] but that does not mean he abandoned the syllogism. His sense of the limits of rationality did not turn him into a misologist like Kierkegaard who rejected the value of seeking reasons for beliefs or taking seriously the reasons advanced by others. In everyday discourse he exhibited a sincere if conventional respect for logical thinking: in a letter to his exasperating stepson Pavel he chided the young man for being "illogical" (29/1:366); in *A Writer's Diary*, praising an article by N. P. Peterson, he wrote: "Rarely have I read anything *more logical*" (22:83; Dostoevsky's emphasis). And Dostoevsky demonstrated respect for the rational argumentation of his philosophical ad-

---

15. On this text see Heinrich Stammler, "Dostoevsky's Aesthetics and Schelling's Philosophy of Art," *Comparative Literature* 7 (1955): 314–15.

16. Arsenii Gulyga, *Russkaia ideia i ee tvortsy* (Moscow: Soratnik, 1995), 75.

versaries, as we shall see in many contexts, by avoiding straw men, acknowledging that his opponents, too, had a case to make, and confronting the full
force of their arguments—the very features of his work that cause some confusion as to where his own sentiments lay. Like other Russian thinkers of his
time, Dostoevsky brought intense moral passion to his philosophizing, but unlike many he did not scorn questions of the logic and epistemological grounding of philosophical convictions.

Critics who consider Dostoevsky a thoroughgoing irrationalist are fond of
citing an apparently blatant burst of antirational sentiment in a letter he wrote
in Siberia in 1854, after his release from prison, to Natalya Fonvizina, one of
the Decembrists' wives who had presented him and his fellow convicts with
copies of the Gospels on their way to the camps early in 1850. In a heartfelt
confession of his religious searchings, he sought to convey to Fonvizina the
depth of his Christian faith with these paradoxical words: "If someone were to
prove to me that Christ is outside the truth, and it *really* were the case that the
truth is outside Christ, then I should rather remain with Christ than with the
truth" (28/1:176; Dostoevsky's emphasis).[17] Although this statement suggests a
total abandonment of rational standards in matters of religious belief, it is interesting to focus on its second, often overlooked clause: "and [if] it *really*
[*deistvitel'no*] were the case that the truth is outside Christ."[18] To say that a
proposition "really" is the case is simply another way of saying that the proposition is *true;* it is to assert categorically the truth of the proposition. Hence by
this second clause Dostoevsky reveals himself as a rationalist *malgré lui:* he requires that it genuinely be *true* that the truth lies outside Christ before he will
choose the latter—a confused and no doubt unconscious bow to the authority
of rational standards even when, in a transport of religious enthusiasm, he
sought to dramatize his devotion to faith by sacrificing rationality to it. And of
course, as we shall see, he did *not* think that the truth lay "outside Christ."
Thus the statement is far from an unqualified rejection of rational demands.

Those who make a point of denying that Dostoevsky used rational argumentation tacitly contradict themselves when they come to describe his strategies in dealing with ideas. There is broad agreement, for example, that he
often sought to demonstrate the unsoundness of his opponents' views by
drawing out all of their implications—that is, by showing what they entail and
what, if adopted, they would mean in practice. Thus, the same critic who

---

17. See also Dostoevsky's use of this point in *Demons* (10:198).

18. Konstantin Mochulsky, in quoting the passage, simply leaves out the clause in question, with no
indication of the omission. See his *Dostoevsky: His Life and Work*, trans. Michael A. Minihan (Princeton, N.J.: Princeton University Press, 1971), 152.

stated that Dostoevsky did not employ "logical persuasion" goes on to describe the writer's procedure of "carrying 'the logical presuppositions and possibilities of ideas to their consistent conclusion'."[19] Reinhard Lauth, too, speaks of Dostoevsky's "methodical process" of rejecting an idea because it has negative "practical and logical consequences."[20] But this is simply a form of the argumentative strategy, well known in logic, of reductio ad absurdum, or arguing against a proposition by showing that it entails an unacceptable conclusion; certainly the use of that strategy qualifies as an attempt at logical persuasion. Dostoevsky's relentless pursuit of the implications of opposing views shows that his thought is not altogether alien to the demands of rationality and hence is subject to philosophical analysis, "antirationalist" though he may have been in some respects. And reductio, as we shall see, is only one of the logical strategies he employed to support his philosophical convictions.

Thus, as severely as Dostoevsky castigated his philosophical opponents for their "rationalism," he by no means ceded to them the right to use logical reasoning. Much of his criticism is directed against their pretensions to total, perfect rationality—pretensions he found ludicrous; "the most fanatical progressives," he wrote in 1863, "lay claim to logic more and more, and lay claim to it precisely at the moment of the greatest manifestation of their fanaticism, when there is really no question of logic at all" (20:54). On another occasion, mentally addressing an imagined "liberal" who argued that individuals would willingly give up their freedom in a socialist order, he observed that "your rationality is completely irrational."[21] In accepting reason without giving it a monopoly on human thought, Dostoevsky adhered to a distinguished Russian philosophical tradition that, in the words of A. A. Ivanova, "consists not in denying reason [razum] but in denying absolute rationalism [ratsionalizm]."[22] The discursive, rational dimension of his philosophical thought is one that has been sorely neglected; it is well worth examining on its own merits despite its secondary importance for his art.

A final misgiving about the value of studying Dostoevsky's contributions to philosophy has to do with the episodic character of his attention to the subject. As someone who made his living by writing fiction—a trade to which he was bound by lifelong, often urgent financial need—and whose other published

---

19. Joseph Frank, *Dostoevsky: The Stir of Liberation, 1860–1865* (Princeton, N.J.: Princeton University Press, 1986), 345; see also 125.

20. Reinhard Lauth, *Die Philosophie Dostojewskis in systematischer Darstellung* (Munich: R. Piper, 1950), 37–38.

21. *Neizdannyi Dostoevskii: Zapisnye knizhki i tetradi, 1860–81 gg.*, ed. V. R. Shcherbina et al. (Moscow: Nauka, 1971), 294.

22. A. A. Ivanova, *Filosofskie otkrytiia F. M. Dostoevskogo* (Moscow: n.p., 1995), 181.

writings, also undertaken with an eye to income, were largely journalistic and topical, Dostoevsky had no time for philosophical system-building. Thus even if it is admitted that much of his writing has a philosophical component, we may wonder whether his "philosophy" amounts to anything more than a miscellany of incidental views without unifying character or direction.

This book will try to show that Dostoevsky's philosophy, though not constituting a "system" in the traditional sense, has a strong single focus. Like that of most Russian philosophers, it is decidedly anthropocentric: it was prompted not by abstract cosmological and epistemological concerns but by an obsession with humanity. More precisely, Dostoevsky wished to understand the condition of being human, or as he put it in a late notebook, "to find the man in man" (27:65). Intellectually this absorption in philosophical anthropology was so intense as to co-opt and transform all his other concerns. Whatever subject he took up—religion, art, the state, history, morality—he was interested above all in its human significance and specifically in what clues he could find in it to the question of what it means to be human.

At an early age Dostoevsky announced his view of humanity as a puzzle to be solved and committed himself to the work of solving it. In a letter written when he was seventeen to his older brother Mikhail, he speaks of studying "what man and life mean." "Man is a mystery," he goes on. "The mystery must be solved, and if you work at solving it all your life, don't say that you have wasted your time. I occupy myself with this mystery because I wish to be a man" (28/1:63). These words could easily be dismissed as juvenile romanticism but for the fact that he *did* work at it all his life, incorporating the quest in some way in virtually everything he wrote.

How well he succeeded is of course another and a still debated question. He did not manage to complete the belletristic version of what he believed he had learned about the human mystery; *The Brothers Karamazov*, his last novel, was only the first part of a projected longer work. And, of course, he decided that there are limits to the human ability to penetrate the mystery. Nonetheless, his writings suggest that over the years he grew increasingly confident that he had solved the puzzle of humanity to the extent that anyone could solve it in this world. By the end of his life, his searchings had produced a substantial body of philosophical doctrines concerning the human condition, including highly controversial doctrines about national identity that some see as his glory and others as his shame.

The primary aim of this book is to do something Dostoevsky himself might have done had he not lacked the opportunity, and perhaps in the end the inclination—namely, present a comprehensive account of his philosophical reflections in the areas to which he turned his attention, which in practice means the results of his exploration of what it means to be a human being. Essentially, I propose to examine the conceptual structure of his philosophical beliefs and try to identify whatever grounding he believed he had for them. Overall the effort will be to present a portrait of Dostoevsky's philosophical thought that he himself, in a generous mood and without expectation of flattery, might recognize as tolerably faithful to both its letter and its spirit.[23]

A secondary but still important aim requires a transition from philosophical ghostwriting to philosophical critique. Because many of his views are controversial, after laying them out as sympathetically as possible it will be worthwhile to consider the soundness of his assumptions and premises and the strength of his arguments. Some critics may be inclined to dismiss the bulk of his arguments as rationalizations for beliefs irrationally held. But that would be to make a claim about the *psychology* of Dostoevsky's convictions, whereas my perspective is philosophical: it has to do with the conceptual and logical structure of his convictions and not their psychological genesis or function. I shall argue that on the whole Dostoevsky's positions are philosophically more sophisticated, better grounded, and more cohesive than is usually suspected. For a proper estimate of the value of his philosophical legacy, however, flaws and vulnerabilities must also be considered. Here I cannot count on even hypothetical agreement from my subject, though I shall try to base my critique on principles that he himself might be willing to regard as appropriate.

These two aims, analytical and critical, are pursued in six chapters, each devoted to an area in which Dostoevsky advanced and defended philosophical positions. If for the sake of simplicity we phrase his dominant philosophical concern in the language of Immanuel Kant's blunt question, "What is man?", we can say that Dostoevsky's philosophical views, taken as a whole, form a set of complementary answers to that question, each reflecting a different perspective on the nature, capacities, and prospects of humanity. Each incorporates views that fall under traditional rubrics of philosophy such as metaphysics, ethics, and aesthetics, but Dostoevsky himself did not formulate them in that way. To him what was important was that they captured some significant aspect of human life and work.

The answer that appears most fundamental to Dostoevsky's philosophical outlook, and hence is explored in chapter 1, is that human beings have immortal souls as well as mortal bodies and hence are residents of two realms—

---

23. Such an effort presupposes the possibility of establishing (always subject to correction) what E.D. Hirsch Jr., in his *Validity in Interpretation* (New Haven, Conn.: Yale University Press, 1967), 8, called the "meaning" of a text in the sense of what the author himself meant—a procedure employed admirably by Joseph Frank throughout his study; see Frank's convincing defense of the procedure in *Dostoevsky: The Stir of Liberation*, 387.

the temporal material world and the eternal spiritual world. In elaborating this familiar Christian dualism in ontology he addressed himself to many topics in metaphysics, theology, and the philosophy of religion, including the opposition between materialism and idealism, the existence of God, the problem of evil, the nature of religious faith, the immortality of the soul, the essence of Christianity—all from the point of view of their bearing on the question of "what man and life mean."

Second, there was no conception of human nature to which Dostoevsky was more adamantly opposed than that of Nikolay Chernyshevsky, Dmitry Pisarev, and other representatives of the positivistic Russian intelligentsia of his day, who held that all human actions not only inevitably are, but should be, rationally directed toward the maximum satisfaction of one's own best interests. Direct or implied criticism of this theory, later dubbed 'Rational Egoism', can be found throughout Dostoevsky's corpus, but his most sustained attack on it is found in a single much-debated work, *Notes from Underground*. The second chapter of this book is devoted largely to a new interpretation of that work as a comprehensive and philosophically astute critique of Rational Egoism, along with the argumentation in another, shorter work in which he also attacks the simplistic psychology and mechanistic materialism of the "Nihilists," as he typically called them.

The conception of human beings as free moral agents that Dostoevsky advanced against the Rational Egoists is examined in chapter 3. Although he viewed individuals as complex, rational-irrational personalities endowed with the ineradicable but demanding faculty of free choice and with an inherent need for self-expression, he also saw them as moral creatures whose standards of both personal conduct and social relationships were provided by the New Testament image of Jesus Christ. With the Christian ideal of brotherly love as his foundation, he explored the moral life of humanity with attention to a surprisingly broad range of topics in personal and social ethics. Among the themes he discussed are altruism, egoism, and their relations to good and evil; the impossibility of perfect adherence to the moral ideal; the role of consciousness, suffering, and sacrifice in moral life; the relationship between freedom, moral responsibility, and environmental influences; and the defects of utilitarianism as an ethical and social theory.

As an artist, Dostoevsky was of course closely attuned to aesthetic values, and a major component of his philosophical outlook, taken up in chapter 4, was his view of human beings as creatures with inborn aesthetic needs. He saw these needs as not only related to moral needs but at the highest level indistinguishable from them. Needs of both sorts are rooted in human spirituality, and he believed that the term 'beauty', as used in speaking of the ideal beauty of

Christ, ultimately can serve as the name of both the highest aesthetic value and the highest moral good; he attributed to such beauty a redemptive role in human life: "Beauty will save the world." Closely related elements of his aesthetic theory are his reflections on the nature of artistic creativity and on the character of aesthetic experience and value—themes developed most effectively in his witty and cogent attacks on the "realist" theories of art advanced by his philosophical opponents.

Another subject to which Dostoevsky was powerfully drawn was the sociopolitical dimension of human existence, particularly as it related to the Russian Nihilists' commitment to revolution. He regarded as profoundly antihumanitarian their view that "advanced" thinkers such as themselves were entitled and even obliged to destroy the existing order of society by direct action, not excluding violence and tyranny. The Russian revolutionary movement of his day provided him with an abundance of evidence on which to base his critique; he developed it not only in his letters and essays but in *Crime and Punishment, The Brothers Karamazov* (especially the "Legend of the Grand Inquisitor"), and *Demons*. The latter work in particular served Dostoevsky as a vehicle for attacking the revolutionaries: "I want to express a few thoughts, even if my artistry perishes in so doing," he wrote in a letter while working on the book; "even if it proves to be a lampoon, I'll have my say" (29/1:112). (Fortunately for both his message and his readers, his artistry was up to the challenge.) In chapter 5 I shall examine the philosophical premises and implications of his critique of the revolutionary mentality and consider his positive social and political doctrines. No small part of the continuing attraction of Dostoevsky's antirevolutionary outlook in post-Soviet Russia is attributable to its prophetic anticipation of the Bolshevik revolution and Communist rule in Russia.

The final dimension of Dostoevsky's search for what it means to be human, taken up in chapter 6, is the most heavily criticized feature of his intellectual outlook. He early became convinced that human beings, although sharing universal traits that bind them together in the great family of man, are also *national* creatures, differentiated by their distinctive national or ethnic heritages, which profoundly affect their characters and their destinies. In developing this thesis, particularly later in his life but beginning already in the early 1860s, he presented a sweeping philosophy of history that culminates in the assignment of a messianic role to Russia as the only "God-bearing" nation. Here the humanistic universalism of his Christian moral and social philosophy is seemingly abandoned (despite his protestations to the contrary) in favor of a narrow nationalism and ethnic chauvinism. He called his nationalistic conception "the Russian idea"—an expression destined to play a fateful role in Russian intellectual and political life down to the present day. Some interpreters of his thought defend his form of nationalism as a new, benign variety, perfectly compatible with universalism. Other sympathetic critics hurry over it as a regrettable but incidental lapse of judgment on the part of a great Christian humanist, stemming from an excusable excess of patriotic feeling. In any event, it is worth closer examination. Dostoevsky himself believed he was on solid theoretical ground in asserting it, and far from being incidental it is an integral part of his conception of humanity—a part in which he had an intense and enduring interest.

Dostoevsky's nationalism made him a representative of one of the major intellectual orientations in Russia in the second half of the nineteenth century—namely, religious conservatism with a distinctly Slavophile cast. A Petersburger, he had been hostile toward the Moscow-based Slavophiles during his "radical," pre-Siberian period and was still critical of them during his early post-Siberian years. But as he learned more about their ideas he came to recognize his affinity for them, and he eventually pronounced himself "a true Slavophile" (28/2:154). Along with his high-ranking government friend Konstantin Pobedonostsev, he was one of the most interesting and influential neo-Slavophile thinkers of the late nineteenth century, and his outlook richly reflects what Slavophilism became in Russia after the reforms of the 1860s, the Franco-Prussian war of 1870–71, the upsurge of Russian patriotism that accompanied the Russo-Turkish war of 1876–77, and the growing Westernist radical movement in Russia that led in 1881, just a few months after Dostoevsky's death, to the assassination of Alexander II. Furthermore it was largely through Dostoevsky's influence that Slavophile themes crossed over into the twentieth century in the thinking of later Russian philosophers, such as his ardent champion Nikolay Berdyaev. Thus Russian philosophy of the early twentieth century, too, can be illuminated by an examination of Dostoevsky's philosophical outlook.

Finally, it is above all through his nationalism that Dostoevsky's thought has special appeal in Russia again today. "The Russian idea," which he identified and named, though downplayed throughout the Soviet period, has regained remarkable ideological strength in post-Soviet Russia. Public figures as disparate as Orthodox church leaders and officials of the Communist party now freely invoke "the Russian idea" and the authority of Dostoevsky in support of their nationalistic agendas. Thus an analysis and critique of the conceptual structure of his nationalism may also help us to understand contemporary Russian nationalism.

CHAPTER I

Matter and Spirit

Dostoevsky's conception of human nature is grounded in the traditional Christian ontology to which he subscribed from an early age: reality is bifurcated into realms that come together in humanity—a tangible, material realm and an intangible, spiritual realm. His effort to understand the intersection of the two is already evident in a flowery, philosophizing letter written at the age of seventeen to his brother Mikhail:

> If we were [pure] spirits, we would live and float within the sphere of that thought above which our soul floats when it wishes to divine it. We ashes, however—humans—must work at divining the thought but cannot embrace it all at once. What guides thought through the impermanent shell into the makeup of the soul is the mind [*um*]. The mind is a material capacity. . . . The soul, on the other hand, or spirit, lives on thought that the heart whispers to it. . . . The mind is a tool, a machine, prompted by the fire of the soul. (28/1:53–54)

Neither fully spirit nor fully "ashes," human beings have spiritual souls that are dependent, however, on a material instrument for the comprehension of reality.

The human conjunction of these two realms as affecting both thought and action remained a central theme of Dostoevsky's philosophy throughout his life. He frequently invoked it with Christ's pronouncement, "Man does not live by bread alone." Bread nourishes the aspect of human nature that Dostoevsky variously describes as animal, physical, material, earthly, fleshly, finite, or temporal; another form of nourishment is required for the spiritual, immaterial, heavenly, infinite, eternal side of humanity. Matter and spirit are the strictest of binary opposites for Dostoevsky, mutually exclusive in essence and sharing no properties.[1]

The two realms are by no means equal in value or ontological status. The spiritual realm, as the wise old monk Zosima proclaims in *The Brothers Karamazov*, is "the higher half of the human essence" (14:284); matter is only the "outer form" of reality (20:175). This same relative evaluation marks another youthful letter of Dostoevsky's, in which he portrays the human spirit as hobbled by its tie to earthly flesh: "One condition alone has fallen to man's lot: his soul's atmosphere is comprised of the confluence of heaven and earth; . . . the law of spiritual nature has been broken. . . . It seems to me that our world is a purgatory of heavenly spirits beclouded by sinful thought" (28/1:50).

This beclouding was important to Dostoevsky not only ontologically but epistemologically, for he came to believe that the alien character of the merged natures prevents the human soul from fully understanding either. At times he saw reality as a realm of unfathomable superfluity that transcended all efforts to embrace it. A notebook entry of 1876 captures the sense of intellectual futility that sometimes overcame him:

> It's certainly true that reality is deeper than any human imagination, than any fantasy. For all the seeming simplicity of phenomena, it is a dreadful riddle. . . . Nothing in reality is completed, just as it is impossible to find a beginning— everything flows and everything *is*, but you can't lay hold of anything. And what you do lay hold of, comprehend, mark with a word, at once becomes a lie. "A thought spoken is a lie." (23:326)[2]

Although at other times Dostoevsky is not quite so despairing of the human mind's ability to understand the world, he always retained the sense of an earthly estrangement that prevents the soul from fully grasping reality. Presumably he considered the human "mind," the soul's intellectual "tool," to be compromised epistemologically by its dependence on a material brain and sensory apparatus. This estrangement was perhaps best expressed in *The Brothers Karamazov* in the words of Zosima, who in effect repeats Dostoevsky's youthful complaint about the breaking of the law of spiritual nature by the soul's materialization. The soul, blessedly but dimly aware of its own spiritual origins, finds itself in, but not of, the material world, and is cognitively limited for

---

1. For an interesting comparison of the views of Dostoevsky and Vladimir Solovyov on this opposition, see Judith Deutsch Kornblatt and Gary Rosenshield, "Vladimir Solovyov: Confronting Dostoevsky on the Jewish and Christian Questions," *Journal of the American Academy of Religion* 68 (2000): 69–98, especially 82–84.

2. The sentence quoted at the end is a famous line from F. I. Tyutchev's poem "Silentium" (1833).

that reason: "Much on earth is hidden from us, but in its place we have been given a secret, mysterious sense of our living bond with the other world, with the lofty, higher world, and indeed the roots of our thoughts and feelings are not here but in other worlds. That is why philosophers say that the essence of things cannot be grasped on earth" (14:290).

As we shall see, such sentiments did not lead Dostoevsky into a total alogism, such as would cause him to reject reason and science altogether as sources of knowledge of reality; he accepted both within their limits. But his reflections on the material hobbling of spirit did leave him with a settled skepticism. In this respect his thought was akin to that of an earlier thinker to whom he often referred—Blaise Pascal, who wrote that "the end of things and their beginning are hopelessly hidden from him [man] in an impenetrable secret." And it also brought him close to a more unlikely predecessor he never mentioned and probably never knew—David Hume, who held that even the most perfect natural philosophy only "staves off our ignorance a little longer."[3]

As for the makeup of the spiritual world in which the soul is "rooted," Dostoevsky never described it in so many words. Yet he left no doubt that included within it are an eternal, spiritual deity and the immortal souls of human beings. The existence of God and of life after death are the two questions that dominated his reflections about the spiritual world until the end of his life, and for that reason they constitute the dual focus of this chapter.

Dostoevsky appears to have believed in both the existence of God and the immortality of the soul in some form throughout his life. His Christian upbringing, guided by a devout and demanding father, gave him an initial faith in the basic dogmas of Russian Orthodox theology, but it by no means led to mechanical acceptance of those dogmas or approval of all the policies of the Orthodox church as an institution. His reading of "liberal" Western literature in the 1830s and 1840s shook some, but not all, of the religious convictions of his youth; the George Sand he knew, as he indicated later, was not an atheist or agnostic but a true Christian who believed "unconditionally" in the immortality of the human person (23:37). Answering a letter from a skeptic in

---

3. Blaise Pascal, "Thoughts," in *The European Philosophers from Descartes to Nietzsche*, ed. Monroe C. Beardsley (New York: Modern Library, 1960), 101; David Hume, *Enquiries Concerning the Human Understanding and Concerning the Principles of Morals*, 2d ed. (Oxford: Oxford University Press, 1902), 31. Although Pascal's *Pensées* (1669) was not translated into Russian until 1843, the work was known earlier from the original French text. Dostoevsky quotes it in a letter of 1838 to his brother Mikhail, and he mentions Pascal again in a letter of 1839 to his father (28/1:50, 59). Furthermore there are significant quotations from, or allusions to, Pascal in *The Idiot, Demons*, and *The Brothers Karamazov*. The question of Dostoevsky's indebtedness to Pascal is explored by G. Ia. Strel'tsova in *Paskal' i evropeiskaia kul'tura* (Moscow: Respublika, 1994), 330–55.

1877, Dostoevsky wrote that he was familiar with all the writer's arguments against the existence of God and life after death by the time he was twenty (that is, by 1841); but there is no evidence that he ever fully succumbed to them, even in the socialist-radical phase leading up to his arrest and mock execution in 1849 (29/2:141). Facing what he and the other "condemned" men believed to be imminent death, he reportedly cried out, "We shall be with Christ!"[4]

Still, however central and persistent were his beliefs in God and immortality, they were not always beliefs that freed him from doubt; indeed, in a letter of 1870 he spoke of the question of God's existence as "one that has tormented me consciously and unconsciously all my life" (29/1:117). In his mature years he longed for his Christian faith to be immediate, certain, and unquestionable, as it was in childhood, but he found that after exposure to critical secular thinking he could enjoy such unreflective confidence at rare moments only. He confessed his longing for certainty in the same letter of 1854 to Natalya Fonvizina that I cited in the introduction:

> Not because you are religious, but because I have experienced and felt it myself, I'll tell you that at . . . moments you thirst for faith like "withered grass,"[5] and you find it, precisely because the truth shines through amid misfortune. I'll tell you about myself that I am a child of the age, a child of disbelief and doubt till now and even (I know it) to the grave. What dreadful torments this thirst to believe has cost me and continues now to cost me, a thirst that is all the stronger in my soul the more opposing arguments there are in me. And yet God sometimes sends me moments at which I am perfectly at peace; at these moments I love and find that I am loved by others, and at such moments I have composed within myself a creed in which everything is clear and holy to me. (28/1:176)

Although some have taken this text to mean that Dostoevsky at times rejected the existence of God and life after death, there is no indication that the "opposing arguments" he mentions ever actually prevailed. Evidently he often doubted in the sense of being unsure; but he does not say that he ever actually *disbelieved*, only that he is "a child" of disbelief and doubt. A plausible reading of the text is that he is lamenting his frequent lack of confidence in his religious beliefs, not the absence of the beliefs themselves. His "thirst for faith" is

---

4. F.N. Lvov, "Zapiska o dele petrashevtsev," *Literaturnoe nasledstvo* (Moscow: Izdatel'stvo Akademii nauk SSSR, 1956), 63:188.

5. Dostoevsky's reference is to the lament of the biblical psalmist, "I am withered like grass" (Ps. 102:11 [101:12 in the Russian Orthodox Bible]).

a search for the kind of perfect certainty in which "the truth shines through," vanquishing all doubt.

Similarly, when in a late notebook Dostoevsky writes of his Christian convictions that "my *hosanna* has come through a great *furnace of doubts*" (27:86; Dostoevsky's emphasis), we need not interpret that statement as indicating a loss of belief at any time; the hosanna may have weakened, but it survived the furnace. And when in *A Writer's Diary* he speaks of having taken Christ into his soul "anew" through his contact with the common people in prison, he qualifies the renewal by referring to "the Christ whom I had known . . . as a child and *almost* lost [*utratil bylo*] when in my turn I became a 'European liberal'" (26:152; emphasis added). As Robert Louis Jackson has suggested, Dostoevsky's "mature" belief, fervent but often uncertain, recalls the plaintive cry of the father in the Gospel of St. Mark: "Lord, I believe; help thou mine unbelief!"[6]

For Dostoevsky the unreflective certainty of faith, when it is "naturally" present or can be attained through grace or effort, is the purest, most direct consciousness of the truth of his Christian beliefs. In the letter to Fonvizina he associates this consciousness with the feeling of *love* ("I love and find that I am loved by others"). A quarter-century later in *The Brothers Karamazov*, Madame Khokhlakova, the "lady lacking conviction" (*malovernaia dama*), distressed by her doubts about life after death, asks the monk Zosima, "How can I prove it? How can I become convinced?" He responds with advice reminiscent of Dostoevsky's 1854 letter:

> "There is no proving it, but one can be convinced."
> "How? In what way?"
> "By the experience of active love. Strive to love your neighbors actively and tirelessly. To the extent that you succeed in loving, you will become convinced both of the existence of God and of the immortality of your soul. If you attain complete selflessness in loving your neighbor, then you will indubitably be persuaded, and no doubt will even be able to enter your soul. This has been tested, this is certain." (14:52)

When Zosima speaks of conviction attained not through "proving" but through a form of moral effort ("strive to love"), the epistemological suggestion would seem to be that he is simply discarding ratiocination in favor of faith, as one might expect of a Russian Orthodox monk. Indeed, neither he

---

6. Robert Louis Jackson, *Dostoevsky's Quest for Form: A Study of His Philosophy of Art* (New Haven, Conn.: Yale University Press, 1966), xi; Mark 9:24.

nor any other of Dostoevsky's saintly figures sought to argue logically for the tenets of faith; rather, they urged the alteration of moral attitudes and behavior. Note, however, that it is specifically *complete conviction* in the sense of certainty that Khokhlakova is seeking, and it is certainty that Zosima is telling her how to achieve. Decisively rejected, in other words, is not ratiocination as such but ratiocination as a source of perfect confidence regarding immortality and the existence of God.

Dostoevsky's own commitment to the view that "there is something higher than the conclusions of reason [*rassudok*]" (29/2:139) did not prevent him from using rational arguments to support religious truths. The presence of such arguments in his writings despite the epistemological priority he assigned to faith is perfectly understandable if we accept the distinction between certainty and something less. Dostoevsky recognized, as logicians have for centuries, that an argument need not yield deductively necessary or indubitable conclusions in order to have force. Inductive conclusions and explanatory hypotheses, though always open to question, may be based on solid evidence.

Particularly prominent in Dostoevsky's writings are arguments for the immortality of the human soul. They are noteworthy not only as cases of his use of reasoning in dealing with religious questions but as indications of other important features of his philosophy, and for that reason they warrant close scrutiny before we proceed to his reasoning concerning the existence of God.

The Question of Immortality

Between 1864 and 1880, in fiction and nonfiction alike, Dostoevsky referred repeatedly to the immortality of the soul, writing of its great importance for spiritual and even material life. The idea of immortality, he proclaimed in 1876, is "the fundamental and highest" idea of human existence. It is "humanity's chief source of truth and correct consciousness"; all other lofty ideas for which a person might live "*simply flow from it alone*" (24:46–50; Dostoevsky's emphasis). The subject figures prominently in all the great novels after *Crime and Punishment*, and his correspondence, notebooks, and published *Writer's Diary* are dotted with discussions of it.

At most of these points, of course, Dostoevsky is not constructing philosophical arguments. Yet he typically treats immortality as a belief that makes sense even apart from other tenets of religion and faith. Ippolit in *The Idiot*, for example, finds it easy to doubt some claims about the supernatural, but not the claim of immortality: "Never, despite all my desire to do so," he confesses, "have I been able to imagine that there is no future life or Providence" (8:344).

A fascinating notebook entry, related thematically to Ippolit's statement but written by Dostoevsky a decade later, is reminiscent of Descartes's "Meditations," wherein the French philosopher was attempting to find some proposition that could not be doubted, so as to have an indisputable foundation for a structure of knowledge. Descartes, as every beginning philosophy student knows, settled on the assertion of his own existence as such an indubitable proposition. Dostoevsky, for his part, tries to extend that indubitability to the assertion of immortality, claiming that it, too, is impossible to doubt:

> The word *I* is such a great thing that its annihilation is unthinkable. No proofs are needed here. Every proof is inadequate [*nesoizmerimo*]. The idea that *I* cannot die is not proved but sensed. Sensed like living life. My finger is alive, and I cannot deny that it exists. Exactly so with the *I*: having said "I am," I cannot conceive that *I shall not be*, cannot in any way. (24:234; Dostoevsky's emphasis)

The weakness of this extension of Descartes' strategy, compounded by Dostoevsky's apparent conflation of the personal pronoun with the real self, may account for his failure to develop it in a published work. But at least it shows that, although he contended that no "proofs" are needed in the matter, he regarded the immortality thesis as a reasonable belief rather than a paradox or absurdity that could only be accepted on faith. Presumably he viewed it at this point as a product of immediate intuition (something "sensed," to use his expression), not unlike the intuition to which Descartes appealed for his fundamental truth.

More than that, from the mid-1860s to the end of his life Dostoevsky ignored his own disclaimer and offered proofs.[7] In at least five other passages, three of them published, he gave *arguments* for immortality—that is, processes of discursive reasoning in which, either in his own voice or in that of a fictional character, he presents premises as logical support for the conclusion that the soul is immortal. Although the passages themselves are quite diverse in form and context—they are found in two novels, a working notebook, a personal letter, and a published essay—I shall treat each of them equally as containing an argument constructed by Dostoevsky and offered for rational acceptance in its context.

---

7. The ambiguity of the word 'proof' has dogged discussion of Dostoevsky's attitude toward the immortality thesis. When Robert Louis Jackson writes that "Dostoevsky believed in immortality, but he recognized that proofs were impossible," Jackson is quite correct if by 'proof' is meant a rationally unassailable, conclusive demonstration. But in the weaker sense of 'proof' as rational substantiation that is not necessarily conclusive, it is beyond question that Dostoevsky thought proofs of immortality possible. See Robert Louis Jackson, *Dialogues with Dostoevsky: The Overwhelming Questions* (Stanford, Calif.: Stanford University Press, 1993), 297, 302, 335–36.

Reflections on His Wife's Death (1864)

Dostoevsky's earliest case for an afterlife came in a notebook entry of April 1864 in which he jotted reflections on viewing the body of his first wife, Maria Dmitrievna, to whom he had remained deeply attached despite a troubled relationship. "Masha lies on the table," he began. "Will I ever see Masha again?" (20:172)

His reasoning in this text, which I shall call his *argument from the demand for moral perfection*, begins with acceptance of the Christian commandment to love one's neighbor as oneself; the bereaved widower takes the binding character of this moral law as given. But in earthly life, he continues, human egoism prevents us from following the commandment fully: "The *self* stands in the way." Still, in the figure of Christ we are presented with *"the ideal of man incarnate,"* and humanity's task on earth is to strive toward this ideal—to strive to be morally Christlike (20:172; Dostoevsky's emphasis). He goes on:

> All history, both of humanity and in some degree of each person separately, is nothing but development, struggle, striving, and attaining this goal [moral perfection].
>
> But if this is the final goal of humanity (having attained which, humanity would no longer need to develop—that is, to strive, to struggle, to keep the ideal in sight through all its failures and eternally strive toward it—so that it would no longer be necessary to live), then, consequently, a person in reaching this point would end his earthly existence. . . .
>
> But, in my judgment, to attain such a great goal is completely meaningless if, once it is attained, everything is extinguished and disappears—that is, if a person has no life though the goal has been attained. Consequently, there is a future life in paradise. (20:172–73)

Remarkable parallels exist between Dostoevsky's reasoning here and Immanuel Kant's case for the immortality of the soul. Although Kant had affirmed in the *Critique of Pure Reason* that immortality cannot be demonstrably proved, in the *Critique of Practical Reason* he contended that it could justifiably be assumed as a "postulate of pure practical reason" on the grounds that our moral experience would be meaningless without that assumption. Our "practical reason" presents us with a categorical moral imperative, which requires us always to treat others as ends in themselves, never as mere means. But in this life, perfect accordance of the human will with that imperative is impossible. Thus, Kant concludes, there must be a future life in which the struggle for perfection is continued, or the moral commandment would make no sense, for there can be no moral obligation to do the impossible.[8]

Although there is no reason to think that Dostoevsky was familiar with the details of Kant's argument,[9] he shares with the German philosopher two important premises: he accepts the binding character of an absolute moral imperative, and he affirms the impossibility of observing that imperative fully on earth. But Dostoevsky's argument takes an original turn—one by which, interestingly enough, he avoids a difficulty in Kant's reasoning. For Kant's argument as abbreviated above does not really establish that the soul is *immortal;* it shows only that the soul, beyond its earthly life, must have another life of some duration in which compliance with the moral law is perfected. But what happens when, as it seems plausible to assume, compliance *is* perfected in the other world? What grounds do we have for thinking that the soul *goes on* living after its moral mission has been completed? To avoid this problem and conclude that the soul will live *eternally,* Kant was forced to buttress his argument with the puzzling assertion that in fact the struggle for compliance never really ends, even in the other world: the soul, without ever reaching absolute compliance, will progress toward it over an infinity of time, moving to ever higher "degrees" of moral perfection.[10]

Dostoevsky, whether through ignorance of Kant's argument or awareness of its weaknesses, strikes out in another direction: he assumes that moral perfection *is* attainable in the other world, and he continues the argument for an afterlife from there. He agrees with Kant that in this life, progress can be made toward the moral goal. But since perfection is not attainable in earthly existence, its attainment must signify transition to a higher state of existence. The soul, no longer earthly, having no need to develop, and thus no longer "human" in the strict sense, is "reborn . . . into another nature" (20:173). But how does this establish that the new, otherworldly being *continues to exist*—that

8. *Kant's Critique of Practical Reason and Other Works on the Theory of Ethics,* trans. T. K. Abbott, 6th ed. (London: Longman's, Green, 1909), 218–20.

9. The extent of Dostoevsky's knowledge of the Kantian philosophy is a matter of dispute. Iakov Golosovker in his book *Dostoevskii i Kant* (Dostoevsky and Kant) (Moscow: Izd. Akademii nauk, 1963), 38–39, 45, 66, 97, 99, insists that the writer had studied *The Critique of Pure Reason* carefully, but there is no credible evidence to support this claim. Joseph Frank in *Dostoevsky: The Seeds of Revolt, 1821–1849* (Princeton, N.J.: Princeton University Press, 1976), 57, notes that Dostoevsky could have learned the basic ideas of the *Critique of Practical Reason,* including Kant's view of immortality, from Nikolay Karamzin's account of his meeting with Kant in 1789. But that account was not detailed enough to allow anyone to reconstruct Kant's actual argument from it; see Karamzin, *Pis'ma russkogo puteshestvennika* (Moscow; Pravda, 1980), 47–49.

10. Kant, *Critique,* 219.

is, that life after earthly death is eternal? As we saw in the text quoted above, Dostoevsky's solution is to argue that the very achievement of the goal would be meaningless if it were followed by the destruction of the seeker—if after perfection is attained "everything is extinguished and disappears." Hence the conclusion: "There is a future life in paradise."

Dostoevsky's argument here is again reminiscent of Kant's in that both arguments, employing what logicians call "indirect reasoning," end with an implicit reductio ad absurdum. Each seeks to establish a proposition—the immortality of the soul—by showing that its denial leads to an absurdity. Dostoevsky's reductio, however, is an original one, significantly different from Kant's. For Kant, the absurdity is that without immortality the person would not have an infinite time in which to pursue perfection. For Dostoevsky, the absurdity is that the person commanded to achieve perfection would be rewarded with extinction for achieving it. In either case, the quest for moral perfection, and hence the command to seek it, would appear pointless; hence immortality must be affirmed.

Each of these arguments is open to criticism, but it is interesting to note that the impromptu reasoning of the emotional Russian novelist, spun out in an hour of intense personal engagement, is not obviously inferior, from a logical standpoint, to that of the quintessentially cerebral and detached German philosopher. Each argument hinges on the acceptance of an absolute moral law for which no justification is provided. Each, furthermore, shares the weakness of all reductio arguments of the sort we may call "casual" as opposed to strict—that is, arguments in which the "absurdity" in question is not a manifest self-contradiction. Short of showing that your opponent has contradicted himself, what you call an absurdity may be perfectly acceptable not only to your opponent but to other reasonable people. For example, it is perfectly acceptable to Dostoevsky (contra Kant) to view moral perfection as fully achievable by a human soul. And it may be perfectly acceptable to another thinker (contra Dostoevsky) to find that moral perfection is followed by personal extinction. One person's "absurdity" may be another's regrettable but understandable bad fortune.

Each course of reasoning, moreover, has specific problems of its own. Kant fails to explain how moral perfection can have "degrees," and how the assumption of an infinity of progress helps us make sense of the moral imperative if complete moral compliance is forever out of reach. Dostoevsky presupposes not merely the attainability of perfection but an entire theory of the historical "task" of the human species. Indeed, perhaps the most serious difficulty with Dostoevsky's argument is its apparent confusion of the immortality of "each person separately" with the immortality of all "humanity" at the end of human history. Although he begins his reflections on a personal note ("Will I ever see Masha again?"), he proceeds to state his argument primarily in terms of the collectives "man" (*chelovek*) and "humanity" (*chelovechestvo*); he refers to moral perfection as "the final goal of humanity," reached, as he says apocalyptically later in the text, at "the end of the world," after which "there will be no more time" (20:173–74). For individuals dying *before* the end of history, it would appear that to achieve immortality they must all (including the greatest earthly villain?) attain moral perfection by (or just after?) the end of their earthly lives—surely an unlikely prospect.

That Dostoevsky was at least dimly aware of this problem, and was unsure whether his argument applied to *every* individual, is indicated when, toward the end of these notebook reflections, he poses the question, "Is there . . . a future life for every self?" The sentences that follow are among the murkiest in the text, and they conclude with an admission of intellectual failure, but they demonstrate that he believed every human being would in some manner be swept into immortality in humanity's grand finale: "How every self will be resurrected then—in the general Synthesis—is hard to imagine. But a living being that has not died before the attainment of the final ideal and has not been reflected in it must be revived into final, synthetic, infinite life. . . . But how this will be, in what form, in what nature—it is hard for a person even to imagine definitely" (20:174–75).[11]

Not fully satisfied with this treatment of the subject, Dostoevsky never returned to it in that form. There are, however, echoes of it in his later efforts to support immortality, as we shall see.

Demons (1871–72)

Dostoevsky's next case for immortality appears in the novel *Demons*, where it is assigned to Stepan Trofimovich Verkhovensky. Short and straightforward, it reads as follows:

"My immortality is necessary if only because God would not wish to commit an injustice and extinguish altogether the flame of love for Him once it has flared in my heart. . . . If I have loved Him and rejoiced in my love, is it possible that He

11. Among the forms that Dostoevsky later considered, one was the possibility of physical resurrection in a new, changed material nature. In a letter of 1878 he writes that both he and Vladimir Solovyov believe in "real, literal, personal resurrection and in the fact that it will take place on earth" (30/1:14–15).

would extinguish both me and my joy and return us to nothing? If there is a God, then I am immortal!" (10:505)

The only trace of the 1864 reasoning in this *argument from divine justice* is that both speak of immortality as in some sense deserved by the individual: its absence would contravene some demand of morality, or at least some legitimate moral expectation. Beyond that, Verkhovensky's case is remarkably different from Dostoevsky's earlier reasoning. For one thing, it patently assumes the existence of God, and a perfectly just God at that. In the 1864 reasoning, the notion of God is merely implicit: God is the presumed source of the moral commandment and giver of the reward for perfection, but the argument itself does not logically depend on the deity's existence. Second, Verkhovensky's argument does not have a reductio form but reaches the desired conclusion by direct deduction from a set of premises that we may state informally as follows: (1) There is a God, Whom I have had the joy of loving. (2) God would not do something unjust. (3) It would be unjust if God annihilated me after I had had the joy of loving Him. Therefore, God will not annihilate me (that is, I am immortal). Given this simple logical structure, the persuasiveness of the argument depends entirely on the acceptability of the three assumed premises—concerning which, of course, there could be furious debate, as Dostoevsky knew only too well.

A third difference from the 1864 reasoning is that the argument from divine justice plainly applies to a portion of humanity only: it says nothing of the fate of those who have *not* experienced the joy of loving God. Strictly speaking it is an egoistic argument, as Verkhovensky's language indicates ("my immortality," "I am immortal"). Dostoevsky's concern in 1864 was his wife's immortality as a member of the human species; Verkhovensky's concern, on the other hand, is his *own* immortality. The argument he voices applies only incidentally to others—and then only to those who have loved God. I am not suggesting that Dostoevsky himself would reject any of Verkhovensky's premises; I believe he would happily accept all of them. But as we know from the 1864 reflections, Dostoevsky had a broader interest in the subject than Verkhovensky exhibits in *Demons*.

"Unsubstantiated Statements" (1876)

Following his work on *Demons*, Dostoevsky again raised the question of an afterlife in *The Adolescent* (1875), where Arkady, Makar, and Versilov all comment on it and other characters allude to it. But neither the novel nor Dostoevsky's working notebooks for it contain a clear effort to provide rational support for immortality, despite a few hints at what was to come in future works (13:49, 16:8–9). For the next explicit argument we must turn to *A Writer's Diary*.

In the October 1876 installment of that work, Dostoevsky had included a "suicide note" purportedly written by a "materialist" who wished to explain the act he was about to commit. Concerned subsequently that some readers were misconstruing the fictitious note (composed, of course, by Dostoevsky himself) as justifying the act, and that it might even foster suicidal inclinations, he felt obliged to clarify his position in his own voice, which he did in the section of the *Diary* for December 1876 entitled "Unsubstantiated Statements."

It is in this text that he makes the extravagant claims for the idea of immortality cited at the beginning of this section; the text begins not as an argument but as an impassioned panegyric. He asserts that the trouble with the "materialist" is that he has lost faith in "the highest idea of human existence"—the idea of immortality. Belief in the immortality of the human soul, he claims, is a "necessity" and an "inevitability"; without it, human existence is "unnatural, unthinkable, and intolerable." Of all the ideas on earth it is the one "supreme" idea (24:46–48).

After this blizzard of unsupported claims, and despite the title he gives his text, Dostoevsky settles down at the end to state quite explicitly an argument for immortality, which I shall call his *argument from the normal condition of humanity*. His immediate object is to counter the notion that belief in an afterlife might have bad consequences, in that it might make one less attached to earthly life and hence more likely to desire to leave it. Dostoevsky's contention, rather, is that it is precisely the *absence* of belief in immortality that creates disenchantment with earthly life. Confined to a purely earthly perspective, thinking individuals find no "higher meaning" that can sustain them in the midst of suffering and unhappiness; they may be told that their suffering is somehow necessary for the harmony of the whole, but they cannot understand such harmony and are sure that they will never be able to share in it. If all the trials of life lead simply to annihilation, what is the point of living? The argument then proceeds as follows:

> Only with faith in his immortality does a person comprehend his whole rational [*razumnaia*] purpose on earth. Without the conviction of his immortality, a person's ties with the earth are severed; they grow weaker, they decay, and the loss of the higher meaning of life (which he senses if only in the form of the most un-

conscious melancholy) indubitably brings suicide in its train. From that, by inversion, comes the moral of my October article: "If the conviction of immortality is so necessary for human existence, it must be the normal condition of humanity; and if that is the case, then the actual immortality of the human soul *indubitably exists.*" (24:49; Dostoevsky's emphasis)[12]

This new argument, quite different from the previous two, has several noteworthy features. First, it depends in no way on moral deserts or expectations; ethical ideas are entirely beside the point. Second, on the face of it, it does not presuppose the existence of God—though, as we shall see, in providing further defense of the argument it may be necessary to introduce that thesis. Third, it is manifestly a universal argument, free both of the ambiguity about scope of application that affected the 1864 reasoning and of the restricted application of Verkhovensky's egoistic argument in *Demons;* the argument from the normal condition of humanity applies to all humanity.

Fourth, this argument introduces an empirical premise, on which its soundness hinges—a factual claim about human psychology, to the effect that loss of belief in immortality promotes suicide. In principle, such a premise is subject to empirical verification: are suicides in fact more prevalent among people who deny the immortality of the soul? Dostoevsky fails to provide any evidence for the claim, other than the casual assertion that suicide has "so increased . . . among the intelligentsia" (24:47).[13] But its presence in the argument shows that he did not deny the relevance of factual premises in reasoning concerning immortality, despite the transempirical nature of the subject.

Finally, over and above its empirical character, the argument is also significant as containing Dostoevsky's first reference to the psychological effects of belief and disbelief in immortality—a theme that will recur in later arguments.

---

12. Dostoevsky's point about the great importance for human existence of the conviction of immortality was foreshadowed in Pascal's *Pensées*: "All our actions and thoughts must take such different courses, according as there are or are not eternal joys to hope for, that it is impossible to take one step with sense and judgment, unless we regulate our course by our view of this point which ought to be our ultimate end" (Pascal, "Thoughts," 110).

13. Dostoevsky no doubt thought the truth of the claim too obvious to require support. As Irina Paperno explains in her informative study of suicide in nineteenth-century Russia, the Russian reading public of the 1860s–1880s was convinced that the rate of suicide in the country had increased to epidemic proportions. The Russian press was full of accounts of individual suicides and statistical analyses of the supposed epidemic, which was widely attributed to the growing influence of positivist and atheist thought. See Irina Paperno, *Suicide as a Cultural Institution in Dostoevsky's Russia* (Ithaca, N.Y.: Cornell University Press, 1997), 45, 53, 73–77. Paperno also points out that as early as the late eighteenth century some Russians linked suicide with the denial of immortality (14–15).

At the same time, it is important to note that he is not content simply with showing the benign consequences of *believing* in life after death—consequences that presumably would be present even if the belief were false, so long as it were sincerely held. As the phrasing of his "moral" shows, Dostoevsky was perfectly aware of the difference between "the conviction" of immortality (i.e., the psychological state of believing in immortality) and "actual immortality" (i.e., immortality as a metaphysical reality), and it is the latter he wished to establish. For that, he had to effect a logical connection between the conviction and the reality, which he did in the last sentence, somewhat abruptly, by introducing the concept of "the normal condition of humanity."

The abruptness of the argument here is a function of its logical status as an enthymeme—that is, an argument in which an assumed premise, though supposedly more or less obvious, is not explicitly stated. No such tacit assumption appears to be required for the first part of the concluding sentence ("If the conviction of immortality is so essential for human existence, it must be the normal condition of humanity"): this says no more than that it is "normal" for people to hold a belief that is necessary for their existence; since they cannot *exist* without the belief, it must be part of their "normal condition."[14] But the concluding hypothetical ("if so [i.e., if the conviction of immortality is the normal condition of humanity], then the actual immortality of the human soul *indubitably exists*") moves from the presence of a belief to its truth, and consequently appears to need some additional support, even if we disregard the over-enthusiastic claim of indubitability.

Unfortunately, however, in this case the identity of the unexpressed premise is by no means obvious. Why does the fact that people "normally" or necessarily believe something, show that it is true? Perhaps the best guess as to Dostoevsky's thinking here, given the general cast of his worldview, is that he assumed that a benevolent Creator would not make our existence contingent on an essential belief (the belief in immortality) that is *false*. We cannot say with any confidence that this is what he had in mind, but the assumption is consistent with his Christian metaphysics and it would complete the enthymematic argument. What we *can* say with assurance, because it is clear from the explicit

14. Like other Russians of his day and later, Dostoevsky used the term 'normal' (*normal'nyi*) very broadly, as meaning "in accordance with a norm or standard," where the "norm" could be anything from an empirical natural law or typical existing pattern of things (whether good or bad) to something ideal or desirable (whether existing or not). In the present case, the norm in question would appear to be of the empirical variety, having to do with factually necessary conditions for people's existence: just as having lungs to breathe is part of the "normal condition" of a human being, so too is belief in the immortality of the soul, for without that belief (Dostoevsky is claiming) individuals are prone to end their existence.

portion of his argument, is that the mere fact that the belief has beneficial consequences does not, in his view, make it true; it is its being the "normal condition of humanity"—along with some such assumption as the one I have proposed concerning divine benevolence—that allows us to assert "the actual immortality of the human soul."

Before leaving this section of *A Writer's Diary*, it is worth noting that in it (though not in the immediate context of the argument from the normal condition of humanity) Dostoevsky once again links the idea of immortality with love for humanity. We have already seen this linkage both in the 1864 reflections on his wife's death and in Zosima's advice to Khokhlakova. In this section of the *Diary* he writes: "I declare (again *for now* without substantiation) that love for humanity is even completely unthinkable, incomprehensible, and *completely impossible without a concurrent belief in the immortality of the human soul*" (24:49; Dostoevsky's emphasis). He will return to the connection between immortality and love in his final argument for life after death in *The Brothers Karamazov*.

Letter to Nikolay Ozmidov (1878)

Dostoevsky's fullest discussion of immortality after his notebook reflections of 1864 is found in a letter he wrote to an admirer, Nikolay Lukich Ozmidov, in February 1878. Ozmidov had written to him asking for his views on the immortality of the soul. Not surprisingly, Dostoevsky begins his reply with a heartfelt bow to faith: "Wouldn't it be better," he asks Ozmidov, "for you to read through carefully all the epistles of the apostle Paul?", adding that nothing finer has ever been written on the subject of faith (30/1:10). Although he asserts that "it is hardest of all to persuade unbelievers through words and arguments," he nonetheless tacitly affirms the possibility of rational persuasion by launching into a discussion in which he offers two separate arguments for immortality.

The first and more complex, which is also the most logically elegant of Dostoevsky's arguments for immortality, may be called his *argument from the law of the preservation of organisms*:

Every organism exists on earth in order to live, and not to destroy itself.
    Science has determined this, and has already put together rather precisely the laws for the confirmation of this axiom. Humanity as a whole is, of course, simply an organism.[15] . . . Now imagine that there is neither God nor the immor-

---

15. George Kline has pointed out to me that Dostoevsky, in thus applying the term 'organism' to something other than an individual biological entity, is following in a Hegelian tradition also repre-

tality of the soul (the immortality of the soul and God—it's all the same, one and the same idea[16]). Tell me, why then should I live properly, do good, if I shall die on earth altogether? Without immortality, surely the whole point would be just to complete my term, and then everything can go to hell. And if that's so, then why shouldn't I (as long as I can count on my adroitness and wit to keep me from getting caught by the law) kill someone, rob, . . . live at other people's expense, just to satisfy my own belly? After all, I shall die, and all will die, there will be nothing! In that way it will in fact turn out that only the human organism fails to fall under the universal axiom and lives only *for its own destruction*, and not to preserve and nurture itself. For what kind of society is it if all its members are enemies of each other? And the result is dreadful nonsense. (30/1:10–11; Dostoevsky's emphasis)

Like the 1864 reflections, this argument uses the logical strategy of reductio ad absurdum: denying the immortality of the soul is said to yield "dreadful nonsense." But, unlike the earlier case, this is no casual reductio in which the "absurdity" is largely in the eye of the beholder. In this argument Dostoevsky presents a strict or pure reductio—one in which the absurdity is a logical self-contradiction on the part of a presumed opponent. First he seeks Ozmidov's assent to the "axiom" that all "organisms" (among which he counts "humanity as a whole") seek their own preservation. Confident that Ozmidov will accept this supposedly scientific law of nature and its application to humanity as a species, he then considers what would follow from the *denial* of the immortality thesis. It would mean, he argues, a war of all against all—hence a human species hurtling toward mutual destruction rather than self-preservation. Thus if Ozmidov believes there is no immortality, he is contradicting himself—he is saying that all "organisms" (species) seek their own preservation, and yet the human "organism" does *not* seek its own preservation—and that, presumably, is the "dreadful nonsense" that completes the reductio.

Despite the purity of Dostoevsky's logical form in this instance, the soundness of his argument depends also, of course, on the truth of its premises. And on that score there is much that an opponent could quarrel with in this argu-

---

sented by Vladimir Solovyov. In this sense the meaning of the term is something like (as Kline formulated it in another context) "an organized, self-constituting, inwardly articulated whole"; see George L. Kline, "The Religious Roots of S.L. Frank's Ethics and Social Philosophy," in *Russian Religious Thought*, ed. Judith Deutsch Kornblatt and Richard F. Gustafson (Madison: University of Wisconsin Press, 1996), 219.

16. This contention that immortality and God are "one and the same idea" will be discussed in a later section of this chapter.

ment, particularly since, like the argument from the normal condition of humanity, it employs some questionable empirical generalizations. Why should Ozmidov admit in the first place, for example, that the so-called law applies to *species* as well as to individuals? And why should he admit that it applies to *humanity* as well as to nonhuman species? Dostoevsky himself believed that humanity, thanks to free choice, was exempt from the natural law of universal causal determinism, so why not from another natural law? Ten years earlier, he had a character in *The Idiot* proclaim that self-preservation, though a law, is not by itself the "normal law of humanity": "it's no more normal than the law of destruction, or perhaps even self-destruction" (8:311).

The argument's empirical assumptions about human psychology are also open to question. Again as in the case of the argument from the normal condition of humanity, Dostoevsky contends that bad consequences will follow from the denial of an afterlife. But in this case a different set of consequences is envisaged: here the undesirable results in question consist not in suicide, as in the 1876 reasoning, but in grasping, rapacious behavior toward others. If individuals have only earthly lives, they will not be concerned about the well-being of others; they will act to maximize their own individual advantage on earth, for the short duration of their lives, by any available means, even at the cost of destructive behavior.[17] Ironically, the prospect of mass suicide would have served his purpose here better than the prospect of mass rapacity, since direct self-destruction would more obviously contravene the law of the preservation of organisms than would the incidental destruction wrought by unrestrained self-serving behavior. But, inexplicably, he does not even raise the prospect of suicide on this occasion. The two arguments can hardly be considered compatible, since from the same cognitive state on the part of individuals (the denial of immortality) they infer contrary behavior—suicide in one case and self-serving rapacity in the other.

Dostoevsky's second, briefer argument for immortality in the letter to Ozmidov, which I shall call his *argument from the unique character of consciousness*, is again quite different from all his other arguments and offers an interesting glimpse into his understanding of consciousness and the human self. Having spoken in the letter of all the objects of consciousness—all the things that an individual may be aware of, including the "universal axiom" that every organ-

17. Vasily Rozanov is among those who have disagreed with Dostoevsky on this empirical question: "To me it is perfectly obvious and known from immediate facts that people entirely devoid of belief in God and an afterlife are also people who lead lives of amazing purity, full of love and kindness toward others" (V. Rozanov, *Okolo tserkovnykh sten* [St. Petersburg: F. Vaisberg and P. Gershunin, 1906], 2:428 n. 2).

ism seeks to maintain its own existence—he points out that over and against them there is the perceiving conscious subject, *"my self [moe ia]*, which has been conscious of everything." He goes on:

> If it has been conscious of all this, . . . then, therefore, *my self* is higher than all this; . . . [it] stands to the side, as it were, above all this, judges and is conscious of it. But, in that case, this *self* not only is not subject to the earthly axiom, to earthly law, but goes beyond them and has a law higher than them. Where is that law? Not on earth, where all come to an end and all die without a trace and without resurrection. Isn't this a hint at the immortality of the soul? If not, would you, Nikolay Lukich, take to worrying about it, writing letters, looking for it? This means that you can't cope with your *self*: it doesn't fit into the earthly order but seeks something else, besides the earth, to which it also belongs. (30/1:11; Dostoevsky's emphasis)

This distinction between consciousness and its object, and hence between consciousness and *everything* of which we may be conscious, became familiar in late-nineteenth- and early-twentieth-century philosophy through the writings of Franz Brentano, Edmund Husserl, and others, who developed the doctrine of the "intentionality" of consciousness, according to which all consciousness is consciousness *of* something.[18] Such a separation between consciousness and object is already implicit in Dostoevsky's view of freedom of the will: in conscious choice the agent stands "to the side" of possible influences, not subject to deterministic earthly laws. In the letter to Ozmidov, however, he goes much further and interprets the unique ontological status of consciousness as evidence that the self belongs to an unearthly realm not subject to the natural law of universal mortality. This conscious self, in other words, is identified with the purely spiritual and everlasting soul, not with the material tool he calls the "mind." Hence it would appear that for Dostoevsky consciousness and the awareness of self-identity are lodged not in the "mind" but in the soul.

Such a grand conceptual leap would not, of course, be acceptable to many other thinkers. A perception of the weakness of the argument is no doubt what moved Dostoevsky to characterize it as only a "hint." But from the broader perspective of his worldview, the argument from the unique character of consciousness has special interest as an indication that he sought to root the thesis of the immortality of the soul in the very nature of human consciousness.

18. See the exposition of Brentano's philosophy by Roderick M. Chisholm in *The Encyclopedia of Philosophy* (New York: Macmillan, 1967), 1:365–68.

The Brothers Karamazov *(1879–80)*

Our final opportunity to observe Dostoevsky's use of ratiocination in support of the immortality thesis comes in his last great work, *The Brothers Karamazov*. The theme makes an early appearance in the novel. As noted above, it is introduced in the conversation between Khokhlakova and Zosima, where the latter speaks of faith in immortality as growing out of love. Not long thereafter, in another conversation with Zosima, an argument for immortality appears. It is part of an account, by the Karamazovs' neighbor Pyotr Miusov, of statements Ivan Karamazov had supposedly made some five days before:

> "He [Ivan] solemnly declared in argument that there is nothing whatever in all the world to make people love their fellows, no such law of nature that people should love humanity, and that, if there is now and has been in the past any love on earth, it was not from a natural law but simply because people have believed in their immortality. Ivan Fyodorovich added parenthetically that the whole natural law consists in this: that if you were to destroy in humanity the belief in its immortality, not only love but every vital force for the continuation of earthly life would at once dry up. Moreover, then nothing would be immoral any more, everything would be permitted, even cannibalism."[19] (14:64–65)

Ivan, pressed to confirm this account, replies, "Yes. That is what I maintained. There is no virtue if there is no immortality."[20] Challenged by Zosima, however, he quickly confesses that he is *not*, in fact, persuaded by this argument, though he insists that in presenting it he was not "altogether joking" (14:65). No doubt Dostoevsky intended this reasoning, which I shall call his *argument from the need for morality*, to have some weight, for it is what demonstrates at this point that the thinking of the "materialist" Ivan is, as Alyosha says, "great and unresolved" (14:76).[21] Furthermore, if we are to accept Nikolay Strakhov's interpretation of *The Brothers Karamazov*, the argument is the key to the novel: its central point is that Dmitry Karamazov's beliefs in God and immortality kept him from yielding to the urge to kill his father.[22]

The echoes in Ivan's reasoning of Dostoevsky's earlier arguments referring to the destructive consequences of disbelief in immortality might tempt us to view it as merely a variant of those arguments. But closer examination reveals

19. The last sentence is an allusion to 1 Corinthians 6:12.
20. For another discussion of Dostoevsky's attitude toward this thesis, see Jackson, *Dialogues with Dostoevsky*, 293–302.
21. Jackson persuasively shows Dostoevsky's probable indebtedness to Châteaubriand in this connection (ibid., 137–43).
22. Linda Gerstein, *Nikolai Strakhov* (Cambridge, Mass.: Harvard University Press, 1971), 99.

substantial differences, for Ivan's argument does not stand or fall on the consequences of what anyone believes. Although Miusov in reporting the argument mixes metaphysical talk about laws of nature with psychological talk about beliefs, Ivan in his "confirmation" says simply: "There is no virtue if there is no immortality." The metaphysical interpretation of the argument, which reads it as having to do with the (supposed) fact of immortality and its connection with morality, seems more in keeping with Ivan's own intention than does a psychological interpretation.

This text in *The Brothers Karamazov* is not, of course, the first reference in Dostoevsky's writings to a tie between morality and immortality. In *The Adolescent* (1875), Arkady says, "Tell me why I must without fail be a noble person, particularly if everything lasts only a minute" (13:49), suggesting that a mortal being lacks motivation to do good. Similarly, in the letter to Ozmidov, Dostoevsky had said that in the absence of life after death people would have no reason to refrain from murder and other crimes, so long as they could get away with them. By way of explanation, he had offered in that letter only the suggestion that the purely mortal creature's perspective would be strictly finite and earthly, restricted to satisfying the "belly" (30/1:10). But as to precisely why, given a finite, earthly perspective, one's interests would be so concentrated and one could find no reasons to eschew crime, he was silent in the Ozmidov text. What is new in Ivan's argument is that for the first time immortality and morality are connected through the explicit mediation of the concept of love. Although Miusov's report of Ivan's argument is highly informal and enthymematic, I believe that the argument is best interpreted as a reductio of the casual variety, concerned with drawing out the logical implications of rejecting the immortality thesis. Without attempting a full formal reconstruction of the argument, we can capture its heart in two brief statements: (1) without immortality there is no love, and (2) without love there is no morality ("everything is permitted"). On the tacit assumption, then, that the denial of morality is an "absurdity," the truth of the immortality thesis follows by reductio ad absurdum. Comments are in order concerning each of the two key statements.

(1) In asserting that without immortality there is no love, Ivan's argument makes a sweeping claim about the purely natural—in the sense of material, fleshly—aspect of the human essence. Ivan is assuming, first, that a purely mortal human being—that is, a being lacking an immortal soul—would belong exclusively to the natural, material world. And he is assuming, second, that in that world there is no motivation to love one's neighbor or to avoid harming or exploiting one's neighbor in the pursuit of self-gratification. If one is earthbound, governed by earthly, material laws alone, there is no law that produces love;

there are only physical and animal forces, and these do not include love: "there is nothing whatever in all the world to make people love their fellows."[23]

Ivan's argument thus hinges on a particularly harsh conception of the earthly natural order. It is a conception according to which there is no instinctive attachment of one human being to another, not even (presumably) of parent to child, or man to woman; no "natural sympathy" among all human beings such as was postulated by the Scottish moralists of the eighteenth century; no purely naturalistic tendency toward altruistic behavior based on its survival value for the species, such as is now claimed by sociobiologists. Man's earthly nature is devoid of any benevolent proclivities and places him squarely in Tennyson's "nature, red in tooth and claw." Natural man is essentially a beast, and a being without an immortal soul is a purely natural man.

Such, at any rate, would seem to be the thinking behind Ivan's argument. But can we attribute these views to Dostoevsky himself? V. V. Zenkovsky has argued that Dostoevsky never really abandoned the "Christian naturalism" of his early radical phase, which gave him a faith in the "natural nobility" of man that was as much Rousseauian as religious.[24] But I believe, rather, that Dostoevsky's mature writings consistently support the same harsh view of nature assumed by Ivan's argument—nature as a loveless and amoral sphere. We find this conception also in Arkady's quarrelsome speech in The Adolescent, in which he upbraids the materialists for allowing him "neither love, nor a future life, nor recognition for my heroism" (13:49). And it is reflected more fully and artfully in Versilov's famous "vision" in the same novel. Versilov imagines a situation in which love exists in a strictly naturalistic setting: the people of Europe have given up "the great idea of immortality" but still seek to love everyone and everything, consoling themselves in death with the thought that others would remain, loving one another. But he associates this scenario of purely mortal love with "the last day of European humanity," thus signaling his belief that it cannot endure. And he acknowledges its lack of viability as a naturalistic scenario when he confesses that he can never complete the vision in his own mind without imagining that at the end a newly resurrected Christ comes to save His "orphaned people" (13:375, 379).[25] In general I see no basis

23. Jackson, in a fascinating discussion of Dostoevsky's relation to de Sade, has shown the strong parallel here with the latter's cynical question: "Have we ever felt a single natural impulse advising us to prefer others to ourselves, and is not each one of us alone, for himself in the world?" (Dialogues with Dostoevsky, 153–54). Something like the same sentiment is also found in Belinsky, who wrote: "A person as an individual naturally sees in other people as individuals something inimical to him" (V. G. Belinskii, Polnoe sobranie sochinenii [Moscow: Izd. Akademiia nauk SSSR, 1953], 3:339).

24. V. V. Zenkovsky, A History of Russian Philosophy, trans. George L. Kline (London: Routledge and Kegan Paul, 1953), 1:412–13.

25. Cf. Jackson, Dialogues with Dostoevsky, 248.

in Dostoevsky's post-Siberian writings for contending that he somehow grounded love or any other source of morality in the natural (material) order.

But although Dostoevsky denies that there is in humankind a natural (in the sense of earthly) ground for love—and thus rejects as plainly as one could wish the Enlightenment thesis of the "natural goodness" of man—he does not, of course, mean that people are incapable of love or of the social cooperation that love makes possible. He means only that such things do not come "naturally," are not products of man's participation in the material order. Man also has a spiritual character, affirmed when one accepts the thesis of immortality. It is on this ground that Dostoevsky could well say, with Ivan, "if there is now and has been in the past any love on earth, it was not from a law of nature but simply because people have believed in their immortality" (14:64).[26]

(2) The second critical statement in Ivan's argument—that without love there is no morality—is for Dostoevsky simply a corollary of his ethical theory. As we shall see in chapter 3, for Dostoevsky it is axiomatic that without love of others there are no moral standards, since love of others is the *sole* moral standard; without it, "everything is permitted." Ivan's argument, then, presupposes Dostoevsky's ethical theory and can be no more convincing than that theory.

This is not to say that Dostoevsky ignored the existence of other claims to the status of supreme moral standard. Indeed he puts one such claim in the mouth of Rakitin just a few pages later in *The Brothers Karamazov*: "'And did you hear recently his [Ivan's] stupid theory: "Since there is no immortality of the soul, there is no virtue either, which means that everything is permitted"? . . . His whole theory is vile! Humanity will find in itself the strength to live for virtue even without believing in the immortality of the soul! It will find it in love of liberty, of equality, of fraternity'" (14:76). Rakitin is questioning Ivan's assumption that moral behavior can be based only on love of other *people*. No one directly responds to Rakitin at the time, but there is little doubt as to how Dostoevsky himself would answer him, and does answer him in the Legend of the Grand Inquisitor, not to mention *Demons*. Dostoevsky's distrust of "abstractions" such as liberty, equality, and fraternity (even "humanity" when treated as an abstraction) is well established in his writings, for

26. Although in these contexts Dostoevsky ordinarily uses the terms 'nature' (*priroda*) and 'natural' (*estestvennyi*) to signify the material, animal dimension of human existence, on occasion he uses them for the dual, material-spiritual "nature" of the human being, so that the spiritual also becomes part of "nature" when speaking of human beings. In a discussion of interpersonal relations, for example, he speaks of there being "a natural, mutual duty of one person to another" and states that "a human, as a human, must feel the need to love his neighbor," adding that for love to be destroyed "a person would have to hate his own nature" (19:130–32). Here "his own nature" is his nature as (in part) a *spiritual* being.

he believed that devotion to them could be and often is used to justify the most inhumane treatment of real human beings. And compared to real human beings, every other proposed value is an abstraction.

The argument from the need for morality in *The Brothers Karamazov* thus brings together some pervasive themes of Dostoevsky's philosophy: the bond between immortality and love, the absence of love from the purely natural world, and the function of love as the supreme moral standard. In doing so it serves as an apt culmination to his reflections on immortality, though it is far from representing the whole range of those reflections. And, like the other arguments, it is by no means immune to rational attack. Its soundness depends on the truth of several debatable premises, including a particular view of the "natural" condition of human beings, a particular ethical theory, and of course an opponent's willingness to regard the absence of morality as an "absurdity." On the latter score, the argument would not persuade the immoralist who sees no "need for morality" in the first place. It is also worth noting, as Jackson has pointed out, that Dostoevsky was not entirely consistent in claiming a connection between morality and belief in immortality, for he credits the unbeliever Belinsky with moral virtues (21:10).[27]

The foregoing examination of the explicit arguments for immortality in Dostoevsky's writings provides the basis for some general observations concerning his philosophical approach to that subject.

First, he did not disdain rational argumentation in defense of the immortality thesis but engaged in it repeatedly. He employed recognized logical forms, marshaled premises in support of conclusions, and did not hesitate to use factual claims, subject in principal to empirical verification, as premises in reasoning about the spiritual world. Thus despite the epistemological preference he gives to faith, he should not be classed with irrationalists such as Soren Kierkegaard and Lev Shestov, who saw no role whatever for logic in the discussion of religious truths. In the epistemological sphere, Dostoevsky's "irrationalism"—if such it must be called—consists entirely in relegating reason to a secondary role and denying it the power of producing certainty on ultimate questions such as the existence of God and the immortality of the soul. It is an "irrationalism" similar to Immanuel Kant's, which did not exclude the use of reason to defend, by indirect considerations, beliefs that it admittedly cannot prove conclusively.

---

27. Jackson, *Dialogues with Dostoevsky*, 310. It is inconsistencies such as this that Aileen Kelly cites as indications of an unresolved conflict in Dostoevsky's moral value system; see her article "Dostoevskii and the Divided Conscience," *Slavic Review* 47 (1988): 250–53.

Second, there is no such thing as "Dostoevsky's argument for immortality" in the sense of a single process of reasoning that he accepted as uniquely or primarily supporting that conclusion. It is tempting to regard the argument in *The Brothers Karamazov* as his settled word on the subject, since it came last and brought together some of his favorite themes; Irina Paperno calls it his "central argument."[28] But he never repudiated any of the earlier arguments, and each of them incorporates ideas that were integral to his thought. The notion that there is a single Dostoevskian treatment of immortality ignores the conceptual diversity to be found in his various approaches to the subject during the last two decades of his life. The six arguments we have examined differ significantly in their premises and structure; each is a fresh attempt, shaped in part by the dramatic or rhetorical context in which it arises, to show what rational support can be found for the immortality thesis. Dostoevsky appears to regard all of them as at least suggesting and at best establishing—to the extent that reason is capable of doing so—the correctness of the immortality thesis. The notion that Dostoevsky followed one particular line of reasoning concerning immortality is particularly misleading when the reasoning nominated does not in fact correspond to *any* of the arguments found in his texts. William Hubben, for example, suggests that he subscribed to the traditional moral view according to which an afterlife is needed in order to provide a "balancing justice after death"—that is, an arena in which good people will be rewarded (and, presumably, evil people punished).[29] But Dostoevsky never makes such a case for immortality. He does offer moral arguments for immortality, as we have seen, and in one of these arguments (1871–72) Stepan Verkhovensky contends that it would be unjust of God to annihilate him once he had come to love God. But in none of his six arguments (or elsewhere in his writings) is the afterlife understood as a device for punishing or otherwise countering evil. His arguments are as interesting for what they do *not* contain as for what they do.

Third, one of the oldest and most persistent inventions concerning Dostoevsky's defense of immortality, and one for that reason worth closer examination, is the notion that he supported the immortality thesis pragmatically, by

28. Paperno, *Suicide*, 138. I. I. Evlampiev, by contrast, regards Dostoevsky's treatment of suicide, and particularly his characterization of Kirillov in *Demons*, as the key to his understanding of immortality—an understanding that, according to Evlampiev, goes well beyond the conventional Christian conception of the immortality of the soul; see Evlampiev, "Kirillov i Khristos: Samoubiitsy Dostoevskogo i problema bessmertiia," *Voprosy filosofii*, no. 3 (1998): 18–34 (translated into English by Taras Zakydalsky as "Kirillov and Christ: Dostoevsky's Suicides and the Problem of Immortality," *Russian Studies in Philosophy* 38, no. 2 [1999]: 25–51).

29. William Hubben, *Four Prophets of Our Destiny: Kierkegaard, Dostoevsky, Nietzsche, Kafka* (New York: Macmillan, 1952), 79.

appealing to the beneficial consequences of believing it. Reinhard Lauth in his study of Dostoevsky's philosophy speaks of the writer's "pragmatism" and states that Dostoevsky "sees it as a plainly valid criterion of an idea whether it affords life new revelations and furthers it or whether it denies, opposes, and destroys life."[30] Without question Dostoevsky thought that believing in immortality had benefits, but he never made those benefits the ground of the belief's truth. Faith and reason are his two modes of access to the truth of an afterlife—one mode elusive (for modern man) but immediate and capable of yielding perfect certainty, the other discursive and ever at hand but always open to doubt. *Neither* of these two modes is reducible for Dostoevsky to the attempt to identify beliefs that have benign results. Faith has nothing whatever to do with results; in faith the loving soul freely accepts its own spiritual essence and acknowledges its eternity. Reason, on the other hand, can range the natural world for evidence and can certainly consider, among other things, the consequences of beliefs; but reason, as Dostoevsky represents it, is not satisfied with calling a proposition true simply because believing it is beneficial to the believer.

The presence in Dostoevsky's writings of arguments for immortality that make no reference at all to consequences (the arguments in the 1864 notebook and *Demons*, and the second argument in the letter to Ozmidov) obviously demonstrates that pragmatic results were not the *sole* criterion of truth for Dostoevsky. These arguments are concerned with the fact of the immortality of the soul as an ontological condition, without attention to the psychological state of the believer. But do the other arguments, in which effects undeniably figure, show that for Dostoevsky the consequences of a belief serve as at least, in Lauth's measured phrase, "*a* . . . criterion" of the validity of an idea, in the sense of something to which he might resort in the absence of other epistemological warrants? Is *any* of the arguments essentially pragmatic?

The first candidate is the argument from the normal condition of humanity (1876). In this case the appearance of pragmatic reasoning arises from Dostoevsky's stress on the "indispensability" of the idea of immortality for human existence. But as we saw above, in that argument he infers the "actual immor-

---

30. Reinhard Lauth, *Die Philosophie Dostojewskis in systematischer Darstellung* (Munich: R. Piper, 1950), 39. This book has been published in Russian translation as *Filosofiia Dostoevskogo v sistematicheskom izlozhenii*, ed. A. V. Gulyga, trans. I. S. Andreeva (Moscow: Respublika, 1996). Earlier, an even stronger claim of pragmatism was advanced by the distinguished British historian E. H. Carr, who wrote in his biography of Dostoevsky that the writer "believed in . . . the doctrine of the Orthodox church because—to put the matter crudely—it worked"; see his *Dostoevsky, 1821–1881* (1931; reprint, London: George Allen and Unwin, 1962), 219.

tality" of the soul not from the consequences of believing in it but from the fact that people "normally" believe in it. The idea's indispensability does not make it true, as a pragmatist would have it; its indispensability shows only that it is a characteristic, "normal" element of the human condition.

Another case in which Dostoevsky's interest in the effects of belief may mislead the analyst into a diagnosis of pragmatism is the argument from the law of the preservation of organisms (the first argument in the 1878 letter to Ozmidov). An essential element of that reductio argument is the premise to the effect that disbelief in the immortality thesis would lead to a war of all against all. But the forecast of negative consequences stemming from the denial of immortality is not made the warrant of the falsity of the denial; it is used as an element in a pure reductio argument to show that the denial contradicts the so-called law of the preservation of organisms, or in other words that Ozmidov would contradict himself if he denied the immortality thesis. The forecast of effects is necessary for the argument, but the truth of the argument's conclusion is not constituted by the *desirability* of those effects.

The final argument for immortality that one might attempt to construe as pragmatic is the argument from the need for morality in *The Brothers Karamazov* (1879–80). Miusov, as we saw, speaks of the effects of beliefs in reporting Ivan's argument, and throughout the novel the question of immortality is discussed by reference to people's beliefs in it. But in this case we are dealing, after all, with a novel, and in that context the dramatic possibilities of a psychological perspective are more attractive than the bare logical and metaphysical relations to which Dostoevsky confined himself in other texts. That the drama of ideas in *The Brothers Karamazov* is chiefly a psychological, not a metaphysical, drama does not mean that Dostoevsky's *argument*, in its logical structure, is essentially concerned with beliefs and their psychological effects. As we have seen above, the argument can reasonably be read as independent of "belief" language altogether, and hence as not hinging on the *effects* of beliefs, desirable or otherwise. Ivan's argument is directed at the real relationships between immortality as an ontological reality and the existence of ethical standards. The "absurdity" to which his implicit reductio leads is not the undesirability of the consequences of disbelief in immortality but rather the nonexistence of ethical standards ("There is no virtue if there is no immortality")—which is absurd because ethical standards *do* exist.

Thus in no case did Dostoevsky adopt what could be called a pragmatic criterion of truth in dealing with the question of immortality. Each of his six arguments is evidence that he regarded truth as independent of the usefulness of beliefs—just as one would expect of a sworn enemy of utilitarianism.

The Question of the Existence of God

In view of Dostoevsky's repeated attempts to show the reasonableness of believing in human immortality by offering arguments for it, we might expect him to do the same with regard to the question of the existence of God. We know that the question concerned him deeply. As a romantic youth of seventeen he wrote to his brother Mikhail that when a poet is engaged in "puzzling out God" he is fulfilling "the purpose of philosophy" (28/1:54). Later, he planned for many years to write a monumental novel called "The Life of a Great Sinner" (realized only partially in *The Brothers Karamazov*), in which the existence of God would be the central theme; it was in describing his plan in an 1870 letter that he referred to the question as having "tormented" him all his life. That enduring torment, one might think, should have led to reflections on divine existence that were at least as sustained and logically focused as those concerning immortality.

At first glance, however, such reflections are hard to find. With regard to the traditional arguments for the existence of God, Dostoevsky is almost entirely silent. Never in his fiction or nonfiction does he so much as mention the time-honored *first cause argument*, which affirms the need for an ultimate efficient cause of the universe; or the related *first mover argument*, which argues for God as the initial source of the world's motion; or the thoroughly *a priori ontological argument*, which seeks to deduce the existence of God from His very essence as a supremely perfect being. These venerable reasonings, much discussed by St. Thomas Aquinas and the other scholastic fathers of the Roman Catholic church, are ignored by Dostoevsky (as they are, for the most part, by Russian Orthodox theology) even in places where one might expect him to bring them up, such as book 6 of *The Brothers Karamazov*, his self-described reply to all the "atheistic propositions" asserted by Ivan Karamazov in book 5 (30/1:121–22).

The only one of the famous scholastic arguments that finds echoes, though not affirmation, in Dostoevsky's writings is the so-called *argument from design* (also known as the *teleological argument*), which does figure in books 5 and 6 of the novel. In its traditional form, the argument appeals to the existence of God to account for the supposedly beneficent order that exists in nature, whereby dumb animals and even inanimate objects appear to act regularly for good ends. Aquinas phrased it as follows in his *Summa Theologica*:

> We see that things which lack knowledge, such as natural bodies, act for an end, and this is evident from their acting always, or nearly always, in the same way, so

as to obtain the best result. . . . Now whatever lacks knowledge cannot move towards an end, unless it be directed by some being endowed with knowledge and
intelligence. . . . Therefore some intelligent being exists by whom all natural
things are directed to their end; and this being we call God.[31]

In *The Brothers Karamazov*, Dostoevsky incorporated the idea of divine direction to an end in Zosima's reflections on the beauty and mystery of "this
world of God's": "Every blade of grass, every little insect, ant, little golden
bee, everything knows its way astonishingly; though without intellect [*um*]
they testify to the divine mystery, themselves ceaselessly enact it. . . . 'For the
Word is for all, all creation and all creatures, every little leaf strives towards the
Word, sings glory to God'" (14:267–68). As Zosima's remarks indicate, however, his use of the idea differs fundamentally from Aquinas's. For Zosima, it is
not an attempt to prove the existence of a benevolent God but rather a celebration of the divine "mystery" of the universe. Nor is it used as an argument
elsewhere in the novel or in any other writing by Dostoevsky. In *The Brothers
Karamazov* Dostoevsky was far more a critic than a defender of the idea of a
thoroughly beneficent natural order; Ivan's passionate indictment of a world
that allows the suffering and death of innocent children is one of the most
gripping statements of the philosophical "problem of evil" in world literature
(14:215–24). If Dostoevsky was at least somewhat sympathetic to Zosima's
paean to the beauty of the natural order, he did not regard that beauty as absolute. He was acutely aware of its imperfections—an awareness that showed,
he suggested in a notebook later, that his religious faith was not held lightly:
"Although philosophy is not my specialty, . . . it is not like a child that I believe in Christ and profess faith in Him" (27:86).

So what *is* Dostoevsky's reply to Ivan's atheism in *The Brothers Karamazov*?
Let us begin by looking away from the novel to the one direct and explicit argument for the existence of God that we find in his writings. It is fragmentary
in character and has only the shakiest of logical credentials, but it provides a
good opening for an examination of the writer's philosophical thinking on the
subject. In a late notebook (1880–81), in a passage apparently penned after he
had become acquainted with the non-Euclidean geometry of Georg Riemann, Dostoevsky wrote that the existence of God can be deduced simply
from the "fact" of infinity:

The real (created) world is finite, whereas the immaterial world is infinite. If parallel lines were to come together, the law of this world would come to an end.

---

31. Anton C. Pegis, ed., *Introduction to St. Thomas Aquinas* (New York: Modern Library, 1948), 27.

But in infinity they do come together, and infinity unquestionably exists. For if there were no infinity, there would also be no finiteness, it would be inconceivable. But if infinity exists, then God and the other world exist, with laws different from the real (created) world. (27:43)

In this *argument from infinity* (assuming that Dostoevsky accepted it, even if he were simply copying it from a book), we see yet another example of his taste for reductio reasoning, though a highly unsuccessful example. Apparently he took the meeting of parallel lines as proving the ontological reality of "infinity"; but since there is no infinity in our material world, there must be another, immaterial world. All of which leads him to the assertion that *God* exists. To think "infinity" and "immateriality," it would seem, is for Dostoevsky all but enough to think "God."

If this tantalizing fragment reflected chance musings with no relation to his other thoughts about God, it could be dismissed as a simple curiosity. But in fact it is quite consonant with other texts in which Dostoevsky associates infinity and immateriality with the concept of God so closely that little else seems required to complete the concept. I believe that by bringing these texts together we can arrive at a good idea of what I shall call Dostoevsky's *philosophical* conception of God (to be distinguished from his *religious* conception) and can determine how far he thought philosophy could go in grounding the existence of God rationally.

The other texts I have in mind are some that, though not always explicitly structured as arguments for the existence of God, nonetheless imply that Dostoevsky found reasonable support for divine existence in evidence of certain sorts. One such was the historical fact of the universality or near universality of religious beliefs among peoples of the world. Appealing to the ubiquity of religious beliefs as evidence of the existence of God is known in philosophical theology as the *argument from common consent* (*consensus gentium*, in the language of the early Roman thinkers who first advanced it). Although Dostoevsky nowhere formally subscribes to this argument, he does suggest on several occasions that the evidence has force; he comes close to calling belief in God part of the "normal condition of humanity," just as he had said of the belief in immortality. He was, of course, painfully aware of the widespread *absence* of religious belief in modern societies, but he regarded that as an unnatural, diseased rather than normal condition. In healthy, pre-civilized societies, he wrote in a notebook, "God is the idea of collective humanity, of the masses, of *everyone*" (20:191; Dostoevsky's emphasis). And he suggests that even in modern societies the popularity of spiritualism is a manifestation of the *consensus gentium* concerning the reality of the supernatural.

A later notebook entry, addressed to an atheistic opponent, verges on an explicit endorsement of the argument from common consent: "Science cannot disdain the significance of religion among mankind, if only as a historical fact that is striking in its continuity and tenacity. The persistent, permanent conviction that mankind has about *contact with other worlds*[32] is also very significant, of course" (27:85; Dostoevsky's emphasis). Notably, there is no specific reference here to "God" as an entity or person, only to "other worlds," without indication of their character. In other passages, however, Dostoevsky goes somewhat further and links the argument from common consent also with infinity, in that it extends to the *eternity*—that is, infinity in the sense of timelessness—of human beings as participants in these "other worlds." Thus in *A Writer's Diary*, citing again the widespread existence of religion, he refers to "convictions that man is eternal, that he is not simply an earthly animal but is connected with other worlds and with eternity." "Always and everywhere," he adds, "these convictions were formulated in religion" (26:165).

To the extent, then, that Dostoevsky can be said to sympathize with, if not endorse, the argument from common consent, it appears to have for him no specifically theistic, much less Christian, content. It supports at best the existence of (and human participation in) other, nonearthly or immaterial worlds, one feature of which is eternity. The connection of these comments with his notebook "infinity" argument, of course, is the common reference not only to "other worlds" but to infinity, now extrapolated from space to time, in the sense that eternity as timelessness is a form of infinity. His interest in the argument from common consent, apparently, is simply that, like his argument from infinity, it provides evidence of an infinite, immaterial reality.

Still another set of texts relevant to Dostoevsky's reasoning about the existence of God are the very same texts in which he is arguing explicitly for *immortality*. Somewhat surprisingly, he appears to hold that the latter arguments are *at the same time* arguments for the existence of God. On more than one occasion he suggests that the reality of God and the reality of immortality are mutually dependent, so that support for one is support for the other. A close connection, at least, between the two is implied in Zosima's advice to Madame Khokhlakova in *The Brothers Karamazov*, which includes the assurance that through love she can become convinced of *both* the existence of God *and* the immortality of her soul (14:52). And in his actual arguments for immortality, he sometimes speaks as if God and immortality are equivalent concepts. Ivan Karamazov, for example, lumps the two together when he main-

32. There is a biblical ring to Dostoevsky's Russian expression *miry inye*, here translated "other worlds."

tains that the danger to moral character posed by the denial of immortality (the heart of his defense of the latter) extends also to the denial of God: immoralism, he asserts in concluding his argument, must be embraced by "each person . . . who believes neither in God nor in his own immortality" (14:65). Smerdyakov, taunting Ivan in their final meeting after the murder of the elder Karamazov, renders Ivan's immoralist thesis not as "there if no virtue if there is no immortality" but as "there is no virtue if there is no infinite God" (15:67), as if the two formulations were interchangeable. The strongest connection between the two concepts comes in Dostoevsky's letter to Nikolay Ozmidov, where, in presenting his arguments for immortality, he remarks parenthetically, "the immortality of the soul and God—*it's all the same, one and the same idea*" (30/1:10; emphasis added). If the two ideas are equivalent, then all arguments for immortality are also arguments for the existence of God.

But does it make any sense to say they are "the same idea?" If we have in mind a traditional religious, theistic idea of God, surely not: that conception, of a personal God who both created the universe and watches over it, has content far beyond the simple notion of the immortality of spirit, or in other words beyond eternal immaterial existence. But if we confine ourselves to what I believe Dostoevsky means *philosophically* by the term 'God', then his identification of the two, if not logically defensible, is at least understandable. For eternity—infinity as timelessness—and immateriality appear to be defining characteristics of God as Dostoevsky sparingly conceives of Him from a philosophical perspective. To the extent that arguments for immortality provide support for the existence of immortal spiritual souls, they establish the existence of the spiritual infinity that is God. For Dostoevsky, arguments for immortality and arguments for the existence of God are equally ways of establishing the reasonableness of the conclusion that such an infinity exists, and in that regard we may forgive him the exaggeration of calling the two notions "one and the same idea." This may also help to explain why he devotes so much attention to arguments for immortality, for they do double duty as also supporting the existence of a reality with two of the deity's defining characteristics—infinity and immateriality.

Those two characteristics do not, however, exhaust Dostoevsky's philosophical concept of God. For he had still another type of evidence on which to base knowledge of the existence and nature of God—evidence that to him must have been stronger than any other. This was the evidence of direct contact with the deity in personal religious experience.

Supposed immediate awareness of the divine has been advanced in various forms through the ages as an argument for the existence of God, generally known now as the *argument from religious experience*. According to this reasoning, some people, at least, have direct experiences of the divine that serve as undeniable evidence of its reality. In the face of such immediate evidence, the argument's supporters contend, it would be unreasonable (assuming that we can reasonably exclude the possibility of hallucination), indeed it would be absurd, to reject the reality of what is experienced, just as it would be absurd to reject the reality of what stands before one's eyes.

We know from Dostoevsky's own testimony that he had such religious experiences, principally in the ecstatic aura that preceded the epileptic seizures from which he suffered throughout his mature life. Furthermore it is clear from his own and others' accounts of those experiences that he considered them veridical. They are presumably what he was thinking of when he had Zosima say in *The Brothers Karamazov* that "we have been given a secret, mysterious sense of our living bond with the other world, with the lofty, higher world" (14:290).

Our only detailed firsthand account of Dostoevsky's mental state in the epileptic aura occurs in a transparently autobiographical passage in *The Idiot* where he is describing it as experienced by Prince Myshkin:

> [His] mind and heart were illumined with extraordinary light; all uneasiness, all his doubts, all anxiety were as if allayed at once, resolved into a kind of higher tranquillity, full of bright, harmonious joy and hope, full of reason [*razum*] and ultimate cause. . . . [There were] gleams and flashes of a higher perception [*samooshchushchenie*] and consciousness [*samosoznanie*] and thus of "a higher existence". . . . [There was] a feeling of fullness, of proportion, of reconciliation and ecstatic, prayerful fusion with the highest synthesis of life. . . . "At that moment," as he once said . . . "I come somehow to understand the extraordinary saying that *there will be no more time.*" (8:188–89; Dostoevsky's emphasis)[33]

Assuming for the moment that the "higher existence" mentioned may be equated with God, we may ask whether an experience of the sort Dostoevsky describes can qualify in any way as an "argument" for the existence of God, which implies that it is grounded in rational considerations of some sort. Is not

33. Although the Russian words translated "consciousness" and "perception" here and in the following passage have the prefix *samo* (self), they should not be taken to mean consciousness or perception of the self *simpliciter*. Dostoevsky is speaking of consciousness and perception of oneself as included in the "highest synthesis of life." The concluding clause—"there will be no more time"—is a reference to Revelations 10:6. Dostoevsky's statement in this passage that the experience is "full of reason [*razum*]" must be kept in mind in interpreting Prince Myshkin's statement in *The Idiot* that "the essence of the religious sense falls under no sort of reasonings [*rassuzhdeniia*]" (8:184). The Prince is referring to discursive processes of reasoning in the sense of *rassudok* rather than to the immediate grasp of truth by reason in the sense of *razum*.

the cited "higher perception" simply a mystical experience? Unquestionably it is such an experience, but as presented by Dostoevsky it does not exclude reason: he describes it as "full of reason." Significantly, the Russian word he uses here for reason is *razum*, the term for the epistemologically superior application of the rational faculty, comparable to the German *Vernunft*. For Dostoevsky the experience represents not an abandonment of reason but extraordinary access to its higher form. As he describes it, it corresponds to what philosophers have called "rational intuition"—the apprehension of a truth not on empirical grounds or as the result of a process of reasoning from premises to conclusions but as a direct, immediate act of the rational faculty.

Furthermore, and more germane to the question of argumentation, the mystical "higher perception" or rational intuition is not in itself a guarantee of the reality of what is perceived. For that, a process of judgment must take place to authenticate the "gleams and flashes" of the perception, as Dostoevsky recognizes full well. In the novel, Myshkin immediately raises the question of whether these experiences are simply illusory products of his epilepsy. But he decides that even if they were in fact prompted by his illness, their veracity can be established by a cognitive process:

> That this actually was "the highest synthesis of life"—of that he could not doubt or even entertain doubts. It was not as if at that moment he were having abnormal and unreal visions of some sort, as from hashish, opium, or wine, degrading reason [*rassudok*] and distorting the soul. *He could judge of that correctly after the attack.* These moments were purely and simply an extraordinary intensification of consciousness—if it is necessary to express the condition in a word—consciousness and at the same time perception, in the highest degree immediate. (8:188; emphasis added)

Myshkin's confidence in the correctness of his judgment may seem excessive, but the significant point for our purposes is that Dostoevsky acknowledges the need to "judge" the experience in the process of inferring a conclusion from it, a process in which, as in all rational argumentation, mistakes can be made. The experience itself may be mystical, but the judgment that it was not a matter of "abnormal and unreal vision of some sort" requires the operation of the rational faculty. Of the validity of his own experience Dostoevsky states that he "could not doubt," but the fact that he raises the issue and subjects the experience to judgment shows that he did regard it as susceptible to doubt.

A substantive question remains: did Dostoevsky regard the experiences in question as experiences of *God*? Much has been made of these passages in *The*

Idiot by interpreters of his thought. Reinhard Lauth, for example, uses them as the basis for a highly speculative formulation of the writer's religious epistemology and of his conception of God. Joseph Frank, on the other hand, judiciously points out that no specific religious doctrines (not even a generalized theism) are affirmed in the passage, and he raises the question of whether Dostoevsky himself actually saw a connection between the experience and his belief in God.[34] For our purposes, although in fact the passage does not explicitly mention God, it provides content that ties the experience firmly to a conception of God, though not so elaborate and articulated a conception as Lauth constructed.

First, it repeats the references to immateriality (a "higher existence," inaccessible to ordinary perception or awareness) and to infinity as eternity or timelessness ("there will be no more time") that are central to the other arguments. But, second, it goes beyond the other arguments by specifying further content that the experience discloses. In the experience as Dostoevsky describes there is, over and above the perception of "other worlds" and eternity, a euphoric consciousness of "the highest synthesis of life," and of his own inclusion in ("fusion with") that synthesis. The intense "consciousness" that he describes is not simply an awareness of self as such but an awareness of one's union with the all. Consistent with that description, though less specific, is an account of the aura that Strakhov says Dostoevsky gave him in conversation: "For a few moments," Strakhov reports Dostoevsky as saying, "I experience a happiness that is impossible in an ordinary state. . . . I feel a complete harmony in myself and in all the world, and this feeling is so powerful and so sweet that for a few seconds of such bliss one would give ten years of one's life, perhaps all of one's life."[35] Here the synthesis is described as a "harmony," but it is still one that is comprehensive and includes the individual.

For Frank, what Dostoevsky describes is simply an example of a common type of mystical experience in which "the personal ego is obliterated and fuses into a harmony with the cosmos," which is why Frank is reluctant to read the passage as presenting religious experience to support a belief in God.[36] Further grounds for pause may appear when we read Dostoevsky's description in *Demons* of a very similar mystical experience that he assigns to the atheist Kirillov. Like Myshkin, and using much the same language, Kirillov reports hav-

---

34. Lauth, *Die Philosophie Dostojewskis*, 431–42; Joseph Frank, *Dostoevsky: The Years of Ordeal, 1850–59* (Princeton, N.J.: Princeton University Press, 1983), 196–97.

35. *Polnoe sobranie sochinenii F. M. Dostoevskago* (St. Petersburg: Izd. A. G. Dostoevskoi, 1882–83), 1:214.

36. Frank, *Dostoevsky: The Years of Ordeal*, 196.

ing moments of almost unendurable joy in which he feels "the presence of an eternal harmony, completely achieved." Yet he is far from equating that harmony with God; he resists even calling it spiritual (10:450).

In the case of Dostoevsky himself, however, there are other considerations that suggest a close connection between his mystical experiences and the existence of God. Kirillov, blinded by materialism, may not have recognized the spiritual significance of his own experiences. But Dostoevsky labored under no such handicap.

For one thing, we have a report of an occasion on which he explicitly identified a comparable experience (though not in an epileptic aura) as a perception of God. According to Sofya Kovalevskaya, who as a child in the mid-1860s knew Dostoevsky when he was courting her older sister (after the death of his first wife), the writer told her that on one occasion, just as he was insisting to an atheist that God does exist, church bells rang out nearby. She asserts that he described his reaction as follows: "I had the feeling . . . that heaven had come down to earth and swallowed me up. I really perceived God and was permeated by Him. I then cried: Yes, there is a God!" Here not simply a "highest synthesis" but God Himself is said to be directly apprehended in the experience.[37]

Although Frank and others have questioned the reliability of Kovalevskaya's account,[38] it deserves a second look in light of what else, albeit little, we know about Dostoevsky's conception of the deity. There is only one passage in all of his writings in which he explicitly and directly speaks of the nature of God—namely, the same notebook entry of 1864, reflecting on the death of his first wife, that we examined above in the context of immortality. In that passage he describes God in the same terms he used for the object of his mystical experiences—that is, as a full "synthesis" of being:

> The nature of God is the direct opposite of the nature of man. Man, according to a great finding of science, goes from multiplicity to Synthesis, from facts to their generalization and comprehension. But the nature of God is different. It is *the full synthesis of all being*, contemplating itself in multiplicity, in Analysis. (20:174; emphasis added)

37. A. Dolinin, comp., *F. M. Dostoevskii v vospominaniiakh sovremennikov* (Moscow: Khudozhestvennaia literatura, 1964), 1:347. James L. Rice's exhaustive study of Dostoevsky's epilepsy—*Dostoevsky and the Healing Art: An Essay in Literary and Medical History* (Ann Arbor: Ardis, 1985)—touches at several points on the religious overtones sometimes present in an epileptic aura (10, 31, 68, 85, 207).

38. Frank, *Dostoevsky: The Years of Ordeal*, 196–97. Rice (*Dostoevsky and the Healing Art*, 84) supports the trustworthiness of Kovalevskaya's report.

On the basis of this parallel between Dostoevsky's religious experience and the general conception of the nature of God in the 1864 notebook, the statement reported by Kovalevskaya need not be considered an uncharacteristic leap from the experience to God. For the complete synthesis reached in the experience as he describes it in *The Idiot* is precisely the ontological characterization of God that he presented in his notebook. Thus the absence of the word 'God' from his description of the experience does not rule it out as intended to suggest the existence of God, broadly conceived.

From the evidence of this notebook passage, together with his other reflections on the existence of God considered in this section, I believe it is possible to sketch Dostoevsky's "philosophical" conception of God, meaning by that the conception of a supreme being whose existence can be comprehended and supported on reasonable grounds, as distinct from faith. The historical fact of "common consent," the infinity argument, and the arguments for immortality all provide support for the reality of an eternal (timelessly infinite) immaterial reality. Religious experience—which is not "faith" but a rationally defensible form of direct experience—powerfully confirms those conclusions and adds the critically important ontological characterization of God as the "full synthesis of being."

Beyond those broad features of the deity Dostoevsky does not go in seeking to conceive of God philosophically or find rational support for God's existence. I believe he regarded the theistic, personal traits of the Christian God, Creator of the universe and its providential ruler, to be beyond the ken of philosophical reasoning. They are the elements, rather, of a more robust, *religious* conception of God, resting entirely on faith. The God to whom one prays, who gave the world His Only Begotten Son and with Him a moral code, *can* be comprehended philosophically and approached rationally, but only as a supernatural, eternal synthesis of being; beyond that, His attributes are the stuff of mystery, revelation, and faith. Speaking, for example, of Christ as the ultimate test of the morality of one's own convictions, Dostoevsky adds, "but this is no longer philosophy, but faith" (27:56).

Actually the abstract, philosophical conception of God is rarely his main interest, even in a context such as the reflections on his wife's death, where he seems to focus on it. When he speaks in that text of the divine nature as being the "direct opposite" of human nature, we might expect the God presented there to be fully impersonal. Yet the reference to "contemplating" in the last sentence ("*the full synthesis of all being*, contemplating itself in multiplicity . . .") hints at a personal feature, and in a multitude of other passages throughout his writings Dostoevsky consistently goes beyond the philosophical conception to a religious conception of the deity as a supreme, eternal person, possessed of intellectual, volitional, and active capacities. From a religious standpoint Dostoevsky's God, for all His philosophical status as "universal synthesis," is a *person* who created nature and human beings, knows their needs, guides them providentially, issues commandments to them, hears their prayers, judges their actions, and pardons their transgressions. Dostoevsky's old Prince Sokolsky in *The Adolescent*, even in one of his skeptical moods, indicates that he prefers the personal conception of God to thinking of the deity "in the form of some sort of spirit flowing through creation, in the form of a liquid"—a parody of Dostoevsky's own philosophical conception; the Prince dismisses the abstract notion as "still more difficult to understand" than the idea of God as a person (13:31).

Dostoevsky found belief in the existence of God to be rationally supportable up to a point—the point at which God can be conceived philosophically as an infinite, otherworldly synthesis of being. But there is no rational support for the reality of God as *religiously* conceived—that is, as an omnipotent, personal creator and benevolent Father of mankind. Those are the attributes of God that humanize the deity, that give solace and hope. But no arguments, not even religious experience, can yield such a God; belief in His existence is entirely the province of faith.

Returning now to the question of answering Ivan in *The Brothers Karamazov*, the distinction between two conceptions of God may be helpful in understanding why Dostoevsky does not try in book 6 to present some direct refutation of Ivan's principal argument. Ivan, it will be remembered, had cried out against the injustice of a world in which innocent children suffer terrible agonies and death. The only explanation for these atrocities offered by defenders of the argument from design, he observed, is that somehow the overall harmony or well-being of the universe would not be possible without them; despite these evils, say the defenders, the world as it exists is, in Leibniz's memorable phrase, "the best of all possible worlds." Ivan refused to accept this explanation: " 'What kind of harmony is there, if it is hell? . . . And if the sufferings of children are part of the sum of sufferings needed to buy truth, then I affirm in advance that the whole of truth is not worth such a price. . . . They have priced harmony too dearly; we can't afford to pay so much for admission. And therefore I hasten to give back my entrance ticket' " (14:223).[39]

Ivan's version of the familiar "problem of evil" in philosophical theology alludes, without formal statement, to the typical appeal to the presence of evil in the world as an argument against the existence of an all-powerful and benevo-

---

39. See Victor Terras's discussion of Dostoevsky's possible indebtedness to Schiller in this connection, in *Reading Dostoevsky* (Madison: University of Wisconsin Press, 1998), 134–35.

lent Creator such as the Christian God. Popularly the argument is often stated in the form of a logical dilemma: If God were benevolent, He would have wished to create a world without evils such as the suffering of innocent children. And if He were omnipotent, He would have been capable of creating such a world. But these evils are present in the world. Therefore, either God is not benevolent or He is not omnipotent; in other words, the Christian God does not exist.

We might expect Dostoevsky to show some interest in the structure of atheistic arguments such as Ivan's, given his obvious desire to combat their conclusion. But he does not respond directly to Ivan's argument (or any specifically atheistic argument, for that matter) in the novel or elsewhere in his published writings or personal notebooks and letters. The novel itself, of course, may be viewed as an extended *literary* response to Ivan's position. Victor Terras has sensitively pointed out what he calls "counterarguments" to Ivan in the novel, including little Ilyusha's spiritually meaningful death, uplifting episodes such as "Cana of Galilee," and (the most effective, Terras believes) the ad hominem arguments by which Ivan himself is discredited as a person and a thinker.[40] But none of these is literally an argument against Ivan's *position* as such, which logically is not vulnerable to anecdotal descriptions of incidents or attacks on his character. And in general, there seems to be no evidence that Dostoevsky sought to "rationalize" or explain away the problem of evil at all. Why was he silent on the conceptual structure of so important a problem for him as the problem of evil?

A possible explanation for this failure to respond argumentatively to the problem, I suggest, is that Dostoevsky's conceptions of God made it unnecessary to do so. Given the two conceptions as I have sketched them, the problem of evil, however disturbing and however engaging dramatically, has no logical bearing on the question of God's existence. It is irrelevant to belief in God as Dostoevsky conceives the deity *philosophically*, for the object of that rationally supportable belief is an infinite, otherworldly synthesis of being, not a benevolent Creator who could be called into doubt by evidence of gross injustice in His handiwork. And it is irrelevant to God as conceived *religiously*—that is, as the Christian, theistic God—because the object of that belief is a being in whom one has faith regardless of supposed "evidence" to the contrary, or in other words against whom rational considerations do not prevail.

---

40. Ibid., 113–14. The British philosopher Stewart R. Sutherland, in a monograph devoted to careful analysis of Ivan's atheism and Dostoevsky's response to it in *The Brothers Karamazov*, also argues that the response must be approached as "an artistic picture" rather than a discursive refutation (*Atheism and the Rejection of God: Contemporary Philosophy and "The Brothers Karamazov"* [Oxford: Blackwell, 1977], 82).

Dostoevsky himself suggested as much in a letter to N. A. Lyubimov in which he wrote of Ivan: "My hero has chosen a theme that *in my opinion* is irrefutable: the senselessness of the suffering of children" (30/1:63; Dostoevsky's emphasis). It is no accident that the only direct response to Ivan's posing of the problem of evil in *The Brothers Karamazov* comes from Alyosha, who speaks simply of the need to believe in Christ and proclaim His mysterious justice: "Just thou art, O Lord, for thy ways have been revealed" (14:224).

Thus if I am right that two different conceptions of God have their place in Dostoevsky's metaphysical thinking, he could have countered the atheists' concerns about the problem of evil with a dilemma of his own: If God is conceived philosophically as an abstract, immaterial, infinite synthesis of being, then the existence of God is rationally arguable, but arguments based on anthropomorphic characteristics such as benevolence and providence are not germane to the issue. If, on the other hand, God is conceived religiously as an anthropomorphic being endowed with benevolence and providence, then the existence of God is not amenable to rational proof or disproof of any kind but is entirely a matter of faith. In either case, the problem of evil as an attempt to disprove God's existence has no bearing on the question. Positively, Zosima's "answer" to Ivan consists, on the one hand, in affirming the openness of human beings to the religious experience that reveals the God of the philosophers, and, on the other hand, in presenting in his own life a model of the intense faith and love that reveal the God of Christianity despite the undeniable evils of this world.

Faith and Reason

In this chapter I have examined the metaphysical framework within which Dostoevsky's philosophy developed. The bifurcation of reality into a "higher," more fundamental spiritual realm and a derivative, inferior material realm is characteristic of the dualistic ontology of Christianity, and it provided the conceptual structure within which Dostoevsky explored the nature of man as a compound being, a spiritual soul immersed in matter, a disjointed creature with roots in one world but stranded in another. The spiritual realm is the ground of reality and value for Dostoevsky, and for that reason his attention is concentrated on that realm, and above all on what for him were the two metaphysical questions of most profound human concern—the immortality of the human soul and the existence of God.

There is little in his writings to suggest a coherent philosophy of nature, in the sense of a systematic theory of the material world; that world as such held little philosophical fascination for him. He found it an amoral, loveless place, mute and blind to human concerns, devoid of human values. But there is also nothing to suggest that he saw the material world as either illusory or as hopelessly alogical and chaotic, alien to reason and order. As we shall see more fully in subsequent chapters, he accepted (though not without protest) the reality of observable facts and discoverable laws of nature. Though "much is hidden from us" in both the material and the spiritual worlds, he does not deny either an objective material reality or the efficacy of science in dealing with it empirically and rationally. In short, he was a metaphysical realist who accepted, with great regret, the objective, systematic impediments to spirit thrown up by the material world.

Because the rational devices of science and the observation of fact are applicable to the material world, there is a temptation to interpret Dostoevsky as confining them to that world and excluding them from the understanding of the spiritual realm. The temptation is encouraged by his own seeming condemnation of reason in spiritual contexts; he sometimes scornfully dismisses "science" in favor of "faith," as when he writes in a notebook for *Crime and Punishment* that "the calculations of arithmetic destroy, whereas spontaneous faith saves" (7:134). But the situation is not as clear-cut as the total banishment of reason and science from the spiritual world.

Admittedly, faith is for Dostoevsky the only source of perfect certainty concerning such spiritual truths as immortality and the existence of God. But as we have seen in this chapter, he also offers reasonable arguments for those conclusions, in the apparent conviction that such arguments, far from being out of place in the spiritual context, also provide support for the beliefs in question; he certainly thought that belief in immortality and God (in the less robust, philosophical meaning of the term) made rational sense. Some of the arguments, moreover, proceed from empirical premises about the objective, observable material world; typically, these are just the arguments that come to play in his fiction. Finally, none of his reasoning is based on purely subjective, utilitarian considerations of the sort often called "pragmatic."

And if one of his principal grounds for believing in the existence of God is personal religious experience, he describes even that experience as having a rational dimension and as reasonably distinguishable from hallucination. Reinhard Lauth acknowledges the rational component of religious experience as Dostoevsky conceived it and accepts such experience as a form of cognition. But Lauth elevates it to a hyperrational state he calls "the "superconscious" and appears to attribute greater cognitive power to it than I believe was intended by Dostoevsky, who actually says little about it beyond what has been quoted in this chapter. He made no claims to a profound or extensive revelation of reality through mystical experience, beyond the revelation of one's union with the eternal, spiritual synthesis of being.[41] The "much that is hidden from us" is on the whole inaccessible to us mystically as well as rationally. There is in Dostoevsky's metaphysics nothing remotely resembling the articulated conceptual structure of "the higher synthesis" that was erected by the speculative reasoning of his friend Vladimir Solovyov.

The spiritualism craze in Russian society in the 1870s interested Dostoevsky greatly, but he viewed the phenomenon as dangerous because of its "mystical" character. He was put off from the start, he wrote, by "the mystical sense of its doctrine" (22:127). Its "mystical significance," he went on, is "the most harmful thing there can be" (22:130). He did not indicate precisely what he meant by 'mystical' in this context, but his uses of the term were almost always pejorative, and there are enough hints in his writings to allow us to surmise that he would apply the term in a negative sense to the invocation or acceptance of any kind of supernatural power other than the Christian God. He accepts such Christian "mysteries" as the Incarnation, but he not only distances himself from "mysticism" ("I have not presented you with a single mystical idea" [24:256]), he also distances the Orthodox faith from it: "I define Orthodoxy," he wrote in a notebook, "not by mystical beliefs but by love of humanity, and I rejoice in this" (24:254). In A Writer's Diary he all but dissociated Orthodoxy from mysticism altogether: "In Russian, genuine Christianity, there is no mysticism at all; in it there is only love for humanity, only the image of Christ—at least that is the main thing" (23:130).[42] The Grand Inquisitor berates Christ precisely for His refusal to use the power of "miracle, mystery, and authority" to hold men in thrall (14:232). In general Dostoevsky saw little room for mystical vision except in the single case of the revelation of the higher synthesis of being.

Critics have tried to make Dostoevsky an irrationalist in metaphysics by suggesting that he believed reason to be on the side of atheism and materialism, both of which he detested, and to be antithetical to faith. In fact he believed

41. Lauth, Die Philosophie Dostojewskis, 319–22, 326–27. For an extreme case of imputing mystical doctrines to Dostoevsky, see the fanciful exposition of his "hidden theology" in Ellis Sandoz, Political Apocalypse: A Study of Dostoevsky's Grand Inquisitor (Baton Rouge: Louisiana State University, 1971), 66–72.

42. See also the corresponding entry at 24:264. For a comprehensive and insightful discussion of spiritualism in nineteenth-century Russia, see Maria Carlson, "No Religion Higher than the Truth": A History of the Theosophical Movement in Russia, 1875–1922 (Princeton, N.J.: Princeton University Press, 1993), 22–28.

that reason, too, is on the side of God and immortality, but that it is not immune to question and cannot provide certainty. God and immortality can be
supported by reasons, but the reasons are not unassailable.

Ironically, Dostoevsky's position on faith and reason in matters of religious
belief is in some ways similar to that of the Roman Catholic church he so despised. The church's canonical position as codified by St. Thomas Aquinas,
and affirmed with great emphasis by Pope John Paul II,[43] denies the incompatibility of faith and reason. Aquinas argued that some truths such as the existence of God are equally knowable by reason and by faith, but that the essence
of God and divine mysteries such as the Incarnation transcended reason and
were exclusively the province of faith. Dostoevsky held the same views concerning the consistency of the two (in their ideal form, at least), the possibility
of some rational knowledge of the divine, and the need to rely on faith beyond
the limits of reason.

There are, of course, differences as well. For one thing, the "God" whom
reason can know for Dostoevsky (what I have called his philosophical conception of God) is simply an eternal, spiritual principle of the synthesis of being,
not the intelligent creator inferred by Aquinas. The personal characteristics
Aquinas saw in his rationally provable God are for Dostoevsky matters of faith.
Furthermore, Aquinas believed his arguments to be rationally unassailable and
conclusive, whereas Dostoevsky was unwilling to invest such confidence in ratiocination concerning spiritual truths.

Much that has been said here about Dostoevsky's rejection of alogism appears to fly in the face of his dark, absurdist classic *Notes from Underground*,
which is sometimes considered his most important, if not his only, strictly
philosophical work. To judge the compatibility of the foregoing analysis with
that work, we must turn from the arena of ontology to another dimension of
Dostoevsky's lifelong search for an understanding of what it means to be
human.

43. See the papal encyclical "Fides et Ratio," issued on 15 October 1998.

CHAPTER 2

The Case against Rational Egoism

Notes from Underground (1864) was Dostoevsky's most sustained and spirited philosophical attack on the theory of human nature championed by Nikolay Chernyshevsky, Dmitry Pisarev, and other representatives of the materialistic, socially radical Russian intelligentsia in the third quarter of the nineteenth century—the theory later given the name 'Rational Egoism'.[1] Interpretation of his attack on the philosophy of these "Nihilists" (as he and others called them) has been clouded, however, by the fact that it is voiced in a work of fiction by one of the darkest, least sympathetic of all his characters—the nameless narrator and protagonist known as the Underground Man. Was this repellent creature speaking for Dostoevsky?

The Underground Man can easily be viewed as a sheer irrationalist whose rejection of Rational Egoism is a tortured emotional outburst with no logical credentials. Robert Louis Jackson, in his groundbreaking study of 1958, describes the Underground Man's thinking at one point as follows: "It is impossible to argue with the rationalists: reason is on their side. All that remains is irrationally to negate reason."[2] If those words were to be taken not simply as a moment in Jackson's rich analysis but as a comprehensive description of the Underground Man's attitude, it would be senseless to expect philosophically

---

1. Chernyshevsky is often credited with introducing the term 'Rational Egoism' (in Russian, *razumnyi egoizm*) for this nineteenth-century version of the eighteenth-century theory of "enlightened egoism"; see, for example, V. Prilenskii, "Razumnyi egoizm," in *Russkaia filosofiia: Malyi entsiklopedicheskii slovar'*, ed. A. I. Aleshin et al. (Moscow: Nauka, 1995), 435–36. In fact, however, the term itself is a later coinage that does not appear in any of Chernyshevsky's or Pisarev's writings.

2. Robert Louis Jackson, *Dostoevsky's Underground Man in Russian Literature* (The Hague: Mouton, 1958), 40.

nuanced arguments from him. And then we would have no grounds for thinking that Dostoevsky's own treatment of Rational Egoism went beyond sheer
emotional rejection.

Critics from Vasily Rozanov to Joseph Frank have debated the Underground Man's stance toward Rational Egoism and its relation to Dostoevsky's,
with no sign yet of a definitive resolution. Frank's discussion of the question,
presented in the third volume of his monumental literary biography of Dostoevsky, offers a helpful history of the dispute in addition to his own finely elaborated interpretation of the Underground Man as an irrational opponent of
Rational Egoism. Frank reads *Notes from Underground* as satire, and he contends
that the Underground Man is caught in an agonizing self-contradiction: intellectually, he *accepts* the basic premises of the Rational Egoists' outlook, such as
the denial of free will; but he finds, "despite the convictions of his reason,"
that he cannot live with the amoral and dehumanizing implications of those
premises, which strip human beings of moral responsibility.[3]

From a rational point of view, of course, rejection of the implications
should force the Underground Man to reject the premises, too (by the hoary
logical law of *modus tollendo tolens*), and indeed he does at times passionately
condemn them. But according to Frank these condemnations simply show the
depth of his predicament: his "intellectual acceptance" of Chernyshevsky's determinism is conjoined with "simultaneous rejection of it with the entire intuitive-emotional level of personality identified with moral conscience," causing
him to respond irrationally in a multitude of instances.[4] Frank's Underground
Man, then, is an intellectual disciple but an emotional critic of the Rational
Egoists. And he is triply an irrationalist: his thinking is mired in self-contradiction, he acts irrationally as a result, and his opposition to Rational Egoism has
not a rational but an "intuitive-emotional" basis.

But where does this leave Dostoevsky? Must we conclude that he, too, is
somehow suspended between acceptance and rejection of Rational Egoism,
and for that reason has created in *Notes from Underground* a dialogical equilib-
rium in which neither position is privileged? For Frank, certainly not. It follows from Frank's analysis that Dostoevsky himself, unlike the Underground
Man, is a fully *consistent* opponent of Rational Egoism, for that theory is the
target of the inverted irony at the core of his satire; "the more repulsive and
obnoxious he [the Underground Man] portrays himself as being," Frank

3. Joseph Frank, *Dostoevsky: The Stir of Liberation, 1860–1865* (Princeton, N.J.: Princeton University
Press, 1986), 320.
4. Ibid., 322.

writes, "the more he reveals the *true* meaning of what his self-confident judge [the Rational Egoist] so blindly holds dear."[5] And yet, if the only evidence of Dostoevsky's opposition to Rational Egoism is that he subjects it to satirical parody and depicts "intuitive-emotional" responses to it, we might well conclude that his own opposition to Rational Egoism, like the opposition Frank attributes to the Underground Man, cannot be considered "intellectual" or "rational."

This chapter will offer a reading of *Notes from Underground* from a different perspective, one that focuses on the philosophical significance of what the Underground Man says and does in opposition to Rational Egoism rather than on the tangled psychological dynamics of his stance or the literary aspects of Dostoevsky's satire. I am struck by a number of facts about the work that are not adequately accounted for in Frank's or other existing readings. For one thing, the Underground Man often appears to reject Rational Egoism directly and unambivalently, with no suggestion of violating some prior intellectual commitment.[6] Moreover, discursive arguments are discernible in the Underground Man's feverish monologue, and they are invariably directed *against* Rational Egoism, never in favor of it. Again, the "irrational" behavior that the Underground Man engages in, or reports having engaged in (including his fabled inertia and masochism), is often precisely the behavior that someone arguing against Rational Egoism might reasonably adduce as evidence to support his case. On the strength of these facts and others, I shall argue that the Underground Man, for all his supposed "intellectual" acceptance of Rational Egoism, is far more a critic of the theory than its disciple, and that his criticism is logically both well-developed and compelling.

In keeping with this reading, I shall try to show that part 1 of *Notes from Underground* is richer in logical structure than its highly emotive tonality and seemingly rambling form suggest. Let us grant that, as Frank contends, the Underground Man is in some sense committed, inconsistently, to the principles whose consequences he deplores; on the psychological and literary levels such inconsistency certainly provides Dostoevsky with the opportunity for a gripping, dramatic, and wickedly witty portrayal of his protagonist. Yet in the anguished retorts the Underground Man hurls at imagined followers of Chernyshevsky (the "gentlemen" he repeatedly addresses), and in his aberrant

---

5. Ibid. (Frank's emphasis).

6. See, for example, chapter 7 of part 1 of *Notes from Underground* (5:110–13). In this portion of the work in particular there is no evidence that the Underground Man agrees on *any* level with the premises of Rational Egoism.

behavior itself, he is in fact advancing a consistent, logically judicious, perfectly reasonable case against Rational Egoism. It is, moreover, a case to which Dostoevsky himself would subscribe—though only up to a point, as we shall see.

Dostoevsky, I am convinced, did not believe that the Rational Egoists had "reason . . . on their side" or that only an irrational response could be made to their theory. Rather, he invested the Underground Man with arguments against it that are logically responsive to its specific claims—arguments that, from a philosophical point of view, add up to a devastating rational critique of Rational Egoism.

Central to this philosophically oriented reading, which draws also on what we know and what we may reasonably assume about Dostoevsky's intellectual interests at the time of writing *Notes from Underground*, is an interpretation of the Underground Man as a confirmed egoist but not an egoist of the variety championed by Chernyshevsky and Pisarev.

An Egoist but Not a Rational Egoist

That Dostoevsky should make egoism the subject of a major work in 1864 comes as no surprise to anyone familiar either with tendencies in Russian literature at the time or with Dostoevsky's own earlier career, which reflected a continuing interest in the topic.[7] Egoism was a principal theme of one of his three addresses to the radically minded Petrashevsky circle in the late 1840s (he spoke, as he reported later, "*about the person* and *about human egoism*" (18:120; Dostoevsky's emphasis).[8] In his first novel, *Poor Folk* (1846), he treated "self-love" and the inability to put oneself in another's place as character defects, and in some of his stories of the 1840s and 1850s he created pointedly egoistic figures, such as Mr. M. in "A Little Hero" (published in 1857, but written in 1849), and Maria Aleksandrovna in "Uncle's Dream" (1859). In the latter work we find Dostoevsky already grappling with the distinction between egoism and altruism and the dialectic whereby the former is sometimes rationalized as the latter. A year later, he included "egoism" in a notebook list of topics under the heading "future critical articles" (20:153).

In the 1860s Dostoevsky's interest in the phenomenon of egoism was pow-

7. Caryl Emerson has pointed out to me the extent to which Russian writers from the 1840s to the 1860s were concerned with the problem of "self-love." The theme is evident, for example, in Herzen's *Who Is to Blame?*, Turgenev's *Rudin*, and Tolstoy's *Family Happiness* and *The Cossacks*.

8. The activities of the Petrashevsky circle and Dostoevsky's role in it are examined by J.H. Seddon in *The Petrashevtsy: A Study of the Russian Revolutionaries of 1848* (Manchester: Manchester University Press, 1985).

erfully fed by his conviction that a narrow focus on the ego or self—something he considered endemic in *Western* civilization—was a plague that increasingly threatened Russia. We know from many sources that he regarded the spread of egoism in his homeland as a direct consequence of Russia's Westernization and a prime moral, even mortal, danger. A tour through Europe in the summer of 1862 confirmed his negative opinion of the Western character, and in *Winter Notes on Summer Impressions* (published in 1863, one year before *Notes from Underground*) he gave his most explicit and critical analysis of the egoistic principle, virtually equating it with immorality; it is, he writes, "the personal principle, the principle of isolation, of intense self-preservation, of self-solicitousness, of the self-determination of one's own ego, of opposing this ego to all of nature and all other people as a separate, autonomous principle completely equal and equivalent to everything outside itself" (5:79). And just as such self-absorption was a cardinal moral failing, so the selfless love of others— to the point of self-sacrifice, if need be—was the height of moral nobility. In the same work Dostoevsky stated that a sign of the highest development of personality was "voluntary, fully conscious, and completely unconstrained self-sacrifice of one's entire self for the benefit of all." To be genuine, the giving of oneself cannot spring from any calculations of self-interest: "One must love," he insisted (5:79–80).

Given this attitude, we can imagine Dostoevsky's reaction when in the same year of 1863 the leader of Russian radical opinion, Nikolay Chernyshevsky, published his novel *What Is to Be Done?* in which he not merely endorsed "egoism" but made it the model of admirable individual behavior and the key to harmonious social relations.[9] Chernyshevsky's principal characters see themselves as complete egoists, claiming to be guided in their behavior by nothing but informed calculations of their own interests; at the same time, however, they bring great benefit to others and in general behave like paragons of virtue, thus exhibiting the magically benign effects of an "enlightened" or "rational" egoism. To Dostoevsky this picture must have seemed the grossest distortion of reality. These virtuous fictional creations were not the genuine, flesh-and-blood egoists whose growing presence in Russia he feared. Yet the doctrine the pseudo-egoists advanced—Rational Egoism—*was* a genuine danger, because by glorifying the self it could turn the minds of impressionable young people away from sound values and push them in the direction of a true, immoral, destructive egoism.

The hypothesis I wish to propose is that Dostoevsky set out in *Notes from*

---

9. Nikolai Chernyshevsky, *What Is to Be Done?* trans. Michael R. Katz (Ithaca, N.Y.: Cornell University Press, 1989).

Underground to create, in contrast to Chernyshevsky's sham egoists with their contrived goodness, the figure of a genuine, believable Russian egoist—an authentic, nonaltruistic, morally repugnant egoist, someone who by his person and his attitudes would show the reality of egoism in Russia as Dostoevsky had described it in the Western context in *Winter Notes*. We know that, before writing *Notes from Underground*, Dostoevsky had suggested to his brother Mikhail some topics that he thought would help to generate interest in their new journal, *Epokha* (Epoch): "An analysis of Chernyshevsky's novel and Pisemsky's," he wrote in late 1863, "would have a great impact and, the main thing, would serve our purpose" (28/2:57). We know, too, from direct echoes of *What Is to Be Done?* in *Notes from Underground*, that Dostoevsky had Chernyshevsky's work in mind at the time he was writing; the most obvious echoes are the Underground Man's references to the "Crystal Palace" (5:113, 120–21), the figure of the prostitute Liza in part 2, and above all the extended episode of bumping the officer on the Nevsky Prospekt (5:128–32).[10] We know, finally, that Dostoevsky believed novelists should strive to create characters that are both new and typical—characters not previously found in literature but representing significant human types in contemporary society.[11] My surmise, then, is that Dostoevsky used *Notes from Underground* to create such a character as part of an attack on the then-fashionable conception of egoism advanced by the Rational Egoists. This interpretation is consistent with Dostoevsky's enigmatic annotation in which he wrote that people such as his Underground Man "not only can but even must exist in our society, considering the circumstances under which it has generally been formed" (5:99).

The Underground Man displays all the earmarks of egoism (not Rational Egoism, but the real thing) as Dostoevsky had sketched it in *Winter Notes*. Unlike Chernyshevsky's gregarious heroes, the Underground Man isolates himself, festering in his corner with little social connection; he has lost contact with his Russian "soil," with the Russian people, even by and large with educated society. He carries what Dostoevsky in *Winter Notes* called "the self-determination of one's own ego" to the point of obsession. In solitude or in society he is "self-solicitous," preoccupied with his own ailments, concerns,

10. I believe that the Underground Man's request to the reader to "excuse the example from Roman history" (5:112)—he had been speaking of Cleopatra—is also an arch allusion to Chernyshevsky, who used several such examples in his chief philosophical work, "The Anthropological Principle in Philosophy" (1860). See the excerpts from that work in James M. Edie et al., eds., *Russian Philosophy* (Chicago: Quadrangle, 1965), 2:50–51.

11. This is confirmed by a great many comments in Dostoevsky's correspondence concerning his own work and that of other writers. See, for example, 28/1:311–12; 28/2:23; 29/1:19, 142, 232; 30/1:63, 68.

fears, choices, aims, intentions, and gratifications. But perhaps the deepest sign of the Underground Man's egoism, confirmed with full dramatic force in part 2 at the end of the story, is his inability to love, even when presented with an outpouring of love from another person. "She fully understood," he says despairingly of Liza, "that I was a vile person and, most importantly, incapable of loving her" (5:176).

That the Underground Man was not merely egoistic but morally reprehensible in general has not seemed obvious to some readers, who have cited as redeeming features his apparent search, at one point in part 1, for a moral ideal of community, and in part 2 his wish to evoke noble feelings in Liza and his tearful collapse into her arms.[12] But he announces himself as bad in the opening lines of the work ("I am a sick man . . . I am a wicked man [*zloi chelovek*]")—a point perhaps obscured for many readers of the work in English translation because most translators have used not the clearly ethical terms 'wicked' or 'evil' but the primarily psychological term 'spiteful' to translate the Russian *zloi*, which has both ethical and psychological connotations (5:99).[13] The Underground Man, looking back on his story in its closing pages, remarks that "here are *purposely* collected all the features for an anti-hero" (5:178; Dostoevsky's emphasis), and the essential truth of that statement can be shown by a catalogue of the moral deficiencies he exhibits: he is self-indulgent, malevolent, envious, vain, imprudent, inconsiderate, boastful, rude, domineering, sadistic, vengeful, cowardly, manipulative, inconsistent, impudent, ungrateful, lazy, stubborn, destructive, capricious, mendacious, tyrannical—and the list could go on, without ever including a single trait of Chernyshevsky's improbable heroes. It is convincing evidence of Dostoevsky's artistry that he could create a figure with such a farrago of moral flaws who is yet more believable than the heroes of *What Is to Be Done?*

But of course the Underground Man is not a melodrama villain; he would not be a believably wicked human being if he were a caricature of evil. Dostoevsky was convinced that human depravity is ordinarily not so profound as to extinguish all conscience and all recognition of morality. Yet he portrays the Underground Man as someone who did not follow and could not even adequately conceptualize the promptings of conscience to which he, like all human beings, was subject. The Underground Man does display a murky awareness of moral ideals in chapter 10 of part 1, where he speaks of his desire

---

12. See, for example, Frank, *Dostoevsky: The Stir of Liberation*, 329; and Robert Louis Jackson, *Dialogues with Dostoevsky: The Overwhelming Questions* (Stanford, Calif.: Stanford University Press, 1993), 263.

13. See the discussion of this point by Richard Pevear and Larissa Volokhonsky in the foreword to their translation of *Notes from Underground* (New York: Vintage, 1993), xxii–xxiii.

for a social edifice more worthy than the "chicken coop" offered by the radicals. But in the heavily censored text of that chapter (more on this later) there is no indication of what a better structure might be, and he does not rise above an egoistic approach to it, calling it "my wanting" (*moe khotenie*) and "my desire" and insisting on his own right to accept or reject whatever definitions of it are proposed (5:120). He remains to the end a bad person who would like to be good—but only on his own, egoistic terms. In the last chapter of part 1, as he contemplates the effort of going on to write the narrative that forms part 2, he muses: "Writing things down really looks like work. They say that work makes a person good and honest. Well, here's at least a chance" (5:123). Though he did not succeed in becoming good, he sometimes saw it as a desideratum and a possibility.

There is more to the Underground Man, however, than his egoistic, morally repugnant nature. He is also an exponent of philosophical views, and in particular a passionate debater against Rational Egoism. Dostoevsky, I believe, realized that in addition to fashioning a *genuine* egoist he could use his new character to demonstrate conceptually, and not simply through the example of his attitudes and behavior, what is wrong with the theory of *Rational Egoism*. By making the Underground Man an egoist but one who has serious doubts about the teaching of Chernyshevsky and company, Dostoevsky was free to use him as a critic of their theory, and in that way he was able to bring together both personal and conceptual refutations in a neat synthesis of image and argument.

The Underground Man, as a child of his time, was of course familiar with the ideas behind Rational Egoism; perhaps, as Frank contends, he could not entirely free himself from their lure. Certainly none of his arguments were directed against *egoism* as such. Rather, he criticized the particulars of *Rational Egoism* from a position that he considered authentically egoist. Let us proceed, then, to an analysis of the Underground Man's case.

The Two Sides of Rational Egoism

Critics often overlook the logical density and structure of the Underground Man's argument in part 1, not only because they underestimate Dostoevsky's philosophical skills but because they fail to analyze what the Underground Man was arguing against. The Rational Egoism of Chernyshevsky and his followers was a relatively simple theory, but it was not quite so simple as critics maintain when they reduce it to a formula such as "people always act to benefit themselves." It was composed of disparate elements, though even its champions did not always make that clear; indeed, they did not explicitly formulate Rational Egoism as a structured "theory" (in part because of censorship), though their writings presupposed it at every turn. Dostoevsky, to his credit, appears to have understood the architecture of the theory, and his understanding is reflected in the complexity of the Underground Man's response to it. To follow that response, it is essential to reconstruct the elements of the theory as Chernyshevsky and Pisarev expressed them in the early 1860s.[14]

Coexisting somewhat uneasily in the thinking of the Rational Egoists were a descriptive thesis and a normative (prescriptive) thesis—a view of how human beings actually behave and a view of how they ought to behave. What is usually meant by the expression "Rational Egoism" is the two theses together, along with the assumptions on which they rest.

The descriptive side of Rational Egoism was a deterministic theory of human motivation that is sometimes called "psychological egoism." The Rational Egoists, denying free will, contended that human beings are necessitated by their nature to act as they do, and that their choices are always governed by their own interests. Chernyshevsky and Pisarev were sufficiently observant, however, to note that people sometimes appear, at least, to act so as to benefit not themselves but others, and even that they sometimes act in a way that is clearly damaging to their own interests (whether benefiting others or not). Cases of the first kind, the Rational Egoists believed, were easy to explain away: on closer examination, we find that the act that benefited others was "really" undertaken to benefit *oneself;* I help you, for example, because doing so pleases me, and the personal gratification is my motivating benefit and my *only* motive; were it not for that, I would never perform the action. Chernyshevsky argued that all so-called "altruistic" acts turn out on analysis to be "based on the thought of personal interest, personal gratification, personal benefit; they are based on the feeling that is called egoism."[15]

Cases of the second kind (damaging oneself) are more difficult, and to accommodate them the Rational Egoists were forced to qualify the simple formula: they admitted that people do at times harm their own interests, but argued that they never do so in full knowledge of better alternatives and how to achieve them. They do so, rather, through ignorance of their own best interests, or through an uninformed, unthinking, or irrational choice of means to promote those interests, or because of objective circumstances that preclude

14. For a fuller discussion of their views and selections from their writings, see Edie, *Russian Philosophy*, 2:3–108. Although there were significant differences of outlook between Chernyshevsky and Pisarev, both of them endorsed the principles of Rational Egoism as reconstructed here.

15. Ibid., 2:49.

better alternatives. In any event, people always act in the way they *think* will provide them personally the greatest benefit (or the least harm) under the circumstances. This is the formula that best captures psychological egoism as Chernyshevsky and Pisarev conceived it. They believed that human beings, controlled by causal influences, are constitutionally incapable of acting contrary to their own *perception* of their self-interest.

Psychological egoism formed the supposedly "scientific" foundation of Rational Egoism—scientific because it expressed the "natural law" that people invariably act in accordance with what they think are their own best interests. But the Rational Egoists were not content with psychological description. Despite the loudly expressed antipathy to all "morality" and "ideals" that was a hallmark of the "Nihilists," they did not hesitate to make ethical discriminations themselves and urge them on others. The ethical content of works such as Chernyshevsky's *What Is to Be Done?* was in fact a rich stew of moral imperatives: calculate your real interests, educate yourself, free yourself of encumbering traditions and customs, be active and energetic in pursuing your interests, work for whatever social changes are needed to promote them, beware of distracting emotions, put off immediate gratification for greater future gains—in short, be relentlessly rational in pursuing your real interests. Chernyshevsky praises his heroine's conniving mother, Maria Aleksevna, as "morally speaking . . . better than most" because she so effectively promoted her own real interests within the limits set by her environment.[16] Thus to their description of human behavior the Rational Egoists added a normative thesis, in the form of their own version of what some philosophers have called "ethical egoism." We may summarize it as the prescription that people *ought* to act in the way that *really will* provide them personally with the most benefit (or the least harm)—that is, they should act in accordance with their own real best interests (or their "true needs," as the Rational Egoists often expressed it).

The difference between perception and reality is the crux of the matter: through ignorance, irrationality, or the constraint of circumstances I may *perceive* my best interests or needs to be different from what they really are. It is the task of personal and social reform, according to the Rational Egoists, to make perceptions of interests coincide with genuine interests and to arrange society so that the latter can be promoted. Once people have been educated to know what their real interests are and how best to achieve them, and once society has been restructured to allow their achievement, the "natural law" of psychological egoism guarantees that people will act rationally to promote them.

The predictability of human behavior implicit in the "fact" of causal deter-

16. Chernyshevsky, *What Is to Be Done?* 169.

minism makes it possible on this basis, the Rational Egoists maintained, to fashion society so that it provides for the full satisfaction of the real needs of everyone. Chernyshevsky and Pisarev were convinced that a society of perfect egoists, all seeking their own best interests, would not be anarchic or torn by conflict. For they assumed—and this was a highly important presupposition of Rational Egoism—that the *genuine* interests of all people are harmonious and hence jointly satisfiable. In fact, a truly "rational" egoism, as Pisarev in particular insisted, is functionally equivalent to altruism: "The personal benefit of new men [i.e., the new, *rational* egoists] coincides with the benefit of society, and their selfishness contains the broadest love of humanity."[17]

The puzzles and questionable assumptions lurking in this effort to combine psychological and normative egoisms into a coherent theory are of course numerous, and the radical writers never adequately addressed them. Psychological egoism, for example, entails that whatever an agent chooses was necessitated by antecedent causes; the agent could not have chosen otherwise. But if that is so, what is the point of offering also a normative thesis—a thesis concerning what *should* have been chosen? It might seem that the problem is avoided because the descriptive thesis is phrased in terms of *perceived* interests and the prescriptive thesis in terms of *real* interests; but it is still the case that "oughts" are being addressed to human beings who are conceived as governed by universal laws and hence cannot act otherwise. Perhaps the Rational Egoists failed to recognize the problem because they tacitly assumed (unjustifiably, of course) that the revolutionaries who would lead the way in rational action—who would obey the imperatives to act vigorously, educate themselves and others, and remold society—were somehow immune from causal necessitation, just as the Russian Bolsheviks seem to have excluded themselves from the iron necessities of Marx's economic determinism.

Dostoevsky, on the other hand, appears to have been fully aware of the complexities of Rational Egoism and of the problems created by the exclusion of freedom of the will from its theoretical structure. The Underground Man addresses both the descriptive and the normative theses and rejects them both, along with their supporting assumptions.

The Underground Man and Psychological Egoism

The Underground Man subjects psychological egoism—the descriptive side of Rational Egoism—to a withering critique. He does not counter the argu-

---

17. Dmitry Pisarev, "Thinking Proletariat," trans. R. Dixon, in Edie, *Russian Philosophy*, 2:108.

ments purporting to show that "altruistic" acts are really selfish, but we can hardly expect him, as an egoist himself, to object to that point. He is concerned, rather, to show what egoistic action really consists in, and he is convinced that it is not simply a matter of responding mechanically to perceived interests. True egoism is something quite different from that, he believes, and from the very first lines of *Notes from Underground* he is engaged in demonstrating that people do not always (or even typically) take action for the sake of promoting what they themselves believe to be their own best interests (except in the case of one very peculiar "interest" not anticipated by the Rational Egoists, as we shall see). The Underground Man's argument takes two forms, direct and indirect.

In direct refutation of psychological egoism, the Underground Man offers observations of his own and others' behavior. Although he believes himself to be ill and respects doctors, he does not consult them (5:99). Although he is convinced that living in Petersburg is both too expensive and damaging to his health, he remains in Petersburg (5:101). These cases of "inaction" on his part are evidence from his own experience that people do not always act to promote their own perceived best interests. And lest anyone doubt the generalizability of that personal experience, he proceeds in chapter 7 of part 1 to claim evidence on a far grander scale:

> What are we to do with the millions of facts showing that people *knowingly*, that is, fully aware of their real advantage, have put it aside and rushed off onto another road, a risk, a chance, not forced to do so by anyone or anything, but just as if they simply did not want the indicated road, and stubbornly, willfully burst onto another one, difficult, absurd, trying to find it practically in the dark[?] (5:110; Dostoevsky's emphasis).

It is not unusual, he contends, to see someone who acts "against the laws of reason [*rassudok*], against his own advantage—well, in a word, against everything" (5:111). The spirit of rebellion noted in these observations will concern us later; but whatever the ultimate explanation for such conduct, the Underground Man obviously believes that there is an abundance of evidence contradicting psychological egoism.

But he does not limit himself to explicit rejection. Much space in *Notes from Underground* is taken up with a kind of indirect argument from the example of his own egoistic condition, which does not lend itself to analysis in terms of "best interests" and which thus tacitly calls into question the value of using such terms in the attempt to understand human behavior. In the early stages, at least, of his egoistic self-absorption as described in part 1, *he generally has no opinion as to what his "best interests" are;* only in a few cases does he suggest having such an opinion—and then, as we saw, he proceeds to violate the supposed interests. In general (until later in part 1!) he simply *has no* perceived best interests; he does not know *what he thinks are his best interests,* and that circumstance obviously vitiates the psychological egoist's claim to trace all behavior to such thoughts.

His condition is one of perpetual reflection on his own reactions, motives, and behavior. This he calls his "heightened consciousness" (5:102–4)—a state of obsessive, anguished introspection, quite different from the complacent single-mindedness of Rational Egoists such as Chernyshevsky's heroes, who were men and women of action. Although this "heightened" consciousness is in one sense pathological, the close and sustained self-examination that it entails is revelatory in that it discloses to him still other faults of Rational Egoism as a theory of human behavior.

Specifically, his "heightened consciousness" brings home to him his freedom as a conscious being—the free choice that Chernyshevsky and Pisarev had rejected. He finds that he cannot be "determined" to act by any particular perception, whether of his own interests or anything else. This leads him into meditations on the indeterminate identity of the conscious being—meditations that twentieth-century existentialist philosophers took as signs that Dostoevsky was an early champion of their philosophical orientation. Proto-existentialist or not, for our purposes the Underground Man's lamentations about his inability to *become* anything, to have a determinate identity, show that he finds nothing on the basis of which to fix *his* best interests: if he cannot define himself, how can he determine *his* best interests?

It is in this regard that the Underground Man's predicament, facing the open field of choice as a free conscious being, makes him a living argument against psychological egoism. His inaction, unlike that of the hypothetical ass of medieval philosophy ("Buridan's ass") who starved to death poised between two equally attractive bundles of hay, is not the result of opposing deterministic influences that are so perfectly balanced that they cancel each other out; it is a result of there being no determining factors at all—no "primary causes," as he calls them (5:108–9). Where he does act, it is not to promote any "best interests": it is simply to express his own will or caprice. His egoism, in other words, is fundamentally an egoism of personal *will* rather than personal *interests,* and it is this conception of egoism, I believe, that he is counterposing to the radicals' thesis of psychological egoism.

But is that the end of the notion of "best interests" in *Notes from Underground*? No, for the Underground Man puts new life into the notion in the later chapters of part 1 as he turns his attention to the normative or ethical side of Rational Egoism—the side that proclaims how people *ought* to act: namely, that they should act in accordance with what really *is* in their own best interests, the assumption being that doing so will maximize both social and individual well-being. The Rational Egoists framed their normative thesis, too, in terms of "best interests," and by a stunning conceptual shift the Underground Man shows that the Rational Egoists' use of the concept is inadequate in that context, too, though for quite a different reason.

The Underground Man and Ethical Egoism

The Underground Man's rejection of the normative thesis does not, of course, stem from any reluctance to entertain ethical prescriptions. He makes it abundantly clear that he views human beings as fit subjects for moral imperatives. But he finds a fundamental flaw in the normative stance of the Rational Egoists.

The shift in the Underground Man's argumentation beginning in chapter 7, as he takes up the normative thesis, results from a decision to give psychological egoism the benefit of the doubt. Although he is convinced that human behavior is not accurately described by the thesis that people act in accordance with what they think are their own best interests (for their own "advantage," as he puts it), he is willing for the sake of argument to adopt the vocabulary of psychological egoism and consider what the implications would be if it were true. Suppose we say that people do always choose to act in accordance with their perceived best interests or advantage—what would be the consequences for them and for social organization? The Underground Man's answer is an effective use of the same logical strategy of reductio ad absurdum that Dostoevsky employed in arguing for the immortality of the soul.

In the Rational Egoist ideology, as we have seen, the consequences of pursuing one's perceived best interests are wholly benign once people have been educated to *know* their true interests and to pursue them rationally, and once society has been reordered to make that pursuit possible. People's true interests or needs are set by their biological and social natures; these interests follow laws of nature, and hence they can be known with precision by the sciences. Furthermore, human behavior, because it flows from perceived interests and there is no free will, is *predictable* in relation to these true interests: we can be sure that people will recognize their own best interests as science reveals them, and we can be sure that they will pursue those interests if permitted to do so by social arrangements. Finally, science reveals that the true interests or needs of everyone are harmonious and mutually satisfiable, so that a perfect social order can be constructed on their basis. Pisarev, for example, contended that there is a fundamental natural need in all people to engage in socially useful labor; in such a case, surely, a society of harmonious mutual cooperation can flourish.[18]

The Underground Man's reflections, however, have prepared him for a radically different answer to the question of real interests or advantage. He begins by questioning the Rational Egoists' conviction that they know what this advantage is, at least to the extent of knowing that it is something on which a utopian social order could be founded. "What is advantage?" he asks. "Will you really take it upon yourself to define with perfect accuracy just what human advantage consists in?" (5:110). Next, he raises the possibility that this advantage, once known, might prove to be something not harmonizing but unmanageable, something that disrupts classifications and predictions and cannot serve as a foundation for social bliss (5:110–11). Finally, he argues that there is in fact such a disruptive, recalcitrant chief advantage, and that it is what everyone needs more deeply than anything else—namely, the exercise of free choice, action according to one's own independent will:

> Man, always and everywhere, whoever he might be, has loved to act as he wants, and not at all as reason [razum] and advantage command him to; and one can want even against one's own advantage. . . . One's own voluntary, free wanting [khoten'e], one's own caprice, even the wildest, one's own fancy, though inflamed sometimes to the point of madness—all this is that same, omitted, most advantageous advantage, which does not fall under any classification and by which all systems and theories are constantly sent flying to the devil. (5:113)

Human beings, on this view, are fundamentally willful creatures who are moved to defy reason, common sense, and the expectations of others in order to express their own wills. This "most advantageous advantage" cannot be assigned a relative weight in some system of ranked advantages, because it will be pursued, if necessary, contrary to *all* other advantages. Free human beings will risk everything, face any danger, and knowingly damage themselves in order to assert their freedom.

Obviously this insistence on willful behavior is a fatal obstacle to the creation of a utopian social order such as the Rational Egoists had in mind. Even if provided with all other benefits but free choice, in the most rationally ordered of societies, individuals will insist on asserting their independence, at the cost of destroying the system.

18. Ibid., 2:97.

I, for example [the Underground Man goes on], would not be in the least surprised if suddenly, for no reason at all, in the midst of the universal future reasonableness, some gentleman should appear . . . [and], setting arms akimbo, should say to us all: "Well, gentlemen, how about knocking all this reasonableness to dust with one good kick, simply in order to send all these logarithms to the devil and live once again according to our own foolish will!" (5:113)

And the Underground Man is confident that this rebel would find followers.

Translating the Underground Man's arguments into the language of Rational Egoism, we can reformulate the normative thesis. If the Rational Egoists wish to say that people *should* act in accordance with their own real best interest, and we find that this best interest consists in free choice, then they are saying no more than that people should act according to their own free will. But of course the Rational Egoists would not be satisfied with that formulation, because it conflicts with their deterministic notions of human behavior and their dreams of building a well-ordered society for predictably acting human beings; the Rational Egoists' prescription was based on the hypothetical imperative that people should act in accordance with their real best interests *so as to achieve happiness in a properly structured society*—but that is far from what the new formulation provides. The implicit conclusion of the Underground Man's reductio argument, then, is that the Rational Egoists cannot subscribe to the theory they themselves have advocated, once the real content of that theory is clarified.

In effect the Underground Man has set before the Rational Egoists a daunting dilemma. If we *exclude* free choice from our list of advantages to be considered in explaining human motivation, then Rational Egoism is descriptively false as a theory of behavior; for people often act contrary to all *other* perceived advantages, simply in order to express their freedom. If on the other hand we *include* freedom in the list of advantages, then we might consider Rational Egoism descriptively true (people do always seek their perceived advantage—freedom), but it will not be *normatively* acceptable to its own champions. For free choice is the greatest advantage, and the Rational Egoists would not be willing to accept the prescription that people should always act in accordance with their own free will. In *either* case, the Rational Egoists would have to admit that human action is radically unpredictable and that their program is doomed to failure.

To escape the horns of this dilemma, a Rational Egoist would be required to modify his stance drastically. He might, for example, admit that free will *is* a genuine capacity of human beings, but deny that its expression is mankind's "most advantageous advantage," or what brings the greatest real good to individuals. What people truly need, he might maintain, is to be fed, clothed, housed, and made content. This is, of course, precisely the stance taken later, in *The Brothers Karamazov*, by the Grand Inquisitor, who condemns Christ for having burdened humanity with free choice and claims that the greatest benefit to people is to be *relieved* of this freedom (14:230–34). The Underground Man is not yet the monomaniacal Grand Inquisitor; he is a less self-assured and far less ambitious egoist.

The Underground Man and Dostoevsky

Such is the Underground Man's reasoned case against Rational Egoism. Simply as a fictional product, it shows the extent of Dostoevsky's philosophical acumen, which deserves greater respect than it usually receives. But from the point of view of philosophical *convictions*, the question remains as to whether the Underground Man's case is also Dostoevsky's, in the sense of being a set of arguments to which Dostoevsky himself would subscribe. I believe that the interpretation of the Underground Man as an egoist is helpful in answering this question. We cannot answer it, however, by remaining within the fictional world of the Underground; the question simply makes no sense in that world, for Dostoevsky is not one of its inhabitants. But, keeping in mind the character and expressed views of the Underground Man, we can approach the question by going outside the work to draw on evidence of the writer's own convictions, as distinguished from the convictions he attributes to others in a fictional setting.

There is no doubt that Dostoevsky shared the Underground Man's opposition to psychological egoism (the descriptive side of Rational Egoism). Psychological egoism as advanced by Chernyshevsky and Pisarev rested on a denial of free will, whereas Dostoevsky repeatedly voiced his disagreement with the deterministic view of human action; his essay entitled "Environment" in *A Writer's Diary*, for example, makes clear his implacable opposition to any theory that, by stripping individuals of free choice, also relieves them of moral responsibility (21:13–23). Virtually all of his writings, too—his other fiction as well as his nonfiction—contain evidence of action that simply does not fit the mold of "perceived best interests" into which the Rational Egoists sought to force all human behavior. The characters who people Dostoevsky's stories are notoriously either ignorant of their own interests and motives, or hopelessly ambivalent, or captious, or prone to spiteful and malicious acts from which they expect no benefit to themselves—all situations that cannot be accommodated by psychological egoism. Given that the Underground Man's case

against the theory is entirely consistent with what we know about Dostoevsky's view of human beings from his other writings, there is no reason to
withhold ascription of that case to the artist who conceived it.

On the subject of freedom, moreover, Dostoevsky would agree with the
Underground Man that it is not only a fact of human nature but a fact of profound importance. In insisting that a human being is not an organ stop or a
piano key, the Underground Man was reflecting Dostoevsky's own firm belief
in the special character of human action as opposed to the law-governed
processes of nature; a fundamental idea of Christianity, Dostoevsky wrote in *A
Writer's Diary*, is "the acknowledgment of human personality and its freedom
(and therefore also its responsibility)" (23:37). His rejection of what he calls
"the doctrine of the environment" in *A Writer's Diary* is a protest, like the Underground Man's in both substance and passion, against the deterministic theory of human behavior: that doctrine, he writes, "reduces the individual to
complete impersonality, relieves him of all personal moral duty and all independence, reduces him to the foulest slavery imaginable" (21:16).

Furthermore the Underground Man's awareness of the brute, irrational
force of the human drive for free expression was shared by Dostoevsky, as we
know from his earlier observations of the behavior of his fellow Siberian prisoners. In *Notes from the House of the Dead* he speaks of the convicts' efforts to
show that they have more power and freedom than is supposed; he describes a
prisoner's violent outburst as resulting solely from "the anguished, convulsive
manifestation of his personality, the instinctive longing for his self, the desire to
assert himself, to assert his humiliated personality, a desire appearing suddenly
and reaching the point of malice, fury, the clouding of reason, fits, and con-
vulsions" (4:67).[19] This description is echoed in the Underground Man's prediction that under extreme circumstances an individual will "deliberately go
mad" in an effort to demonstrate his freedom (5:117).

Finally, there can be little doubt that the very understanding of egoism personified by the Underground Man—egoism as the glorification of self-will
rather than the maximization of personal advantage—is the understanding to
which Dostoevsky himself adhered. We saw the central place occupied by
"the self-determination of one's own ego" in his analysis of the egoistic principle in the West. In molding his fictional Russian egoist in *Notes from Underground*, he powerfully emphasized this self-determination by raising it to the
level of an absolute. The Underground Man absolutizes freedom of the will:
despite an occasional glimmer of conscience he in fact observes no standard

19. Robert Louis Jackson explored the parallels between the two works in *The Art of Dostoevsky:
Deliriums and Nocturnes* (Princeton, N.J.: Princeton University Press, 1981), 159–70.

other than his own whim—his "own foolish will"—so that for him free choice becomes a value limited by nothing outside the agent. He rhapsodizes over even the most absurd and self-destructive expressions of free choice. The celebration of unbounded willfulness that Dostoevsky assigns to his fictional egoist is a clear indication of his own understanding of the essence of egoism.

Where Dostoevsky parts company with the Underground Man, of course, is in the appraisal of this egoistic insistence on boundless freedom. For all the importance of free choice in Dostoevsky's worldview, when the Underground Man proceeds to the normative dimension of Rational Egoism and character-izes freedom itself as man's "most advantageous advantage," we cannot assume that he is still echoing Dostoevsky's own convictions. From our knowledge of Dostoevsky's Christian value system, which will be discussed further in the next chapter, we can be sure that for him man's "most advantageous advan-tage" lies not in free choice as such but in the free acceptance of Christ and His moral message. The normative stance of the Underground Man, far from co-inciding with Dostoevsky's, illustrates the evils of a freedom unstructured by higher values; the Underground Man's egoism is the perversion of a distinctive and precious human capacity by exempting it from all spiritual authority.

For Dostoevsky, the human will transcends natural law but not moral law. The universe of human choice is subject to the moral pattern of Christ's teach-ing, which centers on love of one's neighbor and hence prescribes altruistic, not egoistic behavior. Dostoevsky's description in *A Writer's Diary* of what he calls "the Russian solution" to Europe's (and humanity's) problems in his day neatly summarizes his rejection of the unruly freedom preached by the Under-ground Man:

> In the present shape of the world people think of freedom as license, whereas genuine freedom consists only in overcoming the self and one's will so as in the end to achieve a moral state such that always, at every moment, one is the real master of oneself. . . . The very highest freedom is . . . "sharing everything you have and going off to serve everyone." If a person is capable of that, is capable of overcoming himself to such an extent—is he, after that, not free? This is precisely the highest manifestation of the will! (25:62)

Dostoevsky, as we know, had included in chapter 10 of part 1 of *Notes from Underground* a Christian disclaimer—he called it "the main idea" of part 1—to the Underground Man's apotheosis of personal will, but it was unaccountably struck out by the censors. "Where I mocked everything and sometimes blas-phemed *for appearances*—it was permitted," he wrote in astonishment to his brother Mikhail; "but where I concluded from all of that the need for faith and

Christ—it was prohibited" (28/2:73; Dostoevsky's emphasis). He was distraught because he believed that without explicit presentation of "the main idea" the chapter was left disjointed and self-contradictory. It would have been better, he lamented, not to print it at all than to print it in its mutilated state. He did not explain what he found self-contradictory in it, but we may assume he thought that the Underground Man's vague moral yearnings in that chapter were unexplained without development of "the need for faith and Christ," and that they clashed with the immoral character he had given the Underground Man.

Ironically, the "swinish censors," as he called them in his letter to Mikhail, may have helped him remain true to his artistic vision. In fashioning the Underground Man as a consummate egoist, passionately devoted to his own caprice, Dostoevsky could not at the same time convincingly impute to him developed Christian convictions, and of course he could not insinuate such convictions in his own voice without a jarring authorial intrusion into the Underground Man's first-person narrative. Dostoevsky made no attempt in subsequent editions of *Notes from Underground* to restore the excised "main idea"— but neither did he drop the chapter. We may speculate that he came to accept the glimmers of moral conscience attributed to the Underground Man in what remained of chapter 10 as not really inconsistent with an egoistic character, so long as the Underground Man did not either live up to them or even articulate them clearly. In any event, having used his fictional egoist effectively to discredit the theory of Rational Egoism, Dostoevsky reserved direct attacks on egoism itself for later works.

Beyond the Underground Man: Identifying "Best Interests"

In *Notes from Underground*, Dostoevsky identified human "best interests" exclusively with freedom, as part of a negative, reductio argument designed to show the absurdity of the Rational Egoist's case. He soon had an opportunity, however, to attack that case from another direction, by arguing that there is more to the notion of what is best for human beings than either the Rational Egoist or his underground opponent imagines. In a witty polemical fantasy entitled "Mr. Shchedrin, or a Schism among the Nihilists" (1864), Dostoevsky presented a far more positive picture of human capacities and needs than was possible in *Notes from Underground*, given its structure as a diatribe against Rational Egoism by a person who is an egoist in the true sense, that is, someone who is interested solely in the unfettered play of his own will. "Mr. Shchedrin" continues the attack on Rational Egoism, but now the focus is not directly on the *egoist* dimension of the outlook but on its conception of what constitutes humanity's "best interest," and specifically on its assumption of the primacy of material, physical needs.

An emphasis on physical needs in the understanding of human nature (and in proposals for the reform of society) was, of course, a corollary of the overall materialist philosophy of the Nihilists and as such it molded their conception of what is in someone's "best interest." Chernyshevsky in his seminal essay "The Anthropological Principle in Philosophy" (1860) had laid out the theoretical premises of the outlook. Man, he proclaimed, is "an extremely complex combination of chemicals that undergoes an extremely complex chemical process we call life." Given that fundamental truth, the philosopher should confine his attention to the scientifically describable properties of the human organism, for "philosophy sees in [it] what medicine, physiology, and chemistry see."[20] As analyzed by these sciences, the organism's complexity reduces to a fairly simple set of needs. The most immediately imperative is air to breathe, but fortunately air is plentiful. After air, however, comes the need that is the key not only to the organism's survival but to interpersonal relations and a bright social future:

> Next to the need to breathe . . . a person's most urgent requirement is food and drink. Very often very many people suffer from a shortage of the articles needed to satisfy these requirements properly, and this is the cause of the largest number of bad actions of all kinds, of nearly all the situations and institutions that are the constant causes of bad actions. If this one cause of evil were abolished, at least nine tenths of all that is bad in human society would quickly disappear. Crime would be reduced to one tenth. In the course of one generation coarse manners and conceptions would yield to humane manners and conceptions.[21]

Following Chernyshevsky's lead, when the Rational Egoists urged their fellow Russians to act in such a way as to promote their own best interest, what they had in mind was not an abstract interest like freedom or a luxury like art and literature, but the universal, pressing individual and social interest in an adequate supply of food.

Dostoevsky's response to this idea came in the form of a bitingly satirical attack on the radical's principal journal, *Sovremennik* (The Contemporary). The talented writer Mikhail Saltykov-Shchedrin, who employed his barbed wit generally, though not exclusively, in the service of the radical camp, had al-

---

20. Edie, *Russian Philosophy*, 2:43, 2:29.
21. Ibid., 2:41.

ready been the target of some malicious allusions in *Notes from Underground*. Shchedrin retaliated with a humorous sketch in *Sovremennik* called "The Swallows," in which Dostoevsky's work (under the supposed title "Notes on the Immortality of the Soul") was mocked as "intellectual albinism" and as a rehash of arguments from St. Thomas Aquinas (referring presumably to the Christian notions excised by the censors).[22] Dostoevsky, in his turn, responded with his pasquinade "Mr. Shchedrin," in which Saltykov-Shchedrin, called "Shchedrodarov," is represented as a vain and unprincipled recruit to the staff of *Sovremennik*, dubbed *"Svoevremennyi"* (The Opportunist). The editors are telling Shchedrodarov how he must write. He must understand, they say, that because people are ignorant they cannot discern "where their real advantage lies"; they live "each of them thoughtlessly, according to their own wills, rather than according to the wise books"—an allusion to Chernyshevsky's *What Is to Be Done?* and other scriptural tracts of the Nihilists (20:110). What people really need, the editors go on, is not senseless, useless "luxuries" such as art, science, philosophy, religion, morality, and national politics, but enough to eat, and drastic measures may be required to concentrate people's attention on that rudimentary "real advantage":

> "If someone should say to you, 'I want to think, I am tormented by the unresolved, eternal questions; I want to love, I long for something to believe in, I seek a moral ideal, I love art,' or anything of that sort, answer him immediately, decisively, and boldly that all of that is nonsense, metaphysics, that it's all a luxury, childish dreams, unneeded things, that first and foremost is the belly. And recommend to him, finally, that if he itches so much, he should take a pair of scissors and cut off the part that itches. 'I want to dance'—cut off his legs. 'I want to paint'—cut off his hands. 'I want to pine and dream'—off with his head. The belly, the belly, and only the belly—that, my dear sir, is the great conviction!" (20:110–11)

By offering up these cutthroat sentiments for ridicule and also by attributing some mental reservations to the rather bewildered Shchedrodarov, Dostoevsky managed in this brief lampoon to lay out a remarkably full case against the Rational Egoist's conception of "best advantage." His case has four key elements.

First, he insists that over and above the physical needs of "the belly," human beings have needs of other sorts, intellectual, emotional, and aesthetic—needs, we may note, that are associated (though Dostoevsky does not explicitly make

---

22. M. E. Saltykov-Shchedrin, *Sobranie sochinenii v dvadtsati tomakh* (Moscow: Khudozhestvennaia literatura, 1965–77), 6:493. For a fuller account of the exchange between Dostoevsky and Shchedrin see Frank, *Dostoevsky: The Stir of Liberation*, 354–55.

the point here) with the "higher," spiritual element of man's nature in the dualistic ontology examined in the previous chapter. Some of these "higher" needs—love, faith, a moral idea, art—are enumerated in the passage quoted above; another brief enumeration is found in an excerpt from an earlier draft of the article, in which Shchedrodarov is represented as wanting to retort that "along with [basic] food, man wants freedom, a little cake, wants to be mischievous, to play, and to fantasize" (20:239).

Second, the single-minded pursuit of physical needs, such as the radicals demand, requires at best ignoring, and at worst eradicating ("cut off his legs") the human capacities with which the higher needs are associated, thereby mutilating the human organism. In both the draft and the finished article, Dostoevsky accuses the radicals of seeking to satisfy physical needs by "the preliminary and intentional paralysis of all a man's other human capacities" (20:110, 239).

Third, he does not deny that the physical needs are genuine and in some sense basic. No doubt it would be very useful, Shchedrodarov muses, "to satisfy one's belly first and then go on to everything else." But two considerations militate against this. One is that it might take an extremely protracted effort to reach a social state in which bellies can truly be satisfied, and in the meantime "one would have overlooked life and spoiled everything." The other is the possibility that the very attainment of the goal of a satisfied belly hinges on the development of the scorned capacities, which is impossible if they are paralyzed in advance. As the draft has it, perhaps the full belly will be humanity's final step rather than its first step (20:110, 239).

Finally, returning to a theme familiar from *Notes from Underground*, human beings will insist on engaging in the free expression of their capacities, full belly or no: "On no account will mankind agree to spit on everything else and live only for the belly" (20:239). The implication, of course, is that a social order that sacrifices other capacities to physical needs would not willingly be supported by those whom it is supposed to benefit. Hence it could become a reality only through the imposition of force, as Dostoevsky suggests with the satirical image of the editor who advocated decapitation as the remedy for the stubborn desire to "pine and dream."

Notes from Underground and "Mr. Shchedrin" are Dostoevsky's principal attacks on the psychological and ethical claims of Rational Egoism. His opposition to other aspects of the Nihilists' outlook, such as their views on art (also discussed in "Mr. Shchedrin") and their revolutionary politics will be taken up in later chapters. He faults their descriptive theory of human motivation ("psychological egoism") as empirically false, untrue to its subject; he faults their normative theory ("ethical egoism") first as self-contradictory and incoherent because of its neglect of free will (in *Notes from Underground*) and then as myopic and dangerous in its single-minded concentration on physical needs as constituting men's "best interest" (in "Mr. Shchedrin").

Dostoevsky's reasoned critique in these two works should lay to rest any lingering suspicions about his capacity for a logical response to views he opposed. Indeed the impact of his satire in both works hinges precisely on the insightful and telling character of his objections, which are just as telling philosophically (though far less so rhetorically) when laid out in the dry literal form to which I have reduced them here. Ironically, Dostoevsky's abilities as a thinker may be obscured by the very literary dazzle they are partly responsible for producing.

Although from a philosophical point of view both these works are primarily negative and critical in nature, addressed as they are to the inadequacies of Rational Egoism, they do indicate the outlines of Dostoevsky's view of man as a free being with spiritual and moral as well as physical needs. But neither work yet identifies the moral ideal, shows the limits of freedom and responsibility, or explores the dialectic of egoism and altruism. For those topics we must attempt to reconstruct Dostoevsky's positive conception of human beings as moral creatures.

CHAPTER 3

The Ethics of Altruism

As a consummate egoist, the Underground Man stands at the furthest extreme from moral virtue. For an understanding of his antipode, the morally good person, we must turn to Dostoevsky's positive ethical philosophy.

Dostoevsky's conception of humanity is deeply rooted in an ethical outlook. The central place of problems of good and evil in his thought—what Vasily Zenkovsky called its "ethicism"—is one of the principal sources of his impact on subsequent Russian philosophy and on legions of readers around the world.[1] And as we saw in chapter 1, for Dostoevsky the existence of objective moral norms of human behavior not only gives the lie to the ethical nihilism of "all things are permitted" but is a foundation on which to ground belief in the existence of God and the immortality of the soul.

But what are these moral norms, and how is their validity established? As with the other regions of Dostoevsky's thought, in ethics we have no treatises from his pen that would answer such questions directly and systematically. We do have his answers to them, however, in a rich mosaic of ethically relevant texts. We have, first, a splendid gallery of fictional saints and sinners, personifying moral conditions of great diversity, from private and public villains (the Underground Man, Raskolnikov, Svidrigaylov) to paragons of virtue (Sonya Marmeladova, Tikhon, Zosima, Prince Myshkin—the latter being Dostoevsky's attempt to depict "a positively beautiful person" [28/2:251]). Second, we have a great many discursive texts in which his view of the ethical universe is laid out piecemeal: discussions of the moral imperative of love and the ego-

---

1. V. V. Zenkovsky, *A History of Russian Philosophy*, trans. George L. Kline (London: Routledge and Kegan Paul, 1953), 1:425.

istic impediments to following it; reflections on conscience and religion as sources of moral standards; explorations of the dialectic of freedom and determinism; controversial pronouncements concerning the nature of guilt and the ethical value of suffering. Although Dostoevsky by no means presented the elements of this mosaic as a structured moral theory, together they display in considerable detail a coherent picture of the ethical nature of man.

The Law of Love and the Law of Personality

Dostoevsky's 1864 reflections on the death of his first wife are as important for his moral philosophy as they are for his views on immortality. His case for immortality in the 1864 text, it will be remembered—what I called his argument from the demand for moral perfection—was based on the unconditional acceptance of the Christian law that he, like Belinsky before him and Tolstoy after him, called "the law of love" (24:165), a law that retains its categorical validity despite the inability of any earthly being to live up to it fully. A closer look at the text with an eye to its moral content will show us the basic principles of Dostoevsky's ethical orientation:

> To love someone *as oneself*, in accordance with Christ's commandment, is impossible. The law of personality [*zakon lichnosti*] is binding on earth. The *self* stands in the way.[2] Christ alone could do it, but Christ was an eternal ideal, toward which man strives and must strive, by the law of nature. Meanwhile, after the appearance of Christ, as *the ideal of man in the flesh*, it became as clear as day that the highest, the final development of personality must come to this (at the very end of development, at the very point of attaining the goal): that the person should find, should recognize, should with the full force of his nature be convinced, that the highest use someone can make of his personality, of the full development of his *self*, is to annihilate this *self*, as it were—to give it totally to each and every one, undividedly and unselfishly. And this is the greatest happiness. In this way the law of the *self* merges with the law of humanism, and, in merging, the two—both the *self* and the *all* (seemingly two extreme opposites)—are mutually annihilated for each other, while at the very same time each separate person attains the highest goal of his individual development. (20:172; Dostoevsky's emphasis)

2. The Russian word *lichnost'* is an abstract noun signifying personality in the sense of the state or condition of being a person. 'Self' is used here to translate the Russian first person singular pronoun *ia*, sometimes translated "the I" or "the ego" in such contexts.

The law that commands "Love everyone as thyself," he goes on, is not a fantasy but is the law of "our ideal" (20:174). Because Christ was the perfect embodiment of such altruism, imperfect humans must regard Him as "the great and final ideal of the development of all humanity, presented to us . . . in the flesh" (20:173). The greatest good for man is the annihilation of "self" in the sense of subjecting one's will to the law of love despite opposition from "the law of personality."

The latter expression is Dostoevsky's term for the egoistic principle inherent in a world of individual human persons, each of whom has both an animal and a spiritual nature and in virtue of the former is moved to follow personal inclinations rather than general dictates of morality. To exhibit what Dostoevsky calls "self-will" (*svoevolie*) as the Underground Man does, for example—that is, by the use of human freedom to assert one's will independently of the law of love—is to act egoistically: it makes the self the determinant and warrant of actions and in so doing disregards others. As we saw in chapter 2, Dostoevsky believed that true freedom consists not in egoistic self-expression but in moral self-mastery (25:62).[3]

For Dostoevsky, then, deviation from moral standards has a single name, and that name is egoism. The equation of immorality with egoism follows simply from his conception of the moral law: if we are commanded to love others as ourselves, any departure from the law must consist in loving ourselves more than we love others. The spheres of immorality and egoism are coextensive; one is not present without the other.

The earthly life of humanity thus becomes for Dostoevsky an endless dialectic between good and evil, between the law of love and the "law of personality," both laws rooted in the complex material-spiritual nature of man. According to the 1864 reflections, the law of love never triumphs fully; on earth the greatest saint is still a human person, whose self "stands in the way" of perfect virtue. Some degree of egoism is an inescapable feature of earthly human life, preventing any individual from achieving perfect adherence to Christ's law. But neither does the law of personality ever fully vanquish the law of love in any creature who deserves to be called human.

How exactly does the self "stand in the way"? What is it about being human that causes people to fall short of full adherence to the moral law? In Dostoevsky's fiction, the human failings that lead to deviation from the law of love are presented in stunning variety and depth, amounting to what is perhaps the

3. See also his notebook entry identifying freedom with "mastering oneself and one's inclinations" (24:213).

greatest exercise in the phenomenology of evil ever undertaken by a writer. We can distinguish in his analysis the workings of weaknesses of three types—affective, volitional, and intellectual.

On the affective side, Dostoevsky regarded man's animal nature as an abundant source of desires and impulses that not simply disregard the needs and interests of others but are directly hostile to them. It is outbursts of "*brutal* sensuality," his "Ridiculous Man" observes, that engender "almost all the sins of our humankind" (25:113; Dostoevsky's emphasis). I argued in chapter 1 that for Dostoevsky there is no altruism in man's purely material makeup; love of others is a spiritual ability that enters human nature only through its participation in the divine. As animals, human beings have only impulses that are indifferent to the well-being of others when they are not directly antipathetic to it. The antipathetic side is abundantly evident in Dostoevsky's cast of characters, saints and villains alike.

It is a striking fact that one of the more common motives of Dostoevsky's characters is spite (*zloba*, adjectivally *zlobnyi* or *zloi*)—the malicious desire to hurt or humiliate someone. From his early stories to his last great novels, spiteful characters abound. *The Insulted and Injured* is a carnival of spite, expressed by everyone from Natasha and Nellie to Mme. Bubnov ("eyes gleaming with spite" [3:258]) and above all Prince Valkovsky, behind whose "mask" was seen "something spiteful, cunning, and supremely egoistic" (3:245) and who "wanted to prick, to sting, to bite, to jeer" (3:360).[4] These are animal desires, as Dostoevsky's choice of words suggests—desires of the kind he attributed to his fellow prisoner "A-v" (Pavel Aristov) in *Notes from the House of the Dead*, whom he describes as "a monster, a moral Quasimodo," an example of the extremes to which the physical side of a human being can go when it is "not restrained inwardly by any standard, by any law" (4:63).

Imposing such a standard or law is the work of the human will, and this is where volitional failings enter the picture. Fundamental to the material nature of man as Dostoevsky understood it is the desire for self-expression, the wish to control one's environment in accordance with one's own wants. A person wishes, as Dostoevsky put it, "to live as much as possible according to his own will" (20:239). This desire for "self-will" drew his particular attention in *Notes*

4. Other examples, in addition to the obvious case of the Underground Man, include Andrey Filippovich in *The Double* (1:151); anonymous boarders in "Mr. Prokharchin" (1:240); Katerina in "The Landlady" (1:298); Anna Nikolaevna ("bursting with spite" [2:308]) in "Uncle's Dream"; Pseldonimov's father-in-law in "A Most Unfortunate Incident" (5:37); Nastasya Filippovna and Rogozhin in *The Idiot* (8:137, 180); Trusotsky in "The Eternal Husband" (9:40); Arkady in *The Adolescent* (13:282); and Grushenka and Smerdyakov in *The Brothers Karamazov* (14:396; 15:164).

from the House of the Dead, where he spoke of the convicts' yearning for power and control and their hysterical, destructive response at being deprived of them; conversely, the jailers who flog and beat the convicts are also dehumanized by the possession of essentially unlimited power, presumably because it removes a needed brake on the expression of self-will:

> Someone who has once experienced this power, this unlimited mastery over the body, blood, and spirit of a person like himself, . . . who has experienced the power and the full opportunity to degrade, by the most supreme humiliation, another being who bears the divine image, will somehow, even against his own will, lose control of his feelings. Tyranny is a habit; it is capable of development, and it develops finally into a disease. I submit that the habit can coarsen and stupefy even the best of persons to the level of the brute. (4:154)

The terrible irony is that the resulting brutishness is mistaken for deity, as shown in the triumphant cry of Kirillov in *Demons*: "For three years I have sought the attribute of divinity in me and I have found it: the attribute of my divinity is—self-will!" (10:472). When in the same work Tikhon tells Stavrogin to put aside his pride, he is protesting against the arrogance of self-will that makes a person claim to be the arbiter of right and wrong. When the animal, selfish will is not restrained by the spiritual, moral will, the law of personality defeats the law of love.

Finally, in Dostoevsky's thinking the law of personality owes its impact in many cases to the operation of distinctly intellectual as distinguished from affective and volitional factors. Even "a delightful nature like yours," he has Alyosha tell Kolya Krasotkin in a notebook for *The Brothers Karamazov*, "is already fully corrupted by convictions" (15:309). Dostoevsky devoted a great deal of attention to the ways in which particular cognitive conditions—that is, particular beliefs, deficiencies in knowledge, or processes of reasoning—contribute to the failure of the moral will to restrain our egoistic impulses. At one point or another he identifies many such cognitive conditions as having this effect: they include the belief in philosophical materialism or atheism; the denial of the immortality of the soul; a lack of adequate knowledge of the common people; casuistic reasoning; a Westernist outlook; a bourgeois mentality; erroneous views of freedom—all are condemned by Dostoevsky at least in part because they undermine spiritual, altruistic impulses and promote egoism.

Among the more pointed condemnations of particular cognitive states are those found in the exhortations of the monk Zosima. Consider, for example, his attack on the thinking behind the modern "reign of freedom," as he calls it:

By understanding freedom as the multiplication and rapid satisfaction of needs, people distort their own nature, for they engender in themselves many senseless and foolish desires, habits and fancies of the most ridiculous sort. They live only to envy one another, to gratify the flesh, and to swagger. . . . It is no wonder that instead of freedom people have fallen into slavery. . . . How can one shake off one's habits, where is this slave to go if he is so habituated to satisfying the innumerable needs he himself has invented? He is isolated, and the whole is no concern of his. (14:284–85)

Here a particular conception of freedom—freedom as the ability to do whatever one pleases—is condemned for stimulating the development of purely personal desires and subverting the moral will to the point of egoistic isolation and unconcern for others (shades of the Underground Man).

For Dostoevsky, then, there is an absolute moral good for man: it is the condition of perfect adherence to the law of love, or in other words loving others to the point of a Christlike giving of oneself to them unreservedly. Human beings are morally obligated to observe this altruistic ideal as fully as their composite, material-spiritual nature will allow, and he does not doubt that they *can* observe it to some degree. But because of the affective, volitional, and cognitive limitations of that composite nature, all of which support the egoistic "law of personality," they can never observe it perfectly.

Moral Epistemology: (1) Conscience

Once we have identified Dostoevsky's conception of the supreme moral principle, we are faced with the question of its epistemological ground. From the standpoint of theory, what justification, if any, is there for accepting the "law of love" as categorical—that is, as an unconditionally binding imperative? And from the standpoint of practice, how does an individual moral agent know the right thing to do in a given situation?

Of all the texts in which Dostoevsky touches on moral philosophy, the one that addresses the epistemological questions most directly is a discussion of another writer's fiction. In his *Writer's Diary* for July and August 1877, he devoted many pages to a commentary on Leo Tolstoy's new novel, *Anna Karenina*. He had severe ideological reservations about the work, chiefly because of what he saw as its author's failure to appreciate the Russian people's sympathies with the Balkan Slavs, then caught up in the Russo-Turkish war of 1877–78. Yet he called the novel "perfection as an artistic work" (25:200), and he even found a few good things to say about it from an ideological stand-point.

In particular he applauded the moral faith that the novel's hero, Levin, seemed to derive from a chance encounter with a peasant. In the *Diary* Dostoevsky described this faith approvingly at some length, closely following Tolstoy's text:

> Levin's idea is this: why should one search with one's intellect for what is already *given* by life itself, something every person is born with and every person should and does follow, even involuntarily? Everyone is born with a conscience, with a conception of good and evil, and so everyone is also born straightaway with an aim in life: to live for good and not to love evil. Born with this are both peasant and master, and Frenchman, Russian, and Turk—they all honor the good (N.B.: Though many in a way that is frightfully their own). I, says Levin, wanted to understand all this through mathematics, science, reason [*razum*], or I was expecting a miracle, whereas it was given to me as a gift, born with me. And there are direct proofs that it is given as a gift: everyone on earth understands or can understand that we must *love our neighbor as ourselves*. In this knowledge is essentially contained the whole *law* of humanity, as Christ himself declared it to us. Yet this knowledge is innate and therefore sent as a gift, for reason could never have yielded such knowledge. Why? Because "loving one's neighbor," if you judge it by reason, turns out to be unreasonable. (25:204; Dostoevsky's emphasis))

On one level, all this is a faithful paraphrase of Tolstoy's prose. But Dostoevsky also calls the thoughts attributed to Levin "very true and well expressed" and he goes on to lament what he takes to be Levin's subsequent retreat from them; clearly he found Levin's reflections much to his liking. Moreover, the choices Dostoevsky makes in phrasing his summary show that he is turning Tolstoy to his own uses. His co-opting of Levin's thoughts is evident, for example, in his introduction of such terms as 'innate' and 'conscience', which Tolstoy had not used but which are key concepts in Dostoevsky's ethical thinking. Overall the passage nicely encapsulates Dostoevsky's own approach to some fundamental questions of ethical epistemology, the elements of which we may summarize here under five heads.

First, the absolute moral law to which human beings are subject is ordinarily made known to them by the inner voice called conscience, which commands them to love others as they love themselves. That conscience makes humans aware of the law is no less self-evident to Dostoevsky than is the law's binding character; as Sergey Belov once observed, Dostoevsky may have been plagued by uncertainty concerning the existence of God, but he never doubted the voice of conscience within him.[5] His commitment to the universality of the moral conscience throughout the human race is implicit in his ascription of it to different classes ("master and peasant") and different countries and religions ("Frenchman, Russian, and Turk")—though it will be noted that he acknowledges significant differences in the ways in which the various groups pursue the good.

In other writings Dostoevsky insistently affirms the presence of a moral conscience even in many who act contrary to its dictates. A criminal can be reformed, Zosima asserts in *The Brothers Karamazov*, only by "the law of Christ speaking in the awareness of his own conscience" (14:60). The most inveterate and unrepentant murderer, Prince Myshkin states in *The Idiot*, "knows all the same that he is a *criminal*, that is, in accordance with his conscience he considers that he has acted wrongly, even though he lacks all repentance" (8:280; Dostoevsky's emphasis). Some of Dostoevsky's more dramatic descriptions of the workings of conscience show it confronting evil acts or intentions, as in the words of the prosecutor Ippolit Kirillovich in *The Brothers Karamazov*, describing Dmitry Karamazov's presumed frame of mind after he supposedly had murdered his father: "And there is still something else, gentlemen of the jury, something that cries out in the soul, throbs ceaselessly in the mind, and poisons his heart unto death—that *something* is conscience, gentlemen of the jury, its judgment, its terrible pangs!" (15:144; Dostoevsky's emphasis). Whatever one's sins, it would seem, conscience remains as what Dostoevsky called in a notebook "the judging God within me" (24:109).

Second, knowledge of the law of love is innate in human beings, a "gift" of the Creator in the sense of an initial structural endowment. When Dostoevsky represents Levin as thinking that "every person is born with a conception of good and evil," he is making, more plainly than Tolstoy's original text does, the point that the knowledge is inherent and universal rather than resulting from a divine blessing that might be bestowed on people selectively or at particular points during their lives. As Dostoevsky wrote in another place, it is "because he is a human being" that a person must feel the need to love his

---

5. Sergei V. Belov, "The History of the Writing of the Novel," in Feodor Dostoevsky, *Crime and Punishment*, ed. George Gibian, 3d ed. (New York: Norton, 1989), 493. For an opposing view, see Aileen Kelly's thought-provoking article "Dostoevskii and the Divided Conscience" (*Slavic Review* 47 [1988]: 239–60), in which she argues that Dostoevsky's conscience was riven by an unresolvable conflict between humanist impulses based on "the moral data of empirical experience" and Christian impulses stemming from "the invisible world of faith" (259). On this ground Kelly concludes that Dostoevsky, unlike Tolstoy, did not take an absolutist position with regard to moral choice (260). My own view as developed in this chapter implies that Dostoevsky was every bit the ethical absolutist that Tolstoy was.

neighbor (19:131–32); the need is an integral element of the spiritual component of man's dualistic nature. Dostoevsky also finds in Levin's reflections a
"common consent" argument for the innateness of our knowledge of the law:
"There are direct proofs that it is given as a gift," his creative paraphrase reads:
"everyone on earth understands or can understand that we must *love our neighbor as ourselves*" (25:204; Dostoevsky's emphasis). Although he does not bring
up the point, the inborn character of conscience can also explain how moral
behavior is sometimes found even in people like Belinsky who reject the existence of God and the immortality of the soul, thereby contradicting the thesis
that "there is no virtue if there is no immortality": their false convictions may
not yet have had the full effect of "corrupting" their natures, but the risk is
surely there.

Third, the morally obligatory character of the law of love is not established
by "mathematics, science, [or] reason" (Levin's words, repeated by Dostoevsky), but is something "sensed" or intuited by the individual. In other texts
Dostoevsky elaborates on this point, making clear that he regards the moral
law as known to us through an immediate perception that neither requires not
admits intellectual justification. The term he invariably uses for this perception
is *chuvstvo*, which in Russian covers both the five senses and emotional states or
feelings. Thus the same Russian concept is being employed when he speaks of
an individual's "moral sense" (*nravstvennoe chuvstvo*) (23:37) and of "the feeling
of altruism" (*chuvstvo blagodeianii*) (24:294). Conscience speaks to us in sensory-
emotional rather than intellectual language, as he repeatedly stresses in his
notebooks. To foster morality, he wrote in 1876 or 1877, "you won't get anywhere through intellect" (24:226). Because moral ideas come to us from "feeling," it is impossible to *prove* that they are moral; they "can never be justified
by logic alone" (27:85). Considered as an *idea* (i.e., as an intellectual category),
he writes, love of humanity is "incomprehensible" to us: "The great ideal was
revealed to us only in the form of a feeling" (24:311).

Fourth, implicit in Dostoevsky's view of conscience as commanding adherence to a *law* is the deontological character of his ethical thinking—that is, his
view of moral actions as being obligatory regardless of their consequences.
That conscience tells us directly and immediately what is right and wrong
means that no utilitarian calculation, no consideration of the results of actions
is needed or desirable.

Dostoevsky's principal overt attack on consequentialist thinking is found
not in his ethical reflections but in his discussions of the nature of art, as we
shall see in the following chapter. Some of the points he makes in that context,
however, speak also to the basic theoretical vulnerabilities he finds in utilitarian moral theory. Chief among them is the assumption that the future can be

predicted with sufficient assurance to allow an advance determination of the utility of a proposed action, without which a decision about the morality of the action cannot be made on utilitarian grounds. For Dostoevsky, the future is too uncertain to permit us to make reliable forecasts of consequences:

> The normal, natural ways of usefulness are not completely known to us; at least they have not been calculated to the last degree of accuracy. How, indeed, is one to determine, clearly and unquestionably, what must be done in order to reach the ideal of all our desires and of everything that humanity desires and strives for? One can guess, . . . but it is impossible to calculate every future step of all humanity like a calendar. (18:95)

In particular, Dostoevsky condemns the notion that an action which in itself is morally abhorrent may be justified on the ground that its good consequences will outweigh its inherent evil. This opposition to what he calls the "Jesuit" notion that "the end justifies the means" is suggested already in *The Double* (1:132) and is a dominant theme in both *Crime and Punishment* and *Demons*. One thread in the tangled fabric of Raskolnikov's motivation in murdering the old pawnbroker is articulated by the anonymous student whose conversation he overhears in the tavern: " 'Kill her and take her money, so as with its help to dedicate oneself to the service of all humanity and the common good. Don't you think that thousands of good deeds will make up for one little crime? For one life, thousands of lives saved from corruption and decay! One death, and a hundred lives in return—why, it's just a matter of arithmetic!' " (6:54). Here, as in the parallel case of the justification of violent social revolution, the supposed utility of an action, determined entirely by a forecast of its consequences, is thought to establish its moral acceptability. But how can a radically uncertain forecast justify a certain present evil?

Questions of predictability aside, as a confirmed deontologist or nonconsequentialist Dostoevsky simply rejects "utility" out of hand as inappropriate to the determination of something as categorical as the moral imperatives prescribed by conscience. "Turn the other cheek, love [others] more than oneself," he writes in a notebook, "not because it is useful, but because it is pleasing, to the point of a burning feeling [*chuvstvo*], to the point of passion" (27:57). Another notebook entry concerning the obligation to help someone in need makes particularly clear his deontological conception of moral duty and his rejection of "reasoning" in its establishment:

> NB. The Gospels do not allow searching for reasons to help. Just accept, the Samaritan.

And if you once permit a reason to help
. . . Then right away you get into intellect and reasoning. There is no sufficient reason, no, help him. (24:266)

Finally, it is another implication of the ideas expressed in the Levin passage
that morality needs to be neither learned nor taught, except possibly as rein-
forcement or reinvigoration of what is innately given. One need not be overly
concerned about the moral training of a child, Dostoevsky contended elsewhere, because the moral law is already inscribed in the child's conscience
from birth. This was the central notion of a letter he wrote in 1878 to a concerned mother who had asked him for advice about the moral education of
her son. "You puzzle too much and worry yourself sick," he told the woman:
"The matter can be handled far more simply. Why raise such questions as
'What is the *good*, and what isn't?' They are questions only for you, as for any
inward person, but what have they to do with the upbringing of your child?
Everyone who is capable of *truth*—all such people sense with their own conscience what is the good and what isn't" (30/1:16–17; Dostoevsky's emphasis).
He does go on to give the woman specific advice, but it has to do with encouraging her son's religious beliefs and stimulating his innate moral sense by
providing examples of virtue in her own conduct. "Be good," he writes, "and
let your child himself, without prompting, recognize that you are good, and
let him remember that you were good; then, believe me, you will have fulfilled your duty to him for his entire life, because you will have taught him *directly* that good is good" (30/1:17).

Dostoevsky's insistence, here and in other places, on the importance of setting good moral examples has suggested to some that he viewed the examples
as *instilling* moral ideas in individuals, as if inscribing the law of love for the first
time on the tabula rasa of the moral consciousness.[6] But it is clear from his letter to the mother that he sees examples not as creating moral knowledge but as
stimulating and strengthening the knowledge that is inborn; in the case of the
child, the function of examples is to help him become aware of what he knows
innately to be good. Dostoevsky's belief in the power of examples may also be
connected, of course, with the novelist's preference for images over intellectual formulas; images of Christ and the Christian saints are for him important
heuristic tools of the moral consciousness, personifying and dramatizing what
conscience tells us more abstractly. Russian peasants may not have much

---

6. For a hint of this view see Gary Saul Morson, "Introductory Study: Dostoevsky's Great Experiment," in Fyodor Dostoevsky, *A Writer's Diary*, trans. Kenneth Lantz (Evanston, Ill.: Northwestern
University Press, 1993–94), 1:17–18.

knowledge of Orthodox church dogma, he concedes at one point in a notebook, but they know the lives of the saints (24:191).

Dostoevsky was distressed by widespread violation of the law of love, but he
argued vigorously that such violation did not disprove its inborn character. It
meant simply that people often did not follow the moral truth within them.
From his reflections on the extent to which the human conscience can be suppressed or ignored, while still remaining in some sense present in the heart of
every individual, we can construct a hierarchy of the various moral states that
Dostoevsky recognized in different human beings, or in the same human being
at different times.

The morally highest state is that of the person with a true, strong, and active
conscience whose behavior typically, though never perfectly, follows the law
of love. This is the condition of the individual who, contemplating the Christian ideal, has an "immediate, terribly strong, unconquerable feeling that *this* is
terribly *good*" and acts upon it (20:192; Dostoevsky's emphasis).

The next highest state of the moral conscience is that of individuals who, although they have acted contrary to the law of love, know that what they have
done is wrong *and* repent having done it. Although their moral conscience was
not strong enough to prevent them from acting immorally (Dostoevsky decisively rejects the Platonic contention that to know the good is to do it), it subjects them still to pangs of remorse ranging from simple unease to the "terrible
judgment" that the prosecutor imputes to Dmitry Karamazov's conscience and
the "torments" of conscience to which Alyosha attributes Ivan's illness at the
end of book 11 of *The Brothers Karamazov* (15:89). It is also the condition toward which Raskolnikov is moving at the very end of the epilogue to *Crime
and Punishment*, having been beguiled earlier by the anonymous student's boast
that he could kill and rob the old pawnbroker "without a twinge of conscience" (6:54), and having long insisted that his own conscience was clear
(6:417). Of the various states in the moral hierarchy, this state of the repentant
sinner is the one most characteristic of the human condition as Dostoevsky en-
visages it.

A step below the repentant sinner in the hierarchy is the acknowledged but
unrepentant sinner, or in other words the person, like the murderer mentioned by Prince Myshkin, who knows that it is wrong to violate the law of
love but violates it nonetheless *and* feels no remorse for doing so. The conscience of such a person is still sufficiently alive to recognize culpability but not
to cause repentance for committing the act, much less to deter it. Dostoevsky
found cases of this condition among his fellow prisoners in Siberia, and he used
them, as we saw above, as evidence of the ubiquity of the moral sense, albeit

weakened: the experience convinced him late in life that even the most hardened and unrepentant criminal still acknowledges that he is a criminal (8:280).
Outside prison, too, the common Russian people may be "depraved," but at
least they "do not consider their wickedness good" (24:198).

On each of the levels considered thus far, the Christian conscience is manifested in some way: on each, the law of love is recognized as morally binding,
even when it is callously violated. But on the fourth and lowest level, both remorse and the sense of guilt are absent: conscience is no longer evident at all.
Dostoevsky recognized the existence of such a level at the time he wrote *Notes
from the House of the Dead* (1862), and he assigned to it not only the "moral
Quasimodo" A-v but most of his fellow prisoners: "The majority of them," he
observed, "did not consider themselves guilty at all" (4:147). Some of his notebook descriptions of ordinary Russians as "simply immoral" and as exhibiting
"the naked depravity of egoism" (24:229) also suggest the existence of people
with a total lack of conscience. Although he had second thoughts about the
prisoners later, as we shall see, he did at one point seem to believe that some
individuals are altogether devoid of an active moral sense.

Yet nowhere does he say that any human being was denied the "gift" of
conscience at birth, or that the gift has been *irretrievably* lost. Presumably it is
with individuals such as "A-v", Raskolnikov, Svidrigaylov, and Stavrogin in
mind that Dostoevsky in the Levin text qualifies his assertion about the universality of conscience by saying that everyone on earth either understands or
"*can understand*" that we must obey the law of love. We see such an understanding dawning on Raskolnikov at the very end of the novel; even the thoroughgoing amoralist Svidrigaylov, Terras has argued, has a "deep" conscience
that destroys him.[7] And although Stavrogin claims of himself (in one of Dostoevsky's drafts of the suppressed chapter "At Tikhon's") that he "lacks the
knowledge and the sense of good and evil," he adds that he had "lost" that
sense, implying that he possessed it at one time (12:113). Rejecting any genetic
grounds for the apparent absence of a moral conscience, Dostoevsky sought to
explain it as the suppression or deadening of the inborn moral sense.

Thus although Dostoevsky did believe that there is such a thing as absolute
evil—namely, violation of the law of love—he apparently refused to believe
that any individual human soul is absolutely evil; each contains the divine
spark. We must reject the false dichotomy of asking whether man for Dostoevsky is good or evil; he is both. When Dostoevsky wrote that evil is "more
deeply rooted in humanity" than the socialists believe (25:201), he was not

7. Victor Terras, *Reading Dostoevsky* (Madison: University of Wisconsin Press, 1998), 71.

saying that people are unqualifiedly evil. Thanks to the law of personality, short of utopia no one is absolutely good; but thanks to the gift of conscience, no one is absolutely evil.

Moral Epistemology: (2) Faith

Still, the fact that an individual's conscience may or may not be sufficiently alive to recognize a morally good action or condemn an evil one presents Dostoevsky with an epistemological problem. How, in practice, can conscience be trusted? If conscience is the only ground of moral judgments, and if it says different things to different people, or to the same people at different times, are we not caught in a moral relativism quite out of character with the absolutist tenor of Dostoevsky's ethical philosophy?

Furthermore, despite his persistent recourse to an inborn human conscience as the purveyor of moral truth, Dostoevsky also frequently appears to make religious faith the ultimate court of moral appeal, as if 'the good' were not defined simply as what conscience commands but requires some other sanction. Writing in a notebook about the source of moral ideas, he identifies it as "religious feeling" (27:85). He often suggests, as we have seen, that loss of morality follows loss of faith in God; the character Keller in *The Idiot*, for example, anticipating the famous aphorism of *The Brothers Karamazov*, claims that "disbelief in the Most High" left him "without a shadow of morality" (8:256). Another notebook entry reads, "If we are without the authority of faith and of Christ, we shall lose our way in everything" (27:85). Still more pointed is this entry: "All morality proceeds from religion, for religion is simply the formula of morality" (24:168). In regard specifically to the Russian Orthodox faith, Dostoevsky stated that "Orthodoxy—that is, a form of confessing Christ—is the principle of our morality and our conscience" (21:266).

So which is, in fact, the ultimate source and warrant of our moral judgments—conscience or faith? Until the last year of his life there is no evidence that Dostoevsky gave much thought to choosing between them, convinced as he was that conscience is a divine gift, so structured that its dictates and the Christian law of love coincide in every respect. Ordinarily, whether one looks to the inner voice of conscience or to the pronouncements of Christ as the ultimate test of human behavior, the result will be the same, so that there is no reason to raise the question of a conflict between them. In 1880, however, he was prompted to reflect at length on just such a conflict, and when he did he resolved it decisively in favor of faith.

On June 8 of that year Dostoevsky had delivered an address in Moscow honoring Alexander Pushkin on the occasion of the dedication of a monument to the great Russian writer. His impassioned speech, praising Pushkin as the embodiment of a unique and superior Russian spirituality that could be a light to the world, created a sensation and added fuel to the enduring Slavophile-Westernist controversies in the Russian press. One of the many liberal-minded Westernists who responded to the speech in print was the legal historian Alexander Gradovsky, who criticized the writer's moralistic condemnation of the reform movement in Russia.[8] Dostoevsky, in turn, devoted much of the final chapter of his *Writer's Diary* for 1880 to rebutting Gradovsky's criticisms. He challenged Gradovsky to explain how social progress could be achieved without a moral rallying point: "How will you unite people to reach your civic goals if you have no basis in a fundamental, great moral idea? And the only moral ideas are those based on the idea of personal, absolute self-perfection in the future, on an ideal. For self-perfection contains everything within it, all aspirations and all longings, and consequently all your civic ideals proceed from it as well" (26:164).

This response drew a philosophically more sophisticated critique of Dostoevsky's position from the prominent liberal jurist and historian Konstantin Kavelin, whose "Letter to F. M. Dostoevsky" was published later in the year. Kavelin questioned not simply his opponent's evaluation of the reform movement but the very conception of morality on which it was based. In particular, Kavelin contended, the expressions 'moral ideas' and 'social morality' make no sense, for morality is a purely nonconceptual, emotional affair and furthermore pertains only to individuals, not societies. As for Dostoevsky's beloved "conscience," Kavelin went on to elaborate a relativistic conception of morality that made conscience a purely social construct; he identified morality with faithfulness to whatever ideas happened to form the content of conscience in a particular society:

> Moral is he who in his thoughts and deeds remains always true to the voice of his conscience, which tells him whether they are good or bad. Morality consists only in the relation of a person to himself; moral truth consists only in the agreement of thoughts and deeds with conscience. *What* exactly conscience says, why it approves some thoughts and deeds and condemns others—this is already outside the realm of morality and is determined by concepts or ideas formed under the influ-

---

8. A. D. Gradovsky, "Mechty i deistvitel'nost' (Po povodu rechi F. M. Dostoevskago)," in *Sobranie sochinenii A. D. Gradovskago* (St. Petersburg: M. M. Stasiulevich, 1899–1904), 6:375–83.

ence of social life and which for that reason are quite different at different times and under different circumstances.[9]

It is because the voice of conscience is formed by social influences, Kavelin went on, that what it says to Christians today is different from what it said to the pagans of ancient Greece. And, in any event, personal morality as determined by faithfulness to one's conscience has nothing to do with the public good: although Charlotte Corday (who murdered Marat) and Felice Orsini (who tried to assassinate Napoleon III) were executed for their crimes, they were "people of lofty morality"—meaning that they acted in full accord with their consciences.[10]

All this was too much for Dostoevsky, for whom *what* conscience required was a matter of the utmost moral and social importance, and it led him to reformulate his views of the nature of conscience and its relation to morality. In the few months left to him before his death in January 1881, he did not complete a reply to Kavelin, but his last notebook contains the main points of his proposed response, written as if in an answering letter. In these private notes he does not conceal his scorn for Kavelin, whom he calls "comical," "pathetic," and "a nihilist" (though he adds "not a nihilist that needs to be hung" [27:61, 63]). The notes, however, also represent one of Dostoevsky's most sustained efforts to come to grips with the foundations of morality, and they make clearer than ever before the religious basis of his moral philosophy.

Dostoevsky begins his answer by charging that Kavelin is seeking to deny "the spiritual nature of the Russian people." He then makes the cryptic accusation that "you have never looked at the red light [*krasnyi tsvet*]," presumably meaning by the use of that Russian expression that Kavelin has avoided confronting what was a sore subject in the Russian cultural life of the day.[11] "I shall tell you about it," Dostoevsky writes (27:55).

Moving directly to the moral sphere, Dostoevsky focuses on Kavelin's identification of morality with acting on conviction. "I do not acknowledge your thesis that morality is agreement with inner convictions," he writes; "that is merely *honesty* (the Russian language is rich), not morality" (27:56; Dostoevsky's emphasis). Characteristically, he goes on to marshal reductio arguments to support his case, seeking to show the contradictory or otherwise absurd implications of Kavelin's views. He points out, for example, that on Kavelin's position, telling a lie would be both right and wrong—right if done "from

9. K.D. Kavelin, *Nash umstvennyi stroi: Stat'i po filosofii, russkoi istorii, i kul'tury* (Moscow: Pravda, 1989), 467–68 (Kavelin's emphasis).

10. Ibid., 469.

11. I am indebted to Diane Thompson and V.N. Zakharov for clarification of this expression.

conviction," wrong if not (27:85). It would be similarly absurd, Dostoevsky implies, to call "moral" such actions as bombing the Winter Palace or burning heretics at the stake, even if those actions were inspired by conviction (27:56). These arguments reflect Dostoevsky's deontological view that actions are right or wrong in themselves, independently of their motives or intended consequences. In *Notes from the House of the Dead* he had used a kind of common-consent argument for this view: "Everyone will agree that there are crimes which, since the beginning of the world, always and everywhere, by laws of every sort, have been considered indisputable crimes, and will be so considered for as long as humans remains humans" (4:15). For a moral absolutist like Dostoevsky, the fact that a crime is committed "from conviction" by no means redeems it morally.

But if, as he had contended earlier, conscience is the very voice of morality within us, how is it distinguishable from the "conviction" that may prompt an immoral act? Dostoevsky's notes for his response to Kavelin show him grappling with this question. At one point he attempts to counterpose *conscience* as an emotional-affective category to *conviction* as an intellectual category, and he sketches a hypothetical case in which a felt pang of conscience triumphs over an intellectual belief:

> *The moral* is not exhausted simply by the single concept of consistency with one's convictions, because sometimes it is more moral not to follow one's convictions, and the convinced person himself, fully retaining his conviction, stops because of some feeling and does not perform the action. He curses himself and despises himself intellectually, but emotionally, meaning in accordance with his conscience, he cannot do it and he stops. (27:57; Dostoevsky's emphasis)

He suggests that such an inner conflict between "mind" and "feeling" was present in the revolutionary activist and would-be assassin Vera Zasulich, but with the opposite outcome: she allowed "conviction" to prevail over conscience.

What stands out in the notes, however, is not this effort to preserve conscience as morally pristine but the reluctant conclusion that conscience itself can go wrong. Dostoevsky for the first time explicitly acknowledges that there may be cultural or individual differences in what conscience dictates to different people, and specifically that a human conscience may prescribe something other than the law of love. His reflections on two "moral monsters" in particular appear to be associated with this change of heart. One was de Sade: "Conscience, the conscience of the Marquis de Sade!" Dostoevsky muses, adding "that is absurd." The other is the Spanish Inquisitor: "Enough by itself to make the Inquisitor immoral is that in his heart, in his conscience, the idea of the necessity of burning people could find a place," and for good measure Dostoevsky includes Orsini and Adam Mickiewicz's hero Konrad Wallenrod in the same category. All of them, he apparently believed, represented not conviction defeating conscience but an evil *conscience*, a perversion or distortion of man's original "gift." He acknowledged, in other words, that a distinction between a bad "conviction" and a good "conscience" cannot be maintained in all cases, and he resigns himself to admitting that conscience itself can be evil: "Conscience without God is a horror," he writes, still imagining his response to Kavelin; "it can lose its way, to the point of the greatest immorality" (27:56).

Thus conscience itself must always be put to the test of a higher standard. But what is the test? Dostoevsky finds it not in "philosophy," as he puts it in the notes, but in that very "red light" that Kavelin had avoided: "It is not enough to define morality as faithfulness to one's convictions. One must also continually ask oneself the question, Are my convictions true? There is only one test of them—Christ. But this is no longer philosophy, it is faith. And faith is the red light." The ultimate justification of moral judgments comes from religious faith in Christ as the embodiment of supreme goodness: "For me the moral model and ideal is given: Christ. I ask, Would He have burned heretics? No. So that means the burning of heretics is an immoral act" (27:56). Without God, Dostoevsky implied in a note of 1876 or 1877, we cannot simply rely on love of humanity to ground morality, for people will immediately ask, Why should I love humanity? This point is echoed at the end of the Levin passage in *A Writer's Diary*, discussed above, where Dostoevsky wrote that, looked at rationally, love of mankind is unreasonable. Ultimately no reason for it can be given; faith in the God who commanded love of one's neighbor is the only sure ground.

In this last year of his life, then, Dostoevsky finally gave voice, if only in unstructured notes, to what was perhaps an inchoate conviction behind his ethical thinking all along—namely, that the psychological phenomenon of conscience, however important in everyday life, is ethically secondary to the religious faith that accepts the law of love as Christ proclaimed and lived it. Conscience is real and, Dostoevsky believed, generally trustworthy, but Christ is the ultimate authority, which is why loss of faith can lead to the perversion and loss of morality, to the terrible conviction that everything is morally permissible. He did not accept the prevalent skeptical view that attributed conscience entirely to social conditioning (we know that he was familiar with that view even before Kavelin expressed it, for Ivan mentioned it in *The Brothers Karamazov* [15:87]). But he did believe that the voice could be dramatically and tragically distorted by the loss of faith. Had he not created an unforgettable portrait of just such a crippled conscience in the person of Raskolnikov?

Dostoevsky resorted to the image of Christ as a higher authority than conscience, but he does not seem to have realized that the practical content of that image could be far from clear. In a particular case of conduct, even devout Christians can disagree on the answer to the question, What would Jesus do? Dostoevsky's countryman Tolstoy argued that Jesus would eschew all violence of whatever kind, whereas Dostoevsky accepted some forms of violence, even war, as within the bounds of the moral. Dostoevsky's Jesus might not burn heretics, but it seems He would not shy from the use of force in self-defense or to combat crime and other forms of evil. At this point we reach the limit of Dostoevsky's explicit reflections on the ultimate moral sanction: he saw no need for discursive analysis of what constituted altruism in practice, though his fiction provided implicitly a rich account.

The Scope of Moral Responsibility

Beyond the basic principles of morality discussed in the previous sections, Dostoevsky's ethical thinking was also marked by two themes that gave it a distinctive stamp. One was the extraordinarily broad scope he assigned to moral responsibility, particularly later in his life: he came to regard individuals as morally responsible not only in the conventional sense of answerable for their own free behavior but in a special spiritual sense of answerable for the behavior of others, indeed of all humanity. The second theme was the great importance he assigned to human suffering as both a psychological and an ethical category. These themes are the subjects of the two concluding sections of this chapter.

Each of the two senses in which Dostoevsky used the concept of moral responsibility creates difficulties for the interpreter. As for the conventional, commonsense meaning of the term, Dostoevsky's ardent championship of human freedom—Nikolay Berdyaev called him "the most passionate and extreme defender of the freedom of man which the history of human thought has ever known"[12]—has made it difficult to find reasonable limits to responsibility in his thinking; if all free acts are acts for which one is responsible, responsibility must be as "extreme" as freedom itself. The special, spiritual sense of responsibility for the behavior of all humanity, on the other hand, however

---

12. Nicolas Berdyaev, *The Russian Idea*, trans. R.M. French (Boston: Beacon, 1962), 89.

significant to Dostoevsky from a psychological or literary point of view, may seem conceptually either too mystical to repay analysis or too bizarre to be taken seriously.

In this section I shall try to show, first, that although the scope Dostoevsky assigns to responsibility in the conventional sense is indeed broad, it is not fanatically extreme, in that he does acknowledge reasonable limits to it; and, second, that the idea of responsibility for all humanity, although at bottom a religiously inspired, mystical notion, is provided by Dostoevsky with a discursive defense and makes good sense in the context of his metaphysics and Christian faith.

First, the conventional sense of responsibility. Dostoevsky was, of course, a sworn enemy of universal causal determinism, the mechanistic theory that all events (including human acts of will) are necessitated by prior circumstances and therefore can in principle be predicted by someone with knowledge of the appropriate causal laws. With this feature of the Underground Man's diatribe he was in perfect agreement. No element of the Nihilist outlook was more repugnant to him than this theory, which in his view reduced the human being to the status of "a piano key or an organ stop" (5:112)—that is, a transmitter of outside impulses with no genuine agency of its own. It destroys the notion of moral responsibility, for if all acts of volition are necessary products of circumstances that are ultimately beyond a person's control, then "choice" is meaningless: the person could not have chosen otherwise, and consequently cannot be considered morally answerable for the action.

We saw above that Dostoevsky was particularly scornful of what he called "the doctrine of the environment," by which he meant his socialist opponents' use of the determinism theory to absolve individuals of guilt for crime. The socialists' argument, he explained in the essay "Environment" in his *Writer's Diary* for 1873, was that circumstances such as poverty are the causes of criminal action, and for that reason the structure of society, not the unfortunate individual, is at fault. He contended in the essay that by thinking along that line, "little by little we arrive at the conclusion that there are no crimes at all, that 'the environment is to blame' for everything." We even reach the point, he suggested, of considering crime a duty, "a noble protest against 'the environment'"—though it is no less absurd to praise than to blame individuals whose actions are simply the product of social influences (21:16). And he was equally suspicious of purely psychological (as opposed to psycho-social) explanations designed to absolve individuals of responsibility, such as the plea of "temporary insanity" (in Russian, *affekt*)—a topic that provoked the following outburst in a notebook:

Temporary insanity! For pity's sake, then you can call anything, any impression, temporary insanity. And who knows the borderline (who are such experts?), where can you set the norm so that beyond this line temporary insanity is not responsible. Why, any sort of occurrence is temporary insanity! A sunrise—temporary insanity; a glance at the moon—temporary insanity; and what else! (24:207)

As against "the doctrine of the environment," Dostoevsky offered what in the *Diary* he called simply "Christianity," which considers the individual responsible for his actions and "thereby acknowledges his freedom"; as we saw in the previous chapter, he believed that free will and moral responsibility were essential elements of Christian doctrine (21:16). More than that, like many Russian Orthodox thinkers he was convinced that Orthodoxy places greater emphasis on free will than do other branches of Christianity.[13] Father Tikhon makes the point about responsibility with particular emphasis in his conversation with Stavrogin in the suppressed chapter ("At Tikhon's") of *Demons*. Not relying on faith alone to ground the responsibility thesis, Tikhon offers a reasoned argument in its defense: "Christianity recognizes responsibility regardless of any environment. The Lord has not deprived you of intellect; judge for yourself: so long as you are able to pose the question intellectually, 'Am I or am I not responsible for my actions?' it means that unquestionably you are responsible" (12:116). The point of this subtle argument is that the very ability to entertain those alternatives in thought entails that I am free in regard to the action. If I can objectify a decision sufficiently to raise in my consciousness the question of my responsibility for it, it must be within my power to control the decision itself.

Dostoevsky's further description of the doctrine of "Christianity" in *A Writer's Diary*, however, contains a clear indication that he did not in fact regard free will and moral responsibility as absolutes. He certainly did not reject *all* determining environmental or other antecedent circumstances. Indeed, speaking in *Notes from the House of the Dead* about the so-called corrupting influence of the environment, he remarks: "It is true, let us assume, that it does destroy much in us, but certainly not everything" (4:142). The statement with

---

13. Arseny Gulyga, for example, advances this thesis in his *Russkaia ideia i ee tvortsy* (Moscow: Soratnik, 1995), 16. To say that Dostoevsky regarded free will as essential to Christianity is not, however, to go quite as far as Gary Saul Morson goes when he writes that for Dostoevsky "the essence of Christianity was free choice" ("Dostoevskii, Fëdor Mikhailovich," in *Routledge Encyclopedia of Philosophy*, ed. Edward Craig [London: Routledge, 1998], 3:118). I would say, rather, that the essence of Christianity as Dostoevsky conceived it was the categorical law of love, which makes sense as a moral imperative only if we can freely choose to observe it.

which he first introduces the doctrine of "Christianity" in the essay on the environment is qualified accordingly: it is, he says, a doctrine "which, *fully acknowledging the pressure of the environment* and proclaiming mercy for the sinner, nonetheless imposes a moral duty on the individual to struggle against the environment, imposes a boundary where the environment ends and duty begins" (21:16; emphasis added). Thus he does not deny the reality of environmental influences and, contrary to his skepticism about "temporary insanity," he not only accepts the notion of a "boundary" between responsibility and its absence but even suggests that "Christianity" can define it.

Nowhere does he explicitly draw the boundary, but in his writings, both fiction and nonfiction, he presents a multitude of cases in which he grapples with the effects of environmental and other influences and weighs these influences against the willingness and the capacity of individuals to resist them. His strong inclination is to assign moral praise or blame in any action that is consciously done, but he does allow contrary cases. Speaking of the tendency to excuse a murderer on the ground that "because of the pressure of the environment, the evil-doer *could not* but kill," he comments that "I am willing to grant in this case only the smallest number of exceptions, whereas they have been made the general rule among us" (21:264; Dostoevsky's emphasis).

The most notable exception that Dostoevsky did allow came in the sensational case of a young woman in St. Petersburg named Ekaterina Kornilova, who was charged with attempting to murder her stepdaughter. Kornilova, pregnant with her own first child and ill-treated by her censorious husband, had in his absence thrown or pushed his six-year-old daughter out a fourth-floor window. Although the child survived the fall without serious injury, Kornilova surrendered to the authorities and was duly convicted; her marriage was legally dissolved.

Dostoevsky addressed the case on several occasions in his widely read *Writer's Diary*, finally coming to the conclusion that Kornilova was not responsible for her action. He did not deny that the action was conscious and thus prima facie one for which she should be held responsible, but he argued that under the circumstances she could not help herself: "While fully retaining consciousness, she simply could not resist in the face of the impulse" to push the child (23:139). Contrary to his general contempt for "temporary insanity," he used precisely that defense in this case, arguing that here no expert knowledge was needed to recognize it: "Everyone knows," he claimed, "that a woman during pregnancy (especially with her first child) is very often subject to certain strange influences and impressions to which her psyche strangely and fantastically submits" (23:138). Because of the public sympathy aroused by his well-publicized arguments, the case was reconsidered and Kornilova's conviction was overturned. In his comments on the case, Dostoevsky explicitly stated that his opposition to determinism was not categorical but was directed against the attempt to make it a universal truth: the doctrine that crime stems from a disordered society, he wrote, is "an idea that *in some* particular applications and in certain sorts of phenomena is true to the point of genius, but that is completely mistaken when applied to the whole and the general" (23:137–38; Dostoevsky's emphasis).

Dostoevsky's willingness to consider the facts of individual cases in fixing moral responsibility may give the appearance that his ethics is purely situational or represents a kind of casuistry, in the sense of relying on particular circumstances rather than on "theory" or general laws in making moral discriminations.[14] Certainly a sensitivity to the moral nuances of particular cases of conduct is abundantly evident in *A Writer's Diary*. But Dostoevsky did not reject "theory" in the sense of universally valid ethical laws. His ethical thinking is founded on and dominated by an absolute moral law—the Christian law of love—which is nothing if not universal. "There is one law," he wrote in the preparatory materials for *Crime and Punishment*, "the moral law" (7:142).

The clarity of that categorical law left little doubt in Dostoevsky's mind as to *what* is right and wrong in particular cases; a healthy conscience and faith in the Christian ideal almost always sufficed to make that determination, he believed. He was too much a moral absolutist to engage in casuistry when it came to the moral worth of a particular *act;* that depends not on "circumstances" but on the act's conformity with the objective ideal, which he seems to have regarded as generally quite obvious. Circumstances can, however, be highly relevant to the question of the worth of the moral *agent*, in that they bear on the question of guilt and responsibility for performing what in the abstract would universally and unquestionably be considered a "crime," such as hurling a child out a window when nothing threatened the child inside. It is the question of responsibility that typically concerned Dostoevsky in the *Diary*, with its frequent attention to crime and legal affairs of the day in Russia. Dostoevsky's casuistry, in other words, was typically directed at the determination of *responsibility;* certainly it did not entail the circumstantiality of right and wrong, the rejection of ethical theory, or the denial of a universal, categorical moral law.[15] In the Kornilova case the question was not whether throwing the child out the

14. Morson applies the term "casuistical" to Dostoevsky's approach, arguing that for Dostoevsky "any ethical theory . . . will produce grotesque results when formulated as a universal law" (Dostoevsky, *A Writer's Diary*, 1:43; cf. 1:17, 99–100).

15. This is a distinction that Victor Terras does not draw when he writes that the stories of Luzhin and Svidrigaylov in *Crime and Punishment* imply that for Dostoevsky "guilt and innocence, *and hence right and wrong*, are existentially ambiguous" (Terras, *Reading Dostoevsky*, 71; emphasis added). My ar-

window was right or wrong but whether the young stepmother could be held morally and legally responsible for doing so.

Thus far we have been examining the first of Dostoevsky's two concepts of moral responsibility—the conventional or commonsense concept, which he extended to virtually all conscious activity, excluding only a small number of cases in which it can truly be said that the individuals are not responsible because the actions were not under their control. In the last decade of his life, however, he elaborated a far more dramatic and radical conception of moral responsibility, which extended the notion well beyond its conventional limitation to the moral agent's own deliberate actions. For he began to hold individuals answerable not only for actions they themselves control but for actions and events with which they are not causally connected either psychologically or materially, including the actions of others widely separated from them in space and time. This notion culminated in the thesis that *every* individual bears responsibility for the actions of *all* individuals, so that each is guilty of everyone's sins. I am guilty not only of what in the conventional sense are "my" sins, but also of a murder taking place half a world away and a rape committed by someone else ten years in the future. This doctrine of universal guilt is one of Dostoevsky's most arresting contributions to the discussion of moral responsibility.

Although he did not fully articulate and defend this extension of responsibility until the last years of his life, there is intriguing evidence of its attraction to him much earlier. In his first short story, "Mr. Prokharchin" (1846), the elderly protagonist has a delirious dream in which he is tortured by guilt for supposed sins. Most of these fit the conventional conception of responsibility for sins of omission or commission where there is a clear causal bond between the agent and the behavior—cheating a cabman, ingratitude for help received, failing to share his wealth with a poor co-worker who has seven children. But there is also a mysterious dimension to Mr. Prokharchin's guilt, for it extends to things over which he seemingly had no control, such as the very existence of the seven children; Dostoevsky writes of him, highlighting the irrationality of his guilt: "Although he was completely convinced of his innocence in regard to the troublesome assembly of seven under one roof, in fact it seemed to work out that no one was to blame but [he]" (1:250). He felt responsible for their existence despite being innocent of it in a causal sense.

Some critics find a similarly expansive sense of guilt in other works of fiction

---

gument is that the ambiguity of guilt does not entail the ambiguity of right and wrong; the wrongness of an action may be perfectly clear even though one's responsibility for committing it is not clear.

by Dostoevsky, including *Crime and Punishment*.[16] Before *The Brothers Karamazov*, however, the only other work in which a variant of it becomes obvious is "The Dream of a Ridiculous Man," published as part of *A Writer's Diary* in 1877. In that story, a despondent man is transported in a dream to a utopian "twin earth" in which evil is unknown and universal love prevails. Marveling at the beauty and joy of the new world, the Ridiculous Man watches powerless and in horror as his very presence, a contaminant from the fallen earth, somehow gradually infects the utopia with the same sins and evils he thought he had escaped. Dostoevsky pointedly refrains from providing any causal mechanism for the sad transformation: "How this could have happened I don't know," the Ridiculous Man says. But he has no doubt that he is guilty of their sins, though he neither intended them nor deliberately caused them by his actions: "I corrupted them all! . . . By myself I infected that whole happy earth, which had been sinless before me." He begs them to crucify him and shows them how to build a cross, but they merely laugh at him (25:115, 117). Like some reverse Messiah, he had come from an imperfect to a perfect world, and he is responsible for creating rather than redeeming the sins of everyone in it.

It was Dostoevsky's work on *The Brothers Karamazov* that crystallized his thinking concerning universal guilt. That the idea had by then acquired great importance to him is confirmed by an interesting letter written in June 1880, while he was working on the novel. A St. Petersburg friend with literary pretensions named Yulia Abaza had sent him the manuscript of a story that contained bizarre plot twists, among them that the hero is discovered to have—literally—a block of ice for a heart. Telling Abaza gently that the piece would need revision "from start to finish," Dostoevsky also gave her some specific advice about recasting the hero without recourse to the aberrant anatomy: "Give him spiritual suffering, give him an understanding of his sin as that of a whole generation. Without fail link a woman to him, even if he is a monk of the strictest rite, and make him consciously accept suffering for all his ancestors, and for everyone and everything, so as to atone for human sin. A great idea, if only your artistry is up to it! But what about that block of ice?" (30/1:192). Here, it will be noted, Dostoevsky makes explicit the whole sweep and the noncausal nature of universal guilt as he understands it: since it extends to responsibility for the sins not only of contemporaries and successors but of *ancestors*, it obviously is not based on empirically understandable causal connections.

16. Vyacheslav Ivanov, "The Revolt against Mother Earth," in Dostoevsky, *Crime and Punishment*, 588, 592.

In *The Brothers Karamazov* (1879–80) he assigned to the monk Zosima an exposition of the doctrine of universal guilt. The doctrine is first introduced in book 4, where Zosima, anticipating his imminent death, is sharing with other monks his thoughts on the monastic life:

> When he [a monk] realizes that he is not only worse than all the worldly, but that he is guilty before all people for everyone and everything, for all human sins, collective and individual, only then can the goal of our coming together be attained. For understand, dear ones, that each one of us is undoubtedly guilty for all men and for everything on earth, not merely through common, collective guilt but each individually for all people and for each person on this earth. This awareness crowns the monk's path as it does that of every person on earth. For monks are not a special sort of people, but only what all people ought to be. (14:149)

Zosima dwells on the doctrine at some length in books 4 and 6, and the notion appears once more in the novel, independently of Zosima's homilies, when Dmitry Karamazov, on the eve of his trial for his father's murder, declares himself ready to accept guilt "because we are all guilty for all" (15:31).

Dostoevsky's awareness of the difficulty of comprehending universal guilt is suggested in the novel when he describes the doctrine as simply a "feeling" on the part of Zosima's devout older brother, from whom Zosima himself is said to have acquired it. To his mother's puzzled questions, the brother can only reply "believe me, in truth everyone is guilty before all people, for all people and for everything. I don't know how to explain it to you, but I feel to the point of torment that it is so" (14:262).

Zosima himself, however, does not shy from elaborating the notion, approaching it from several standpoints in an effort to make it plausible to his listeners. On one hand he speaks of the advantages of believing it, contending that it serves as effective psychological preparation and inducement to act morally. Our capacity to love everyone, he states, is increased by the conviction that we are responsible to everyone: only in the presence of that conviction, he tells his auditors, "is our heart moved to infinite, universal, and insatiable love. Then each of you will be capable of gaining the whole world by love and washing away the world's sins with your tears" (14:149). In book 6 he sees the conviction, too, as a psychological antidote against any loss of heart induced by the seeming power of sin and evil over good works: "Children, run from this dejection!" he enjoins the monks. "There is only one way to save yourself here: take yourself in hand and make yourself answerable for all of human sin" (14:290).

To say that believing the doctrine has psychological advantages, however, does not clarify the doctrine itself, and Zosima also seeks to explain on what grounds it makes sense to hold all individuals responsible for the actions of everyone. At first glance, it may appear that he is offering a standard cause-and-effect explanation of universal guilt, for he suggests that one's action or inaction, through the force of example, might have been a contributing cause, even in the conventional sense, for the action or inaction of others. He states: "If I had been righteous myself, perhaps there would be no criminal standing before me," and he soon makes clear that he has in mind the lasting power of the virtue of one person, publicly manifested through good work, to influence others: "Understand that you yourself are guilty, for you might have been a light to evil-doers . . . and were not a light. If you had been a light, by your light you would have illumined the path for others, too, and the person who did evil might not have done so in the presence of your light" (14:291–92). Dostoevsky had made a quite comparable point about the influence of others on the evil-doer in his essay on the environment:

> Actually, if we consider that we ourselves are sometimes still worse than the criminal, we thereby acknowledge also that we are half to blame for his crime. If he has violated the law that the country wrote for him, we ourselves are to blame that he now stands before us. If all of us were better, then he, too, would be better and would not be standing before us now. . . . Once we have made ourselves better, we shall also correct the environment and make it better. (21:15)

Perhaps, then, Zosima is offering in *The Brothers Karamazov* no more than this same diffuse point about possible empirical connections between one's actions and the sins of others. Simply by failing to provide an example of good moral behavior, or perhaps failing to exert myself to exhort and inspire others, I bear some responsibility in the conventional cause-and-effect sense for their actions.

In fact, however, Zosima's understanding of responsibility in this universal sense is anything but conventional. For the "light" of good example of which Zosima speaks is not an empirical causal force but a supernatural one—the "heavenly light," he calls it—in the efficacy of which one must simply have faith. It cannot be judged by its earthly results:

> And even though you were a light, but you see that people are not being saved even in the presence of your light, be firm and do not doubt the power of the heavenly light. Believe that if they have not been saved now, they will be saved

later. And if they are not saved even later, then their sons will be saved, for your light will not die even if you have already died. The righteous man departs, but his light remains. . . . You are working for the whole, you are acting for the future. (14:292)

Although the language of "power" still suggests attention to causal effectiveness, it is not the demonstrable, spatiotemporal effectiveness of the physical world. For Zosima, the world in which the "heavenly light" is bound to have results is not the empirical universe of linear cause and effect but a spiritualized universe in which the mystical connectedness of all things guarantees a timeless universal response to every action. Zosima describes this world by enunciating what is in effect a metaphysical theory of the organic unity of all reality:

My young brother begged forgiveness of the birds. That seems senseless, but it is right, for everything is like an ocean, everything flows and connects; touch it in one place and it responds at the other end of the world. It may be madness to beg forgiveness of the birds, but really it would be better for the birds, and for a child, and for any beast around you, if you yourself were a nobler person than you are now, if only by a drop. Everything is like an ocean, I say to you. (14:290)

Because the world is an organic whole, every element of which is tied to every other, no line can be drawn beyond which I am not responsible for my actions; universal responsibility is established. Since it is a timeless universe, there is nothing to prevent "backward" connections, so that responsibility must be accepted for the actions of one's ancestors as well as successors.

At this point it is appropriate to ask whether we may ascribe to Dostoevsky himself this mystical, extended notion of universal responsibility, complete with the metaphysical theory to which Zosima resorts in expounding it. We know that Dostoevsky often contented himself with the commonsense conception of responsibility that requires linear spatiotemporal connections. His frequent remarks concerning guilt and responsibility in *A Writer's Diary* (setting aside the fanciful "Dream of a Ridiculous Man") and in his letters and notebooks before 1880 remain well within the conventional bounds of the likely and immediate impact of actions on others close by. Indeed, consideration of the consequences of behavior that are remote in space and time goes against the deontological, anticonsequentialist character of his customary moral reasoning. Even in discussing *The Brothers Karamazov*, he could give a perfectly commonsense reply to an impatient reader who asked him, before the serialization of the novel had been concluded, for clarification concerning guilt for the murder of the elder Karamazov. Ignoring the universal responsibility that Dmitry so dramatically assumes later in the novel, Dostoevsky answered:

> Dear Madame,
> Old Karamazov was killed by the servant Smerdyakov. All the details will be clarified in the subsequent course of the novel. Ivan Fyodorovich had a hand in the murder only indirectly and remotely, only by refraining (intentionally) from bringing Smerdyakov to his senses during the conversation with him before his departure for Moscow. . . . Dmitry Fyodorovich is completely innocent of his father's murder. (30/1:129)

Yet Dostoevsky was also perfectly capable of entertaining and using simultaneously the grander, mystical sense of responsibility for the sins of others. I believe he was attracted to it with particular force in the last few years of his life, and not only for its value as a literary theme. We know from his reflections on the death of his first wife that by the mid-1860s he was convinced that the *spiritual* world formed an organic whole—the universal synthesis that is God—though he did not suggest before *The Brothers Karamazov* that he regarded the *material* world, birds included, as forming the kind of universally concatenated, mutually responsive world such as was envisaged by Zosima as the ground of universal responsibility. But in the last novel he allowed Zosima, understandably for a mystically inclined Russian Orthodox monk, to engage in just such a spiritualization of the material world—to picture the world of flesh and blood, of men and birds, as being free of internal boundaries and divisions, like the "ocean" of spirit. The idea was no doubt attractive to Dostoevsky not only for its striking imagery but for its symbolic emphasis on the importance of moral behavior and personal responsibility.

But perhaps even more significant was its correspondence with the ideal image of Christ, who in the atonement took upon himself the sins of all humanity. In Christ, universal responsibility was real and manifest, and if the supreme moral good consists in being Christlike, we must accept universal responsibility, however far-fetched such a notion may seem to those who insist on spatiotemporal causality in moral behavior. And if moral responsibility is to be truly universal, there must be a picture of reality that allows us to conceive of how that universality might be possible. Zosima's picture does not *justify* belief in universal responsibility in any rational way, but something like it must be presupposed if faith in Christ as the moral ideal is not to be merely absurd. We cannot say with any assurance that Dostoevsky fully shared Zosima's metaphysical spiritualization of the material world, but he certainly invoked the monk's vision in his effort to make sense of the universal responsibility that he thought essential to the Christian moral ideal.

The Ethical Significance of Suffering

The second distinctive feature of Dostoevsky's ethical thinking that I marked out for special attention in this chapter is the great importance he attributed to pain and suffering in human life. As early as his novel *The Insulted and Injured* (1861), he introduced the idea that suffering serves as a form of moral cleansing or purification (3:230), and in the later novels this theme is powerfully elaborated, along with other morally relevant aspects of suffering. In this respect Dostoevsky's "ethics of suffering," as Alexander Vucinich has called it,[17] is entirely in keeping with the spirit of Russian Orthodox Christianity, and especially of the ascetic Russian monastic tradition to which Dostoevsky was so sympathetic. G. P. Fedotov writes in his *Russian Religious Mind* that the moral sanctification of suffering lies at the very core of Russian religiosity: "The evaluation of suffering as a superior moral good, as almost an end in itself, is one of the most precious features of the Russian religious mind."[18] Indeed, for Dostoevsky suffering of some types—but only some types—not merely approached but reached the status of an end-in-itself.

It does not require profound study of Dostoevsky's writings to recognize that he did not consider *all* suffering to be morally valuable. He did not defend Kornilova on the ground that in pushing her stepdaughter out the window she was bringing good to the child by giving her an opportunity to experience pain. He did not suggest, pace Ivan Karamazov, that the suffering of innocent children is a good thing. And he did not praise the suffering he saw as nothing more than an attendant or consequence of egoism. The agonies of the Underground Man, for example, are morally worthless because he cannot give himself to others; they are among the worst a human being can experience. "What is hell?" Zosima asks in *The Brothers Karamazov;* "I reason thus: 'the suffering of being no longer able to love' " (14:292).

Far from accepting all suffering as good, Dostoevsky excluded whole classes of it from the moral sphere, including some of the suffering most common in human life. One such is masochistic suffering, which, in the broad if not the sexual sense, he mentions so often in his fiction and for the recognition of

17. Alexander Vucinich, "Introduction," in Berdyaev, *The Russian Idea,* xviii.
18. George P. Fedotov, *The Russian Religious Mind: Kievan Christianity, the Tenth to the Thirteenth Centuries* (New York: Harper, 1960), 341.

which he is justly renowned.[19] That one can find pleasure in suffering by no means changes its moral status for Dostoevsky, for unlike the utilitarians he attributed no ethical value to pleasure. His attitude toward the phenomenon of masochism is for the most part mildly ironical—the detached observer smiling at human foibles—with a pronounced note of disdain where the desire for suffering becomes a form of exaggerated self-assertion, as in what he calls Nellie's "egoism of suffering" in *The Insulted and Injured* (3:386). A similar withholding of moral approval is evident in his famous thesis about the inherent masochism of the Russian character. "I think that the paramount, most basic spiritual need of the Russian people is the need for suffering, constant and unslakeable suffering, everywhere and in everything," he wrote in his 1873 *Writer's Diary;* "the Russian people seem to enjoy their suffering" (21:36). He does find positive value in some of the suffering of Russians, as we shall see shortly, but not in connection with their supposed masochism; that phenomenon is presented simply as a factual thesis about the Russian character, though admittedly not without a hint of perverse national pride.

Still another, even more prevalent type of suffering that is outside the moral sphere for Dostoevsky is the anguish he associates with the very possession of free will. Although he nowhere elaborates this point in his own voice, he does express it through the two fictional characters he most entrusted with pronouncing disturbing truths about the human condition—the Underground Man and the Grand Inquisitor. To the socialists' claim to eliminate suffering in their future utopia, the Underground Man retorts that conscious suffering is a badge of humanity; associated with the ability to doubt and rebel that the utopia would supposedly eliminate, it is essential to human freedom (5:119). The Grand Inquisitor, a champion of just such a structured utopia, makes the same point in mirror image. His argument is that God provided human beings with an essentially flawed nature that, in the absence of external control, makes suffering inevitable. In creating man as a free being, God condemned him to eternal unhappiness, for the responsibility of conscious free choice is an ago-

19. Dostoevsky's novels and stories abound in characters who find pleasure in suffering. Among them are Katerina in "The Landlady," who confesses that "what is bitter and rends my heart is that . . . my shame and disgrace . . . are dear to me" (1:299); Nellie in *The Insulted and Injured*, whose "egoism of suffering" is expressed in the enjoyment of her own pain (3:386); the narrator in *Notes from the House of the Dead*, who derived perverse satisfaction from the thought that only one creature in the world loved him—the dog, Sharik (4:77); the Underground Man, who says there can be enjoyment in a toothache and who takes pleasure in his own humiliation (5:102, 106); the gambler of the eponymous novella, who enjoys the pain that Polina's coldness gives him (5:231); Raskolnikov in *Crime and Punishment*, who found "a kind of pleasure" in tormenting himself with his problems (6:39); Marmeladov in the same novel, who speaks of the pleasure of being dragged into a room by his hair (6:24); Liza in *The Brothers Karamazov*, who cries "I want someone to torment me!" (15:21); and many others.

nizing burden. Upbraiding Christ for these mistakes, the Grand Inquisitor details his objection:

> Perhaps you forgot that peace and even death are dearer to man than free choice in the knowledge of good and evil? Nothing is more alluring to man than freedom of conscience, but nothing is more agonizing, either. . . . Instead of taking control of man's freedom you increased it, and burdened the realm of man's soul with its torments forever. . . . It was impossible to leave them in greater confusion and agony than you did by leaving them with so many cares and insoluble problems. (14:232)

The Grand Inquisitor's solution, of course, is to remove the freedom so as to assuage the torment: "And people rejoiced that they were again led like sheep and that so terrible a gift, which had brought them such suffering, was lifted from their hearts at last. . . . With us all will be happy and will no longer rebel or destroy each other, as they do everywhere under your freedom" (14:234–35). In the statements of neither character is suffering as such exalted; it is associated with something Dostoevsky valued highly—freedom—but as a consequence, not a moral condition. As the Underground Man comments: "I am not here defending suffering as such, or well-being, either; I am defending . . . my own caprice and its being guaranteed to me when necessary" (5:119).

Yet very often a positive evaluation *is* implied when Dostoevsky speaks of suffering, and the distinct impression with which he leaves readers is that suffering is in many cases a great good. Frequently he gives no more than vague and general reasons for his approval; his version of the Russian Orthodox "sanctification of suffering" was broad enough to include different forms and circumstances under which pain is beneficial to humanity. When, setting aside the question of masochism, he asserts in *A Writer's Diary* that the Slavic peoples have "developed only through suffering," doing so "in the slavery of serfdom, in ignorance and oppression," he is finding positive value in their national tribulations, including presumably the more mundane material consequences of serfdom and oppression in addition to purely psychic distress. The experience of suffering had a kind of instrumental value for them: it fortified them both individually and as nations, allowing them to "raise themselves up spiritually in their suffering, to strengthen themselves politically in their oppression, and, amid slavery and humiliation, to unite with one another in love and in Christ's truth" (23:103). He does not explain *how* suffering functioned to serve them in those ways, and my suspicion is that often he had no precise idea about it himself beyond the familiar folk wisdom that suffering is "good for the soul."

Similarly vague are Dostoevsky's suggestions, many cryptic and the majority undeveloped, concerning the functional value of suffering in promoting "awareness" of various sorts. The Underground Man, for example, proclaims that suffering is "the sole cause of consciousness" (5:119); Dostoevsky in *A Writer's Diary* refers to the "higher consciousness" that is aroused both by grief and by the suffering that always accompanies a great happiness (26:110); in a letter of 1870 to his niece Sofya Ivanova he writes (apropos of the Franco-Prussian war), "Without suffering you won't even understand happiness (29/1:137); and he frequently remarks on the educative value of suffering, saying, for example, that impressions made by the experience of suffering in childhood will "lead a child far more deeply into life than the most lenient school" (22:9). All these texts display sentiments at least as old as Aeschylus ("By suffering comes wisdom") and reaffirmed by many in the nineteenth century, including Elizabeth Barrett Browning ("Knowledge by suffering entereth").[20] They all, again, invoke little more than a commonsense approval of negative experiences as having spiritual benefits.

But there is also, especially in the novels and other writings of Dostoevsky's later years, a more developed, focused notion of suffering as an instrumental value of great moral significance. This is the doctrine of suffering as a "redemptive and regenerative" force, as Berdyaev puts it,[21] through the action of which the individual is morally redeemed. E. H. Carr called this doctrine of salvation through suffering "the central truth of [Dostoevsky's] religious and moral belief."[22]

In its simplest, most mundane form, this notion may be seen at work in Dostoevsky's theory of criminal punishment—that is, his justification for the infliction of suffering on people convicted of crimes—as presented in the essay "Environment" in *A Writer's Diary* for 1873. One of his concerns in that essay is what he considers to be the predisposition of Russian juries (following the Judicial Reform of 1864) to acquit or recommend clemency for criminals. Such leniency, he argues, is a disservice to the criminal himself, for it weakens his moral sense: "You only plant cynicism in his soul; you leave him with a corrupting question. . . . Into their soul you pour disbelief in popular justice

---

20. The quotations are taken from Aeschylus's *Agamemnon* (line 177) and Browning's *A Vision of Poets* (line 929).
21. Nicholas Berdyaev, *Dostoevsky*, trans. Donald Attwater (Cleveland: World, 1957), 95.
22. E. H. Carr, *Dostoevsky, 1821–1881* (London: George Allen and Unwin, 1962), 154.

[*pravda*], in divine justice; you leave them confused . . . 'So perhaps I'm not guilty at all'—this is what he thinks *in the final analysis*. You put that notion in his head yourselves" (21:19; Dostoevsky's emphasis). There is no one more unfortunate, Dostoevsky contends, than a criminal who has ceased to consider himself a criminal, for he is no more than a "beast" with a "starved" conscience (21:18). Better for the criminals themselves, then, is "purification through suffering"; they cannot be reformed, he argues, without "strict punishment, the stockade, and penal servitude" (21:19). As he develops his case in the essay we see that this "purification" consists largely if not entirely in the clarification and strengthening of the voice of conscience.

Dostoevsky cites, as examples of the impact of punishment on conscience, the inveterate criminals he came to know so well in his Siberian prison. In that "hard school," he writes, all of them came to recognize their own guilt; perhaps not a single one of them "escaped the long spiritual suffering within him that cleansed and fortified him" (21:18–19).[23] With sustained and onerous punishment, their consciences were cleared of egoistic efforts at self-justification and were thereby "purified" and fortified. His point about the need for reform in the jury system is that the awakened consciences of these hardened criminals, presumably recidivists, could have been aroused and fortified earlier, to the point of turning them from crime, had they not been shown leniency. We see here the great moral significance for Dostoevsky of the admission of guilt. The recognition of their own responsibility for evil that punishment elicited from the confirmed criminals signifies the rebirth of conscience, the return of the individual to the spiritual world of moral truth, which could have taken place sooner if the authorities had had a realistic understanding of the value of punishment.

In Dostoevsky's great novels, we find the same theme of suffering as working to rectify the moral condition of the individual—to set the individual on a sound moral footing, whether by animating and strengthening conscience, effecting "moral purification," or serving as expiation for sins. "Accept suffering

---

23. This is the point, mentioned earlier, at which Dostoevsky contradicts what he said about the convicts and their reaction to punishment in his prison memoir, *Notes from the House of the Dead* (1861–62). In that earlier work, he forcefully and repeatedly remarked on the absence of a sense of guilt and remorse among his fellow convicts: "Over the course of several years," he wrote, "I did not see the slightest sign of remorse among these people . . . inwardly the majority of them considered themselves entirely in the right" (4:15; cf. 4:147). Although he allowed at the time for the possibility that his observations were inaccurate, he testified that he was struck by the absence of a sense of guilt, and he concluded then that the prevailing philosophy of corrective punishment is mistaken: "Prisons and penal servitude do not reform the criminal," he declared; "they only develop hatred" (4:15). By 1873, however, he remembered their attitudes and behavior quite differently, and he drew the opposite conclusion about the possibility of reform through suffering.

and redeem yourself through it," Sonya urges Raskolnikov (6:323). When Dmitry Karamazov, wrongly convicted of murdering his father, nonetheless is reconciled to his impending punishment as morally appropriate, he is attributing to suffering a purely instrumental moral role: "I accept the torture of accusation and my public shame," he states; "I want to suffer and shall be cleansed by suffering! . . . I accept punishment not because I killed him, but because I wanted to kill him and perhaps would in fact have killed him" (14:458).

Joseph Frank has aptly described this instrumental moral role of suffering as one of combating egoism. Frank argues that when Dostoevsky first introduces the theme of earning happiness through suffering—expressed by Natasha in *The Insulted and Injured*—the situation is emblematic of his unwillingness to give a positive moral evaluation to any suffering that is not associated in some way with overcoming egoism: "Natasha, it is clear [Frank writes], is not referring to material hardship or physical deprivation, but rather to the process by which the ramparts of pride, egoism, and wounded self-esteem are battered down and the way left open for forgiveness and love. It is only in this sense that Dostoevsky will ever maintain 'suffering' to be a good."[24] Frank's formula is an insightful analysis of the moral universe of Dostoevsky's mature fiction. All the great novels are morality plays in which egoism is the force to be overcome if salvation is to be found; the "purification" and earning of happiness needed are just those that will work to defeat egoism. The full reanimation of conscience that is implied in Dmitry Karamazov's statement—the recognition that one has done wrong and the penitential acceptance of suffering in consequence of it—is readily described by Frank's formula. For it is directed against egoism, which consists in putting one's own will above the moral law. The overcoming of egoism that Dostoevsky variously describes as strengthening, tempering, elevating, cleansing, or purifying the individual's moral character is essentially what the instrumental value of suffering consists in for him.

Yet it would be the height of irony if for Dostoevsky, a vigorous opponent of the consequentialist ethics of the utilitarians, suffering should have only the same instrumental value they accorded it—that of a necessary evil. Fortunately his "ethics of suffering" does not require us to settle for such an irony, for on further reflection it becomes clear that he regards the act of accepting suffering as often an end-in-itself—a terminal, not merely an instrumental good.

Consider once more the passage in *Winter Notes on Summer Impressions* in which Dostoevsky described the supreme development of personality as consisting in the free act of self-sacrifice: "Voluntarily to lay down one's life for all,

---

24. Joseph Frank, *Dostoevsky: The Stir of Liberation, 1860–1865* (Princeton, N.J.: Princeton University Press, 1986), 129–30.

to go for all to the cross or to the stake," he wrote in that text, "can only be done when one's personality is most powerfully developed" (5:79). There are cases, in other words, in which personal suffering is not prized as a stimulus to the development of morality, for no such stimulus is needed: accepting the suffering of the cross or the stake for the sake of others is a noble act, moral *in itself*, indeed a supremely moral act. Such an act is a direct expression of morality, not a spur to it.

I believe it is beyond question that Dostoevsky considered any act of voluntary suffering for others to be a terminal good, because it is a direct manifestation of the law of love—even if it *also* serves instrumentally to fortify one's own morality or that of others. The willing acceptance of punishment for one's own moral improvement is instrumentally good—a preparation for love; the willing acceptance of suffering for the good of others is terminally good—an act of love.

Much of the morally praiseworthy suffering in Dostoevsky's stories and novels is suffering for the sake of assignable individuals—such is Devushkin's suffering for Varvara Alekseevna in *Poor Folk*, the narrator's for Nastenka in "White Nights," and Sonya's for her family and Raskolnikov in *Crime and Punishment*. But note that in the passage from *Winter Notes on Summer Impressions* Dostoevsky conspicuously speaks of suffering for "all." So he does, too, in sketching the "great idea" for the aspiring writer Yulia Abaza: make your hero, he advises, "consciously accept suffering for all his ancestors, and for everyone and everything, so as to atone for human sin" (30/1:192). In the final chapter of *The Brothers Karamazov*, Kolya cries out, "I should like to die for all humanity" and "I want to suffer for all people" (15:190, 195). Obviously the moral paragon here is once again Christ; at this moral summit, suffering for Dostoevsky is bound up with the mystical notion of universal responsibility for sin and becomes mystical itself. The extension of guilt to all requires a mystical penitence, the acceptance of suffering for all. Such suffering is not valued instrumentally. It is the ultimate act of love. Being Christlike as the moral ideal requires suffering for all. If hell is the suffering of being unable to love anyone, suffering for the love of all is its consummate defeat.

It is wonderfully appropriate to the persona of Dostoevsky's anti-Christ, the Grand Inquisitor, that he, too, views himself as suffering for the love of all, in that he is taking on the onerous burden of freedom that weak human beings cannot endure. But in depriving them of free choice he is destroying their humanity, Dostoevsky believes—just as would any attempt to translate the mystical suffering of Christ into a social order presided over by a secular "redeemer." Still, much of the pathos of the Legend of the Grand Inquisitor is created by his seemingly genuine love for humanity and wish to suffer for it, at least as Ivan Karamazov describes him; these features invest his action with a shadow of moral nobility, despite his egoistic, tragically mistaken notions about what love for humanity requires. Not only Ivan's but Dostoevsky's own understanding of the Grand Inquisitor as an arrogantly deluded lover of humanity is revealed, I believe, in Ivan's achingly beautiful alternative ending to the Legend, in which a wordless Christ, having heard out the Inquisitor's indictment, responds to him only with a kiss . . . whereupon the Inquisitor, who earlier had intended to burn Christ at the stake, allows Him to escape (14:239).[25] They are two figures with an identical sense of universal responsibility, but vastly different notions of what it demanded of them.

Dostoevsky's conception of the moral value of suffering, like his ethical thinking generally, is dominated by the figure of Christ as the supreme ethical ideal and the Christian law of love as the supreme ethical principle. Suffering serves to counter egoism, humbling the individual and enlivening conscience, and in that respect it is instrumentally valuable as promoting observance of the moral law. But suffering has a more intimate connection with the law when, in Christlike fashion, it is freely accepted for the good of others. Then it is itself a manifestation of the law; it is not an aid to altruism but an active instance of it in its most sublime form, the paradigm of which is Christ's suffering for the good of all.

25. For a probing and sensitive discussion of Christ's silence in the Legend of the Grand Inquisitor, see chapter 5 of Bruce K. Ward's *Dostoyevsky's Critique of the West: The Quest for the Earthly Paradise* (Waterloo, Ont.: Wilfrid Laurier University Press, 1986), 135–61.

CHAPTER 4

The Logic of Aesthetics

The preceding chapter explored Dostoevsky's ethical thought without attention to questions of aesthetics. In his opinion, however, the moral and aesthetic natures of human beings are not independent but tightly linked, and for that reason an examination of his ideas on beauty and art will throw further light on his ethics as well.

Aesthetics is the region of Dostoevsky's philosophical thought that has been studied the most, not only because it is closest to his primary identity as a belletrist but because it is intimately connected with his hopes for human salvation, as announced in an enigmatic but much quoted line from *The Idiot*: "Beauty will save the world" (8:317).[1] The primary aim of this chapter is not to repeat or reject the existing studies but rather to complement them by looking at the logic of Dostoevsky's position—that is, at the rationale for aesthetics that he constructed in response to the narrowly rationalistic, utilitarian skepticism about art that prevailed among the Russian intelligentsia of his day.

Almost everything Dostoevsky wrote on the subject was prompted by intense dissatisfaction with the radical aesthetic views of Nikolay Chernyshevsky and his followers. Although he did not formulate a structured aesthetic theory,

---

1. Many Russian-language monographs dealing with philosophical aspects of Dostoevsky's aesthetics were published in the twentieth century, from Ivan Lapshin's *Estetika Dostoevskogo* (Berlin: Obelisk, 1923) and Mikhail Bakhtin's enormously influential *Problemy tvorchestva Dostoevskogo* (Leningrad: Priboi, 1928) to Nadezhda Kashina's late Soviet study, *Estetika F. M. Dostoevskogo*, 2d ed. (Moscow: Vysshaia shkola, 1989). In other languages less has been produced, but nothing in any language, Russian included, can compare in depth or breadth with Robert Louis Jackson's book *Dostoevsky's Quest for Form: A Study of His Philosophy of Art* (New Haven, Conn.: Yale University Press, 1966), which masterfully analyzes the whole sweep of the writer's aesthetic thinking beginning with its Romantic roots.

in the context of polemics against the radicals he vigorously defended his own opinions on the fundamental questions of art and beauty with which such theories deal. In 1861 he published his most significant work in aesthetics in the form of a long critical essay entitled (with transparent allusion to the critic Nikolay Dobrolyubov) "Mr. ———bov and the Question of Art" (18:70–103). And in other works, too, he responded discursively to the ideas put forth by the radicals, advancing arguments against them that were intended to be logically coherent and persuasive.

In these disputes Dostoevsky exhibited no great philosophical originality. His indebtedness to the aesthetic thinking of Schelling, Apollon Grigoryev, and Nikolay Strakhov is well documented.[2] But he marshaled his borrowings effectively, and I believe it can be shown that he had the better of the debate against the Chernyshevsky school. His analyses were more thorough and incisive; his arguments, despite some overreaching, were more apt and compelling. In short, his position was more reasonable than the rationalists', amounting in fact to a comprehensive logical destruction of their case.

To set the stage for Dostoevsky's responses to them it is necessary to sketch the main features of their utilitarian philosophy of art—a philosophy anticipated by Vissarion Belinsky in the 1840s but first formulated and incorporated into a broad theoretical framework by Chernyshevsky in the 1850s, after which it was further elaborated and radicalized by Dobrolyubov and Dmitry Pisarev.

The Utilitarians' Aesthetics

In the worldview popularized by Chernyshevsky and his school, the concept of human needs occupied a central place. Human beings, they claimed, have by nature objective needs that must be satisfied, and the existence of such requirements provides us with an infallible test of the value of every cultural practice and social institution: how well, if at all, does it satisfy natural human needs? The existence of "artificial" or purely subjective demands not rooted in the nature of human beings was also recognized, but the persistence of such false "needs" was attributed to habit, ignorance, or social conditioning; the real question was not what people wanted or thought they needed, but what their

2. Heinrich Stammler, "Dostoevsky's Aesthetics and Schelling's Philosophy of Art," *Comparative Literature* 7 (1955): 313–23; Wayne Dowler, *Dostoevsky, Grigor'ev, and Native Soil Conservatism* (Toronto: University of Toronto Press, 1982), 32–34, 48, 61, 116–17, 123–27; Linda Gerstein, *Nikolai Strakhov* (Cambridge, Mass.: Harvard University Press, 1971), 36–37.

nature as human beings objectively required. The task of social change, then, was resolved into the intellectual effort to identify the authentic needs of human beings and the revolutionary effort to eliminate wasteful catering to false needs and promote the satisfaction of true needs.

To these thinkers, what others called "needs" for beauty and art were by and large artificial—that is, demands corresponding to no natural imperative of the human or social organism. Chernyshevsky's assault on aesthetics was launched in his influential university dissertation, *The Aesthetic Relation of Art to Reality* (1855), in which he denied that art arose out of anything like an inherent demand for beauty. Of the origin of song, for example, Chernyshevsky wrote: "What is the first need that prompts someone to begin to sing? Does a striving for beauty play any part in it? It seems to us that this need is completely different from a concern for beauty. . . . Singing, being in its essence an expression of joy or sorrow, does not at all proceed from our striving for beauty." He did not deny that there is an "aesthetic sense," but he contended that this sense is readily and amply satisfied by the beauty in "real life"—a beauty no art can equal. When singing is turned into an "art," it is only a surrogate, an imitation of "singing as a work of nature."[3]

Although Chernyshevsky did find another raison d'être for some types of art (as we shall see shortly), the overall effect of his attitude was to relegate the specifically *aesthetic* value of art to the realm of the inessential. Even with regard to the beauty in "life," he tended to dismiss it as epiphenomenal and subjective: although "the beautiful" and "the sublime" can be found both in nature and in human life, he wrote, "the enjoyment of whatever objects possess these qualities depends directly on the ideas of the person who enjoys them." For Chernyshevsky and his followers, the true needs of man such as food and shelter depend not at all on "ideas" but entirely on the objective realities of human physiology and the environment.[4]

As Pisarev carried this thought further in the mid-1860s, "aesthetics" stands for what is a purely subjective type of gratification having no ground in real needs:

> The vacuity of all aesthetic judgments consists in the fact that they are pronounced not as the result of reflection but through inspiration, at the prompting of what is called the voice of instinct or feeling. You glance at it, you like it—

---

3. N.G. Chernyshevskii, *Polnoe sobranie sochinenii* (Moscow: Gos. izd. khudozhestvennoi literatury, 1939–53), 2:61, 63.
4. Ibid., 117, 114–15.

well, that means it is good, beautiful, fine. . . . Clearly nature has nothing to do with the matter here; the inner voice of immediate feeling simply parrots what was droned into our ears in earliest childhood. . . . Aesthetics, unaccountability, routine, habit—these are all perfectly equivalent concepts.

Particularly in the midst of poverty and oppressive social surroundings, Pisarev argued, all man's attention should be given to fulfilling the genuine, natural requirements of the human organism—requirements that have "a definite physiological meaning."[5]

What role, if any, might art play in such fulfillment? Chernyshevsky, whose scorn for aesthetic judgments was less intense than Pisarev's, identified a number of limited functions for art in his 1855 dissertation. Art's primary purpose, given the superiority of beauty in nature and "real life," was simply to portray that beauty, which it could accomplish through mimetic faithfulness to reality: "The first purpose of art" Chernyshevsky wrote, "is the representation of nature and life"; works of art "do not correct reality, do not embellish it, but represent it, serve as a substitute for it."[6] In this role art can be useful when people have no access to its real counterpart; a seascape, for example, is useful to those unable to experience the beauty of the sea at first hand. Art, then, must first and foremost be realistic, because only by accurately reproducing reality can it begin to have real value to mankind. The idea of art as a substitute for an absent reality demonstrates that for Chernyshevsky the need for art per se is distinctly secondary to the need for "reality." Art is a stand-in, entirely dispensable in the presence of the original; there is no *aesthetic* need as such.

As his dissertation proceeds, however, Chernyshevsky goes beyond the notion of art as a surrogate to consider other useful functions it may perform, and he begins to speak of the artist as not only a copyist but a teacher and a judge. Although this section of the work is less well developed (no doubt because of Tsarist censorship), the value of art as social criticism for Chernyshevsky comes through very clearly. The artist, who on the one hand can transmit the beauty of a reality to which one has no access, on the other hand can analyze and pass judgment on the reality in which one is immersed. In the latter case, the demand for accurate description remains, but it is augmented by other demands:

5. Dmitry Pisarev, "The Realists," trans. James P. Scanlan, in *Russian Philosophy*, ed. James M. Edie et al. (Chicago: Quadrangle, 1965), 2:86–89.
6. Chernyshevskii, *Polnoe*, 2:77–78.

We have said above that besides representation art has still another purpose—the explanation of life. To some degree all the arts can do this: often it is sufficient to call attention to an object (which art always does) in order to explain its signifi- cance, or to make people understand life better. . . . Poetry [in particular] always of necessity points sharply and clearly to the essential features of an object. . . . [Furthermore] the poet or artist, unable to cease being human, cannot, even if he wished, refrain from pronouncing his judgment on the phenomena he depicts. This judgment is expressed in his work—that is another purpose of works of art, in virtue of which art is numbered among the moral activities of man.[7]

Were it not for the censors, Chernyshevsky would no doubt have argued openly that in portraying social *evils* (depicting social reality without embel- lishment, to use his Aesopian language) the good artist will also explain and condemn them, and in that way will serve the real needs of society both intel- lectually and morally. As it was, Chernyshevsky was limited to concluding that "the fine and lofty mission" of art extended to being not only "a substitute for reality in the event of its absence" but also "a manual of life for man."[8]

Chernyshevsky's followers accepted his realism, his suspicion of the purely "aesthetic," and his stress on social utility as the standard of art, but they tended to see even less connection between art and the satisfaction of real human needs than he did. Pisarev, in particular, found most art entirely devoid of any "fine and lofty mission," and he eventually mounted a full-bore attack on the realm of the aesthetic in his essays "The Realists" (1864) and "The An- nihilation of Aesthetics" (1865). Of all the arts, only literature has a chance of being useful, according to Pisarev, and then only if the writer "hates with a great and holy hatred that enormous mass of petty and rotten stupidities" that exists in contemporary society, and in his passion "depict[s] for us clearly and strikingly those sides of human life which we must know so as to think and act sensibly." Pointedly, Pisarev admits no Russian writers to full membership in this elite circle; Gogol he called an "embryo" poet and Pushkin a "parody" of a poet. The writer who lacks the requisite passion and talent, Pisarev insisted, should change professions; it would be better for him (meaning for society) to "sew boots and bake pies."[9]

Aside from this exception for a small body of literature, Pisarev rejects the arts wholesale on the ground that they have nothing but "aesthetic" value— that is, they are merely titillating, subjectively and trivially. He makes a minor exception for graphic art, acknowledging the limited practical value of archi-

7. Ibid., 85–86.
8. Ibid., 90.
9. Pisarev, "The Realists," 91.

tectural plans and illustrations for popular works in the sciences, but otherwise he sees no redeeming features at all in the nonliterary arts. Referring to figures in music, theater, and dance admired by his Russian contemporaries, he writes sarcastically that "how Mozart and Fanny Elssler, Talma and Rubini could have contrived to apply their great gifts to some rational enterprise, I cannot even imagine." What Russia needs is not art but science, and needs it "not in homeopathic doses but by the bucket and the barrelful."[10]

Dostoevsky's immediate ideological adversary in the early 1860s was neither Chernyshevsky, whose works on aesthetics were already behind him, nor Pisarev, whose vitriol had not yet been fully poured out in print. Rather it was Nikolay Dobrolyubov, the principal literary critic for *Sovremennik* (The Contemporary), the most radical of the intelligentsia journals competing with the Dostoevsky brothers' journal *Vremya* (Time). Ideologically, Dobrolyubov occupied a middle ground between Chernyshevsky and Pisarev. Like the former, he did not dismiss "the aesthetic" out of hand, and he attributed much greater significance than Pisarev did to art, especially literature, as at least potentially a force for good in Russian society. He was the most perceptive literary critic of the three, and by 1861 his critical essays had won him a large audience. Yet, like Pisarev, Dobrolyubov saw little value in the pursuit of beauty or the exercise of artistry per se, and his principal criterion of aesthetic excellence was service to the "true" needs of contemporary Russian society, which he conceived as largely if not entirely material in nature.

Dostoevsky's response to Dobrolyubov in his 1861 essay "Mr. ———bov and the Question of Art" was occasioned by two pieces Dobrolyubov had published in *Sovremennik* during the previous year. One, entitled "Features for the Characterization of the Russian Common People", was a long and highly favorable review of a volume of stories on Russian folk life by Maria Aleksandrovna Markovich (1834–1907), who wrote under the pseudonym "Marko Vovchok." The second, "Poems of Ivan Nikitin," was a briefer, negative appraisal of a volume of lyric verse by the realist poet Ivan Savvich Nikitin (1824–61). Dobrolyubov's explanation of his reasons for lauding the former writer and scolding the latter show us the main elements of his approach to aesthetics as Dostoevsky engaged it in "Mr. ———bov" and subsequent writings.

For Dobrolyubov the primary virtue of Marko Vovchok's stories is that they truthfully portray the dignity, strength, sufferings, and needs of the common people in Russia. Just as for Chernyshevsky the beauty of a painting comes from the beauty of the objective reality it depicts, so for Dobrolyubov a story's value is determined chiefly by the value of the real-life phenomena it

---

10. Ibid., 92, 94.

portrays. The only formal requirements that Dobrolyubov stipulates is that the portrayal be "clear, vivid, and truthful," where "truthful" meant realistically faithful to the phenomena represented. Beyond that, content is everything: the merit of artistic works, he writes, depends on "how important [are] the phenomena of life with which they deal." Dobrolyubov explains this requirement further in a summarizing passage that shows his aesthetic priorities:

> If the phenomena and persons depicted by Vovchok in no way portray for us our people . . . but simply relate exceptional and curious cases having no importance at all, then it is evident that the literary merit of [her book] is absolutely insignificant too. If, however, the reader . . . acknowledges the universality and the great importance of the features we have pointed to in Marko Vovchok's book, then of course he cannot help acknowledging the high merit of a literary phenomenon that so comprehensively, vividly, and truthfully portrays our national life.[11]

In Dobrolyubov's mind, then, the principal question in appraising a work is whether the real-life phenomena portrayed are "universal" and "important" and thus worth portraying. For Dobrolyubov and his circle, the answer in broad terms was obvious: what should be portrayed is what will contribute to the understanding and fulfillment of the "natural" needs of society and its members. In Russia in 1860, that meant above all the elimination of the institution of serfdom (finally achieved by imperial decree in 1861). In depicting "truthfully" the dignity, good sense, and high moral character of the peasants, Marko Vovchok was helping people to understand her subjects' "natural, innate demands," to see that tyranny and coercion are "antithetical to the natural demands of the organism." Literature, Dobrolyubov proclaimed, must respond to "the living demands of nature," and in doing so it is obliged to be "the vehicle of enlightened and not of ignorant ideas." On this basis he issued a stern moral summons to the contemporary Russian writer: "It is now the task of literature to pursue the remnants of serfdom in public life and deal the finishing blow to the concepts it engendered."[12]

That the "natural needs" to be served by art are not primarily aesthetic is made even clearer by Dobrolyubov in his review of Nikitin's book. The son of a poor shopkeeper, Nikitin excelled at portraying the sufferings of the Russian peasantry and lower middle class; the long narrative poem for which he is best known, *The Kulak* (1858), is the story of a peasant whose poverty leads him to exploit others of his class. These interests should have endeared Nikitin

---

11. N. A. Dobroliubov, *Sobranie sochinenii v deviati tomakh* (Moscow: Gos. izd. khudozhestvennoi literatury, 1961–64), 6:286–87.

12. Ibid., 250, 253, 288, 223.

to the radical intelligentsia, but he disappointed them because he was insufficiently single-minded in his attention to social ills. He was drawn also to patriotic and spiritual themes—"metaphysical," Dobrolyubov called the latter—
and, perhaps worst of all, he displayed a disturbing interest in formal values in
his poetry.

Dobrolyubov's critique begins by faulting Nikitin for "taking it into his
head" in his latest book to rewrite, solely with an eye to stylistic improvement,
verses he had published a few years before: "Rhymes and phrases are changed,
a line from one couplet is moved to another, two lines are made into one, and
so on—and all this without any inner necessity, simply according to the demands of the ear!" The exclamation mark demonstrates how low, if at all, the
requirements of euphony rank on the scale of "natural needs" for Dobrolyubov. Unlike Pisarev, he did not deny all value to stylistic refinements;
he admitted that in some cases Nikitin's revisions were for the better. But he
made it clear that what he calls "aesthetic niceties" are insufficient and essentially unnecessary for the production of good art. Let Mr. Nikitin, he writes,
"put aside all thought of the power of his 'plastic' talent. . . . Plasticity in poetry is a luxury, a caprice, an accessory. We may marvel at poets who have
nothing but plastic talent, but we marvel in just the same way at the brilliant
virtuoso whose whole merit consists in the skillful surmounting of the techni-
cal difficulties of a game . . . The task of poetry is life."[13]

Pushkin and Lermontov, Dobrolyubov goes on, did have "plastic" talents,
but more importantly they dealt in their day with "life" in a way that was useful to Russian society at the time. Unfortunately, they have nothing to offer
the society of the 1860s. Nikitin might have filled the void, were he not now
concerned "above all with artistry."[14]

The substantive program for art outlined by Dobrolyubov in the Nikitin
essay is an amplification of the ideas sketched in his appreciation of Marko
Vovchok's work, though his references to serfdom are now oblique. The artist
must depict realistically and sympathetically "the simple, urgent needs of life,"
"the urgent demands of human nature," the struggle to satisfy authentic
human and social requirements. In the present day, he continues, that struggle
is focused on "the organization of social relations" and in particular on "the
distribution of natural goods among people," in consequence of what he calls
the modern "discovery" that all man's troubles arise from "the greater or lesser
injustice of the social circumstances in which he lives." A prime need of soci-

13. Ibid., 155, 168, 176. The Russian word here translated 'plasticity' (*plastika*) connotes grace and
elegance of style.
14. Ibid., 173.

ety, then, is "the *study* of all social inequities" (Dobrolyubov's emphasis), and it is here that literature finds the role that may give it true value. The very origin of the novel, a modern form, is connected, Dobrolyubov contends, with "the new view of the structure of social relations as the cause of the universal discord that now alarms every person who has given so much as a single thought to the meaning of his existence." The epic and dramatic genres, too, have come to depict and study social relations, and it is now the turn of lyric poetry, which is already attempting to "sing of the feelings aroused in the soul by particular phenomena of social life." Were it not for censorship, Dobrolyubov might have recommended not only the study of existing social relations but their radical transformation. In any event, he made clear the utilitarian duty of the artist.[15]

Art and Human Needs

Dostoevsky's polemical response in "Mr. ——bov and the Question of Art" is shaped by the fact that in general terms he accepted several of the radicals' premises. He signals a degree of approval at the outset when, adopting a rhetorical strategy much loved by thinkers through the ages, he presents his own view as a reasonable middle course between two extremes, each of which takes a good point too far—that is, the radicals' utilitarian position at one pole and the doctrine of "art for art's sake" at the other. It soon becomes evident, however, that he is far closer to the latter extreme; virtually all of his arguments are directed against the utilitarians' position. Yet there is a significant area of agreement between Dostoevsky and the utilitarians. They agree, first, that the satisfaction of inherent human needs is an appropriate criterion by which to evaluate art. They agree, second, that realism is essential in art and that in virtue of its realism art can convey knowledge of the world. And they agree, third, that art can have extra-aesthetic, moral and social value.

In light of this concurrence on fundamental points, Dostoevsky treated the radicals' views in aesthetics somewhat differently from the way he treated their denials of immortality and the existence of God and their theory of Rational Egoism. Rather than contending that his opponents subscribed to false principles, he sought to show that they wrongly construed the true principles he shared with them. When these same principles are interpreted properly, he contended, they not only validate but mandate the very forms of art against which the radicals rail. His own interpretations, which constitute his case for

15. Ibid., 165–66, 177.

the importance of the aesthetic realm in human life, will occupy us in the three remaining sections of this chapter, beginning here with the subject of art and the satisfaction of human needs.

In response to the utilitarians' insistence on judging art by its relevance to true needs, Dostoevsky accepted the criterion but mounted a two-pronged attack on their understanding of it. First, he contended that the radicals, because of their impoverished view of human nature, did not adequately identify all of man's true needs. Second, he argued that a utilitarian approach is ill-suited to the determination of the value of art no matter what needs are posited.

The crux of Dostoevsky's first charge is that his opponents, as materialists, ignore the spiritual dimension of man and look only to physiology to find authentic human requirements, thereby inevitably focusing on such basic demands as food and shelter. There are in human nature spiritual and specifically aesthetic needs as well, he insists in "Mr. ——bov":

> Art is as much a need for man as eating and drinking. The need for beauty and the creativity that embodies it is inseparable from man; without it, perhaps, man would not wish to live in this world. Man thirsts for it, finds and accepts beauty *without any conditions*, simply because it is beauty, and bows down reverentially before it, without asking what it is useful for and what one may buy with it. (18:94; Dostoevsky's emphasis)

He is not denying that art can be useful, but he is insisting that it is not valued solely for any extra-aesthetic utility it may have. It directly fulfills, and is sought in response to, a purely aesthetic requirement that is just as important in human life as the "basic" needs acknowledged by the utilitarians.

Neither Dostoevsky nor his ideological opponents ever asked themselves how imperative a requirement had to be in order to qualify as a "true" or basic need. The materialists, however, tacitly took physical survival as the touchstone: air to breathe, water to drink, food to eat, and defense against disease and the elements were unquestionably genuine, physiologically based needs, which must be satisfied for a person to continue in existence. Dostoevsky did not reject this criterion, but he could not reasonably argue that deprivation of beauty and art leads directly to death by some physiological mechanism. As the above passage indicates, however, he did attempt to establish a nexus between beauty and physical survival: without beauty "man would not wish to live in this world." In keeping with his broader view of human nature as incorporating a free spiritual consciousness, he connects such deprivation not with physiologically unavoidable death but with *unwillingness* to continue in existence, just as he also argued (as we saw in chapter 1) that deprivation of the beliefs in

God and immortality leads to suicide.[16] In a letter of 1876 he included suicide among a list of horrors that would follow if people were deprived of the "ideal" of beauty: "If . . . there is no spiritual life, no ideal of Beauty, then man will languish, will die, will go out of his mind, will kill himself or sink into pagan fantasies" (29/2:85).

Whatever we may think of such hypothetical predictions, Dostoevsky was serious about rivaling the claims of the materialists: he wished to put the aesthetic need on the same level of vital urgency as the need for food and drink. It is not a merely "unaccountable" and subjective requirement, as Pisarev had insisted, but a requirement for (endurable) existence. Perhaps Dostoevsky's most telling point in that connection, more convincing than dire talk of suicidal consequences, is his sober observation in "Mr. ——bov" concerning the ubiquity of art in human culture, which suggests a more than accidental connection with human existence: "From the beginning of the world to the present day, art has never left man, has always responded to his needs and ideal. . . . It was born with man, developed along with his historical life, and died together with his historical life" (18:101).

In "Mr. ——bov" Dostoevsky does not attempt a classic definition of the primary object of the aesthetic need—that is, beauty—by genus and differentia, but he does provide an ostensive definition by mentioning specific works of art that he considers beautiful, including the Apollo Belvedere, a statue of the goddess Diana, Afanasy Fet's poem "Diana," and the *Iliad* (all of them works that radical writers had held up as useless, if not socially pernicious, examples of "pure" art). As for what these disparate examples have in common in virtue of which they all deserve the epithet 'beautiful', he makes his point in a clever riposte to the Nihilists' insistence that in difficult times social resources should be directed exclusively to genuine, material needs rather than useless luxuries like art. Just the reverse, says Dostoevsky:

> The need for beauty develops most when people are in discord with reality, in disharmony, in conflict, that is, when they are *most alive*, for people are most alive when they are searching for something and trying to obtain it; it is then that there arises in them the most natural desire for everything harmonious, for tranquillity, and in beauty there is both harmony and tranquillity. (18:94; Dostoevsky's emphasis)

16. Years later, Dostoevsky put a version of the same notion about the vital need for beauty in the mouth of the elder Verkhovensky in *Demons*: "Without science, without bread," Stepan Trofimovich exclaims, "life is possible; only without beauty it is impossible, for there will be nothing left in the world" (10:373).

Of course this attempt to turn the tables on his socialist opponents would hardly be convincing to them, since they would regard the harmony and tranquillity offered by the perception of beauty as no more than escapism, and they certainly would deny that people are "most alive" when they are deprived and seeking. Here again we see a fundamental difference between two conceptions of human well-being: the radicals equated happiness with satisfaction, whereas Dostoevsky equated it with the struggle for satisfaction.

In any event, for Dostoevsky what all beautiful things have in common is that they incorporate "harmony and tranquillity." The aesthetic importance of these qualities in his thinking is further confirmed a few lines later in the essay when he sums up his point: "And thus beauty is inherent in everything healthy—that is, most alive—and is an inescapable need of the human organism," he writes; "It is harmony; in it is the pledge of tranquillity" (18:94). Robert Louis Jackson has given us a full account of the contours of this essentially classical conception of beauty—beauty as the ideal of "harmony, measure, and repose"—as it emerges in Dostoevsky's writings.[17] Although in *The Brothers Karamazov* Dmitry exclaims that beauty is "undefinable" and "a mysterious thing" (14:100), Dostoevsky did not leave us in the dark as to the general contours of the concept. For him the classical conception to which he subscribed is manifested in everything from the sensory perception of beauty in the human form to the perception of metaphysical harmony in mystical experience.

A lucid portrayal of the latter harmony occurs in Dostoevsky's account in *The Idiot* of the aura preceding Prince Myshkin's (and surely his own) epileptic seizures. In chapter 1, I discussed that account in its religious dimension, as offering evidence for the existence of God. Although it did not concern us at the time, the passage also has an aesthetic dimension, for Dostoevsky describes the moment of ecstatic union with "the highest synthesis of life" as a resolution of all conflict and disquiet, and explicitly calls it not only a "higher tranquillity" but the height of *beauty*:

> The result . . . [is] harmony and beauty in the highest degree, and gives a feeling, unprecedented and undivined before, of fullness, of proportion, of reconciliation and ecstatic, prayerful fusion with the highest synthesis of life. . . . That it really was "beauty and prayer," that it really was "the highest synthesis of life," of that he could not doubt, or even entertain the possibility of doubt. (8:188)

17. Jackson, *Dostoevsky's Quest*, 46. On the influence of Schelling in this connection, see Stammler, "Dostoevsky's Aesthetics," 313–23; and Dowler, *Dostoevsky*, 123.

We shall return later to the broader significance of this notion of beauty, and particularly to the question of its connection with moral and social values. For now it is sufficient to note that Dostoevsky ascribes both metaphysical and aesthetic significance to the natural need for beauty.

But beauty is not the sole object of urgent aesthetic need for Dostoevsky. Revisiting the critical passage from "Mr. ——bov," we note that it presents the requirement as twofold: it is a need not only for "beauty" but for "the creativity that embodies it" (18:94). Although he does not lay special stress on the distinction, Dostoevsky appears to recognize here not one but two aesthetic needs—the passive need to experience beauty and the active need to create it.

That the two are in fact distinguishable and separable for Dostoevsky is also suggested by other passages in which he speaks of one without mentioning the other. For example, near the beginning of the article, in summarizing the views of the champions of "art for art's sake," he expresses a point with which he himself agrees, and which he takes to be the core of truth in their position:

> Creativity, the basic principle of every art, is an integral, organic quality of human nature and has the right to exist and develop simply because it is a necessary appurtenance of the human spirit. It is as legitimate in man as intellect, as all the moral qualities of man, and perhaps as two arms, two legs, and a stomach. It is inseparable from man and forms with him one whole. (18:74)

Throughout the article he is arguing for the artistic freedom to create, without the imposition of any norms or standards—including, presumably, the norm of beauty. "In art the first law," he insists, "is freedom of inspiration and creativity" (18:77). And again: "Creativity, the foundation of every art, lives in man as a manifestation of part of his organism, but it lives inseparably with him" (18:101).

The importance of creative activity and its extension beyond the bounds of both art and beauty is suggested at many points in Dostoevsky's writings. Indeed the breadth of the fundamental need is such that even the word 'creativity' is too confining if we restrict it to constructive production only. In an interesting monologue given to the Underground Man, Dostoevsky developed a broader sense of creativity as the expression of power and freedom in striving for a goal, which can also include destruction:

> I agree: man is primarily a creating animal, condemned to strive consciously toward a goal and busy himself with the engineering art—that is, eternally and

ceaselessly to build a road for himself *wherever it may lead*. . . . Man loves to create and to build roads; that is beyond question. But why does he also so passionately love destruction and chaos? . . . Is it perhaps . . . that he himself has an instinctive fear of achieving his goal and completing the structure he is creating? . . . Perhaps, like a chess player, he loves only the process of achieving the goal, not the goal itself. (5:118; Dostoevsky's emphasis)

Particularly significant for our purposes is Dostoevsky's comparison of creativity, broadly conceived, to game-playing, for this comparison finds echoes in other passages in which he conspicuously links art with play. In these passages, the variety of creation we call artistic is traced to a human need to engage in playful, gamelike activity. For example, in an unpublished variant to his 1864 article, "Mr. Shchedrin, or a Schism among the Nihilists," defending the interests of art against its materialist detractors with their emphasis on "the belly," he wrote:

Man, along with [simple] food, wants freedom, a little cake, wants to be mischievous, to play, to fantasize; he has only one life to live, and for that reason everyone wants to live it as much as possible according to his own will. In a word, a full belly may be the final step but not the first step; it may be a worthy product of all vital forces, but not by the preliminary and intentional paralysis of all the other capacities of man. (20:239)

Later, writing *The Brothers Karamazov*, he found an opportunity to offer an explanation of the origin of art along these lines. In book 10, the precocious thirteen-year-old Kolya Krasotkin is reluctant to admit that he plays children's games, but Alyosha reassures him as follows:

Grownups go to the theater, for example, and there, too, the adventures of all sorts of heroes are presented, sometimes also with robbers and fighting; isn't that really the same thing—in its own way, of course? A game of war among young people during recreation, or a game of robbers—this, too, is emerging art, the emerging need for art in the young soul. (14:484)

This is as close as Dostoevsky came to advancing a specific explanation of the need for artistic creativity (as distinguished from the need for beauty), but what he says here demonstrates his affinity with the so-called "play theory" of art soon to be elaborated in Germany and elsewhere by Konrad Lange and Karl Groos, among others. Dostoevsky did not know the writings of these scholars (he died before their principal works were published), but he was certainly familiar with the German idealist conceptions of art that had influenced them. Immanuel Kant in his *Critique of Judgment* (1790) had made a point of comparing art with play, on the ground that each is a free activity "agreeable on its own account."[18] Friedrich Schiller, one of the young Dostoevsky's favorite writers, enthusiastically expanded the comparison and advanced the basic ideas that were carried further by Lange and Groos: namely, that both art and play spring from an excess of human vigor, leading to the expression of human desires and impulses through the imagination in ways that are freer and fuller than those provided by real life.[19] In explaining the human necessity of art, the natural urge to play was at least as important to Dostoevsky as the natural urge to seek harmony and tranquillity.

For Dostoevsky, these two aesthetic needs—the need for beauty and the need to create—come together to prompt activity that produces beauty in the form of art. 'Artistry' (*khudozhestvennost'*) is the term he typically employs for the ability to apply creativity in the service of beauty, and he gave much thought, in "Mr.——bov" and elsewhere, to the values created by artistry itself, independently of any intellectual, moral, or social value that art might have. Artistry has its own "requirements," he tells a correspondent in 1879 (30/1:122). In a notebook entry he calls artistry "the main thing" aesthetically; without it a work is merely boring (24:77).

Dostoevsky never defined 'artistry' in so many words, but consistently with his general idea of beauty as harmony he always discussed it in terms of the distinctive harmonies it produces. For him the creative production of beauty was the production of new entities—works of art—marked by their own harmonies. Unlike Chernyshevsky, for whom artistry merely reproduces the beauties of nature and real life, Dostoevsky believed that artistry itself creates special beauties in the form of specifically aesthetic harmonies.

One such harmony, to which he devoted a great deal of attention, was the conformity of the work of art (he had in mind chiefly literature and painting) to the reality it represents. A distinctively aesthetic value—realism—is created by the agreement between the work and the real world. Hence some degree, at least, of realism is one of the requirements of artistry. In the letter of 1879 quoted above, he worries that his monk Zosima in *The Brothers Karamazov* will not seem sufficiently "sublime" because of the *artistic* need to include petty,

---

18. *Kant's Critique of Aesthetic Judgement*, trans. James Creed Meredith (Oxford: Clarendon, 1911), 164.

19. For further discussion of the play theory, with texts from Lange and Groos, see Melvin M. Rader, ed., *A Modern Book of Esthetics* (New York: Holt, 1935), 3–52.

even comical details of his life: "Because of artistic demands I was compelled to touch on the most banal aspects in the biography of my monk so as not to damage artistic realism" (30/1:122).

Dostoevsky repeatedly affirms that art, however much a product of the creative play of imagination, must be in harmony with reality at some level. "All art consists to some degree in exaggeration," he wrote in 1861, "provided, however, that it does not exceed certain limits"; if a portraitist exaggerates a distinctive facial feature too much, the result is not art but caricature (19:162). Fantasy has its limits, Dostoevsky told the aspiring novelist Yulia Abaza in 1880: "The fantastic must come so close to the real that you should *almost* believe it" (30/1:192; Dostoevsky's emphasis). He insistently demanded "true" characters, meaning in part characters appropriate to the real situations in which they are depicted; in this light he defends his own characters in *Demons* as having been shown by events to be "justified by reality" and "discerned truthfully" (30/1:63). The "beauty" of Pushkin's characters, he said in his memorial speech, "lies in their indubitable truth" (26:144).

Thus although the artwork does not simply copy reality, its aesthetic value is constituted in part by conformity with the real world. Realism is not a device for conveying other values; properly understood, it is itself one of the valued harmonies that artistry produces.

A second type of artistic harmony that Dostoevsky mentions is the accordance between the artist's intention or "idea," as he typically calls it, and the genre selected to express it. That there must be an idea is itself a requirement for artistry, as we shall see in greater detail below; but for Dostoevsky the idea can have aesthetic value only when presented in an appropriate genre.

After the publication of *Crime and Punishment*, the writer Varvara Obolenskaya wrote asking Dostoevsky for permission to adapt the novel for the stage. He willingly agreed, but felt obliged to warn her that attempts to turn other literary forms into drama had often failed: "There is some secret of art according to which the epic form will never find a correspondence in the dramatic form. I even believe that for the different forms of art there also exist sets of poetic ideas that correspond to them, so that an idea can never be expressed in another form, a form not corresponding to it" (29/1:225). He suggested some changes Obolenskaya might care to make in the work, presumably with an eye to developing a new idea that would be appropriate to the dramatic form, but there is no evidence that she pursued the project.

Of greater interest to Dostoevsky was a third type of harmony at which artistry aims—the agreement of the artist's idea with the particular artistic means used within its genre to express it. He referred often to the importance of harmony between form and content, despite his own inability to describe this harmony in detail and despite the fact that he admittedly sometimes failed to find the right form for his own artistic ideas.[20] His most pointed statement of the criterion came in "Mr. ——bov," in the context of literature:

> How does one recognize artistry in a work of art? By the fact that we see the fullest possible accord between the artistic idea and the form in which it is embodied. Let us say it still more clearly: artistry, if only in a novelist, for example, is the ability to express his own idea in the characters and images of the novel so clearly that the reader, having finished it, understands the artist's idea just as perfectly as the writer himself understood it in creating his work. (18:80)

Rather than delving more deeply into what specifically is required for such accordance of form and content, however, Dostoevsky takes refuge in a tautology: "Simply put, then, artistry in a writer is the ability to write well" (18:80). Yet when Dostoevsky lauds Yulia Abaza for what he calls the "true and profound idea" of the manuscript she sent him and then writes, "A great idea, if only your artistry is up to it" (30/1:192), he was undoubtedly thinking not only of the lack of realism in her earlier images (such as the hero with the block of ice for a heart) but of their clumsy, materialistic inappropriateness to her essentially spiritual "idea." The reason he called artistry "the main thing" in the notebook passage cited above is that "it helps to express the idea with a distinct picture and image" (24:77).

Such are the ways in which "artistry" has independent and immediate value for Dostoevsky: it both expresses directly the natural human need to create and it creates products that respond directly to the natural human need for beauty, in the form of the several specifically aesthetic harmonies that the artist produces.

But is establishing that art serves specifically aesthetic needs enough to counter the radicals' arguments against "pure" art? However ardently Dostoevsky may argue that human beings might not *wish* to live without beauty and art, and historically have not done so, are not the needs cited by the radicals— physiological needs without which people *cannot* live—still more urgent? Because he cannot plausibly deny that people have such vital needs, he must find a way to question the reasonableness of using those needs as standards of aesthetic appraisal. This he does in "Mr. ——bov" by wittily casting doubt on the *usefulness* of utilitarian reasoning in determining the worthiness of art. In this way he completes his dual attack on the utilitarians' views of the relation

---

20. On this point see Victor Terras's comments in *Reading Dostoevsky* (Madison: University of Wisconsin Press, 1998), 30–31.

between art and human needs: they ignore man's specifically aesthetic needs, and they unreasonably attempt to judge art on the basis of its tenuous connection with the satisfaction of nonaesthetic needs.

Pursuing the second line of attack, he admits at the outset that there are times in human life when material needs are obviously more pressing than the needs for beauty and creativity. But he suggests that in such cases the needs are appropriately met not by art but by civic action. In the heat of battle, one should aid one's comrades, not withdraw to make sketches; after a natural disaster such as the great Lisbon earthquake of 1755, a newspaper should publish news useful to survivors, not a poem about nightingales and babbling brooks. Even then, however, it is not the *poem* that should be condemned; the fault lies with the poet, who "misused art at an inopportune time. He sang and danced at the coffin of a dead man" (18:76).

Dostoevsky does not deny that, extraordinary circumstances aside, art may be a useful and appropriate instrument for the satisfaction of nonaesthetic needs. But he assumes—justifiably, it would seem—that any such utility will be indirect and deferred. Unlike artistry's immediate satisfaction of the needs for beauty and creativity, the satisfaction of nonaesthetic needs through art depends on the future consequences of producing and exhibiting the art. A novel may help to convince someone that the Russian serfs both want and deserve their freedom. But that is only one step toward the satisfaction of needs. The new conviction must help to create a new mood in society; the new mood must contribute to the elimination of serfdom; and the resulting new social relations must lead to the redistribution of economic goods—all before we reach the actual alleviation of hunger and disease.

Something like such a chain of events is evidently on Dostoevsky's mind when he mounts his most powerful attack on the utilitarian idea in "Mr. ——bov." The problem with utilitarian reasoning, as we saw in Dostoevsky's critique of its use in ethics, is that it depends on the prediction of future consequences; but the "future," at least with respect to the social impact of any given work of art, is notoriously complex and diffuse, and thus impossible to predict with any confidence. Merely on the basis of projected consequences, one cannot convincingly demonstrate that "utilitarian" art will in fact be useful or "pure" art useless:

It is impossible to calculate every future step of all humanity like a calendar. Therefore how is one to determine *absolutely correctly* what is harmful and what is useful? But it is not just a matter of the future: we cannot have precise and positive information about all the paths and deviations—in a word, about the whole normal course—of the useful even in our past . . . Therefore how can you determine, measure, and weigh the benefit that the *Iliad*, for example, has brought humanity as a whole? Where, when, in what cases has it been useful, and in what way? Finally, what exact influence did it have on particular nations at a particular period in their development, and how much of this influence was there (well, let's say in pounds, tons, yards, kilometers, degrees, etc.)? (18:95; Dostoevsky's emphasis)

Thus even in regard to art of the *past*, attempting to draw up a balance sheet of good and bad consequences is fraught with difficulty. Even if the enraged citizens of Lisbon had lynched the insensitive poet in 1755, decades later they might well have built a monument to honor him for his poetic gifts (18:76).

A utilitarian would object that although certainty might be unattainable, reliable judgments can be based on the greater or lesser likelihood of consequences of various kinds: in all human affairs, probabilities, at least, can be established. But Dostoevsky's point is that nothing *more* than probabilities—and rather low-level probabilities at that—can be attained in the charting of chains of consequences, whereas the aesthetic value of *artistry* is assured and unquestionable. Beauty and creativity satisfy needs directly and immediately wherever they are present in art; their value *can* be established "absolutely correctly." Furthermore, the need for beauty is directly satisfied both now and whenever the work is appreciated in the future; of that projection also we can be confident, for it involves no complex forecasting of indirect consequences. It is in this sense that Dostoevsky can write that beauty is "always useful" (18:95), but he means that it is useful as an end in itself, not in the "utilitarian" sense of being a means to an end. It is "useful," he concludes in "Mr.———bov," "because it is beauty, because there is in humanity a constant need for beauty and its highest ideal" (18:102).

Again, this is not to deny that beauty *can* be utilitarian, even in the means-end sense. "The eternal harmony embodied in the *Iliad*," Dostoevsky writes, "can have a highly pronounced impact on the soul. . . . Beauty, harmony and strength can have a great and beneficial impact on [our spirit], a *useful* impact, can instill energy, sustain our strength" (18:96; Dostoevsky's emphasis). He even provides what he admits is a far-fetched example of how the perception of beauty in "pure" art might contribute to social reform. Suppose, he says, that a man in his youth had seen the Apollo Belvedere and "the god had irresistibly impressed himself on the young man's soul by his stately and infinitely beautiful image." Taking a page from the materialists' book, Dostoevsky imagines an actual physiological effect: "Perhaps—who knows!—it may even be that with such sensations of supreme beauty, such a nervous shock, a kind of inner change takes place in man, a kind of movement of particles or galvanic current, in a moment turning what existed before into something different, a piece of ordinary iron into a magnet." He goes on:

> And, who knows? When this young man, twenty or thirty years later, took one stand rather than another at the time of some great social event in which he was a great leading figure . . . perhaps among the mass of reasons that made him act thus and not otherwise there was, unconsciously for him, the impression of the Apollo Belvedere he had seen twenty years before. (18:78)

"You laugh?" Dostoevsky asks his opponents; but "with regard to such facts," he goes on, "you yourselves still know absolutely nothing" (18:78). His point is that the cause-and-effect relations blithely assumed by the utilitarians in rejecting "pure" art in favor of socially committed art are sufficiently complex, indirect, and open that presumed utilitarian value is at best an unreliable standard for discriminating between the two types of art.

Dostoevsky's case for the aesthetic value of art, then, is grounded in disagreements with his materialist opponents as to the character of "natural" human needs and the reliability of utilitarian calculation. Accepting their premise that art should serve needs essential to human nature, he contended that among such needs, no less prevalent and insistent than physiological demands for food and water, are "spiritual" demands for beauty and creative activity. But he also questioned utilitarian reasoning in aesthetics on the ground that the consequences of future actions and events are sufficiently diffuse and uncertain as to mean little in comparison with the certainty that art fulfills the compelling human needs for beauty and creativity.

Realism and the Cognitive Value of Art

The second broad area in which Dostoevsky and his ideological opponents agreed on a basic principle but disagreed on its interpretation is the area of artistic realism and its role in conveying knowledge of the world. Although he viewed aesthetic value as in itself sufficient to justify art, in his arguments against its radical naysayers he was not content with grounding art's right to existence and freedom on its aesthetic merits alone. He also believed that art served other values, among which was the cognitive value of being an avenue to truth, a way of coming to understand man and his world. From his youth onwards, Dostoevsky persistently spoke of artists as seers and prophets, and critics have long noted the importance of artistic cognition in his worldview. Victor Terras comments that Dostoevsky saw art as "a key to understanding life's riddles."[21] Nadezhda Kashina, speaking of Dostoevsky's aesthetics as "highly epistemological," goes so far as to claim that cognition was for him "the meaning and mission of art."[22]

For Dostoevsky what makes art a vehicle of knowledge is precisely one of its *aesthetic* merits—its realism. To the extent that there is a harmony between the work of art and the reality it represents, the work must truthfully correspond to that reality and thus must reflect knowledge of it. Here he was again in fundamental accord with his opponents, who also regarded realism as a truthful correspondence between the work and reality, and who saw some art, at least, as having cognitive value in virtue of its realism; for Belinsky the basic function of art was to enlighten people about reality.[23] But Dostoevsky strongly disputed their understanding of that correspondence and consequently their claim that art meeting their interpretation did actually produce knowledge. Not incidentally, he also disagreed with their contention that his own art, because its subjects often seemed fantastic and unreal, was lacking in such cognitive value.

The tenor of realism as the radical intelligentsia understood it had been set early on by Chernyshevsky's dictum that the first purpose of art was not to "embellish" reality but to "represent it, serve as a substitute for it."[24] Although to his credit Chernyshevsky had tried to distance himself from what he called "Daguerreotype copying" and even to ascribe to art subsidiary functions of explaining and judging the reality it reproduced, his basic injunction to represent reality "as far as possible" and "without correction" had the greatest impact. The tendency in Dostoevsky's Russia to interpret realism as a simple mirroring of reality was no doubt reinforced by such broader European trends as the growing popularity of genre painting and of "naturalistic" literature of the Zola variety. Whatever the causes, the Russian "realists" confronted Dostoevsky with a decidedly photographic conception of realism—realism as a literal transcription of reality.

As Jackson has convincingly shown, Dostoevsky's opposition to realism as thus understood was consistent and intense. For him not photographic faithfulness, not mechanical accuracy, but something else, broader and deeper, was demanded from art.[25] "Disinterestedness and faithful reproduction of reality," he wrote in a notebook, "are worth absolutely nothing and, most important,

21. Ibid., 129.
22. Kashina, *Estetika*, 101.
23. See the discussion of Belinsky's position in Stephen K. Carter, *The Political and Social Thought of F. M. Dostoevsky* (New York: Garland, 1991), 42–43.
24. Chernyshevskii, *Polnoe*, 2:78.
25. Jackson, *Dostoevsky's Quest*, 76–77.

mean nothing" (24:308). Dostoevsky sometimes called his own view "idealism" to distinguish it from theirs, but more often, as in this letter of 1868 to his friend Apollon Maykov, he contended that his outlook is the *true* realism: "Ah, my friend! My conceptions of reality and realism are completely different from those of our realists and critics. My idealism is more real than their [realism]. . . . [My 'fantasy'] is original, real realism! It in fact is what realism is, only deeper, but with them it's shallow sailing" (28/2:329).

The reference to "shallow sailing" is no accident, for it reflects one of a number of charges that Dostoevsky in various places brought against the photographic conception of realism. Each of these charges deserves brief notice, for they all help to flesh out his conception of the cognitive function of realist art.

First, he argues that the photographic reproduction of reality is superficial, confined to surface realities without penetrating to the real nature of things. His contention that his own realism is "deeper" makes use of a spatial metaphor to which he frequently returns: to capture adequately the nature of the subject one must delve beneath the surface, to the depths of the underlying reality. A more adequate understanding of realism requires such probing: "They call me a psychologist," he wrote in a notebook of 1880–81. "Untrue: I am simply a realist in the highest sense—that is, I depict all the depths of the human soul" (27:65).

Dostoevsky employs a related, inner-outer version of the spatial metaphor in *Notes from the House of the Dead*, where he is speaking of the hidden nature of the convicts he encountered in his Siberian prison. However coarse and amoral the men might seem from the outside, he affirmed, in their inner or essential nature they were marked by admirable traits such as a keen sense of justice. "One has only to remove the outer, superficial husk," he wrote, "and look at the kernel itself more attentively, more closely, without prejudice, and he will see in the people such things as he would never have suspected" (4:121–22).

Metaphors aside, Dostoevsky's literal point, and a scarcely debatable one, is that what is directly and plainly obvious about a thing or situation is not necessarily the best clue to its true nature. Confinement to "superficial" or "outer" details without investigation of their invisible or less visible causes and conditions, their "inner essence," is a poor excuse for realism, for it shows little knowledge of the subject. This is perhaps what Dostoevsky had in mind when he dismissed the novelist Aleksey Pisemsky's depictions of the bureaucratic complications of Russian life with the sarcastic comment that "all of Pisemsky's realism comes down to the knowledge of where it is necessary to submit what petition" (20:203).

A second reason why "Daguerreotype" reproduction is incompatible with "realism in the highest sense" for Dostoevsky is that it fails to acknowledge the need for principles of selectivity and hence is undiscriminating. In seeking to portray reality, it does not distinguish between essential and inessential, characteristic and accidental, and consequently it does not convey a truly accurate picture of the nature of the subject. He made this point in 1861 by likening the realist writer Nikolay Uspensky (1837–89) to a mindless photographer who wishes to produce an image of a particular marketplace: passively accepting whatever falls before his lens at the moment, the photographer includes the highly uncharacteristic happenstance of a balloon descent into the square. Far from being required for characterizing the marketplace, inclusion of the balloon descent creates "confusion, not accuracy" (19:180).

What is missing in such an approach, Dostoevsky believed, is a functioning "point of view" or "idea" on the part of the artist, or in other words a principle of selection that would allow the artist to discriminate among and organize the phenomena presented by the reality to be portrayed, and thus provide knowledge of it by calling attention to what is related to its true nature. "It is not enough," he wrote in a review of a new play in 1873, "to represent truthfully all the given qualities of a character; one must resolutely illuminate him with one's own artistic vision" (21:97). The presence of such "vision" or "idea" is essential to artistic realism and also to cognition. Without it, no clear knowledge of the reality can be conveyed, for there is no harmony between the work and the essence of the subject.

Dostoevsky's insistence on the need for an idea or conception of the thing as a principle of selection was elaborated in a section of his *Writer's Diary* for 1873 entitled "Apropos of the Exhibition," in which he reviewed an exhibition of paintings by contemporary Russian artists at the St. Petersburg Academy of Arts. The works, chosen to represent Russia at a coming international exhibition in Vienna, were historical and genre paintings of a supposedly "realist" cast, and Dostoevsky took the occasion to reflect on what he considered the confused aesthetic thinking behind them.

At first glance he appears to suggest that the goal of capturing reality "in itself" is a chimera: " 'It is necessary to portray reality as it is,' they say, whereas such a reality by no means exists or indeed ever has existed on earth, because the essence of things is inaccessible to man. He perceives nature as it is reflected in his idea, having passed through his senses. Thus it is necessary to give somewhat more room to the idea and not fear the ideal" (21:75). Such a comment may seem to render incomprehensible the whole notion of a "faithful" reproduction of reality—an accordance or harmony between a work and reality—in that the "essence" of the latter is unknowable. As Dostoevsky goes on in the essay (and elsewhere), however, it becomes clear that he is not rejecting realism altogether but only considers absurd the interpretation according to which it can be achieved mirror-fashion, without the intervention of the artist's "idea" or "ideal."

Not all such subjective contributions have equal value, he implies. Some (his own among them, he believed) come closer to the "essence" of things than others do, as he indicates when he suggests that in his novel *The Idiot* "man is more real" (9:276). The true artist's responsibilities are, first, to acknowledge the necessity of the ideational element in art and, second, to strive for the ideas that capture as fully as possible the real nature of what is portrayed. To make this point in "Mr. ——bov", he uses for his own purposes a familiar description of how a talented portrait painter works, turning it into an argument for a more adequate understanding of realism:

> The portraitist . . . knows from experience that a person does not always look like himself, and therefore he tries to find "the principal idea of his physiognomy," the moment when the subject most resembles himself. . . . What is the artist doing here, if not trusting more his own idea (the ideal) than the reality before him? Of course the ideal is also reality, just as legitimate as the present reality. (21:75–76)

Dostoevsky's realism "in the highest sense" does not exclude "immediate reality" but acknowledges its interplay with ideal elements that structure and illuminate its true nature. To portray reality "as it really is" is to portray its essential identity, and that cannot be discovered without reflecting on the subject, identifying salient features, going beyond immediate and superficial appearances—in short, without an activity of idealization that allows the artist to penetrate to the core of his subject, be it a person, a society, or an age. "The task of art," Dostoevsky wrote in *A Writer's Diary* in 1873, "is not the contingencies of daily life but their general idea, perceptively discerned and truthfully extracted from the whole miscellany of similar phenomena of life" (21:82).

A third argument Dostoevsky offered against the prevailing interpretation of realism was that by focusing on the banal and the ordinary it excludes attention to unusual or atypical phenomena that may be essential to understanding the subject portrayed. Dobrolyubov, we recall, had rejected the use of "exceptional and curious cases" in literature in favor of portraying what is "universal" in the sense of prevalent and ordinary. Dostoevsky, by contrast, insists that it is precisely the unusual that can provide the key to understanding a subject.[26]

---

26. For a discussion of this idea as an element of romanticism in Dostoevsky's thinking, see Kashina, *Estetika*, 93–94.

In criticizing the realism of ordinariness, Dostoevsky was, among other things, defending his own interest in probing his characters' sometimes bizarre thinking and behavior. He was (and is) often accused of allowing fantasy to exceed the bounds of realism (his artistic method has been dubbed "fantastic realism")[27] because of the particular psychological depths he often chose to explore—those of the criminal, the sociopath, the deviant. But he staunchly defended the realism of his approach, as in this letter of 1869 to Strakhov:

> I have my own special view of reality (in art), and what the majority calls almost fantastic and exceptional is for me sometimes the very essence of the real. The ordinariness of phenomena and a conventional view of them are not yet realism, in my opinion, but even the opposite. In every issue of a newspaper you encounter reports of the most real facts and the strangest ones. To our writers they are fantastic, and indeed they don't deal with them. Yet they are reality, because they are *facts*. (29/1:19; Dostoevsky's emphasis)

Dobrolyubov might well concede that such cases are "factual" and not imaginary, but still contend that to portray them is to misrepresent reality, because they are relatively infrequent and do not characterize reality in a significant way; he had, after all, required the portrayal of phenomena that are not only "universal" but "important." Dostoevsky's contention, to the contrary, is that portraying what is out of the ordinary (in the sense of statistically infrequent) often provides a better understanding of the true nature of something than portraying the banal and ordinary, that it somehow gets at the essence of the reality in question. In his prefatory note to *The Brothers Karamazov* he acknowledges that Alyosha may seem an odd person and thus "a particular and isolated case." But he defends his characterization in the following words: "Not only is an eccentric 'not always' a particular and isolated case, but, on the contrary, it happens sometimes that it is precisely he, perhaps, who carries within him the core of the whole, while the other people of his epoch have all somehow been torn away from it for a time by some kind of rushing wind" (14:5).

By suggesting that Alyosha represents "the core of the whole" Dostoevsky is in effect laying a claim to meeting Dobrolyubov's "importance" criterion. But he is also suggesting that Alyosha's eccentricity has a universal significance because of its broad relevance to the real life under examination in the book,

27. Joseph Frank, *Dostoevsky: The Stir of Liberation, 1860–1865* (Princeton, N.J.: Princeton University Press, 1986), 93.

and this is what is behind Dostoevsky's reluctance in this passage to equate eccentricity with particularity and isolation. "For the story-teller, for the poet, there may be other tasks besides the everyday aspect," he stated in *A Writer's Diary*: "There are the general, eternal, and, it seems, forever inexhaustible depths of the human spirit and character" (21:82). The exceptional, in other words, may be an avenue of access to the universal, to the general nature of the subject. Thus his answer to Dobrolyubov is that what is "exceptional" in one sense may be not only important but even "universal," in another, deeper sense.

The fourth and final charge discernible in Dostoevsky's attack on photographic realism is that it overlooks the dynamic, developmental aspect of the reality portrayed. A significant feature of his idea of realism "in the highest sense" is its concern with the temporal dimension of reality. In "Apropos of the Exhibition" and other writings, Dostoevsky argued that the essential identity of a subject—the "reality" of it that art should portray—is constituted as much by its future as by its present, for it includes the potentialities of the subject, its possibilities, its prospects for development. Because potentialities are inherent attributes of the subject, true realism has of necessity a future orientation.

Dostoevsky's insistence on the future dimension of realism is brought out in a particularly revealing way in "Apropos" where he discusses the supposed realism of the historical paintings in the St. Petersburg exhibition. Historical events, by definition, are events a portion of whose future has already taken place, whose potentialities have at least to some degree been realized. How, then, Dostoevsky asks, can painters claiming to be realists portray such events without reference to their consequences, as he believed some of the exhibition's artists had done? He develops his case by characterizing what he calls the "historical reality" of historical painting as opposed to the "immediate reality" of genre painting:

> Historical reality, for example in art, is of course not current reality (genre), precisely because the former is completed and not current. Ask any psychologist you wish and he will explain to you that if you imagine a past event, especially one long past, completed, historical, . . . the event will *unfailingly* be imagined in its completed form, i.e., with the addition of all its subsequent developments, which had not yet occurred at the precise historical moment in which the artist was trying to picture the person or event. And thus the essence of a historical event cannot even be imagined by an artist exactly as it may have happened in reality. (21:76; Dostoevsky's emphasis)

Yet the superficial "realist" painter, fearing the intrusion of "ideas" in his work, tries to imagine the event "in itself," and in so doing produces an unreality—a portrayal of his subject shorn of its inherent potential. Dostoevsky's critique of a controversial painting by Nikolay Ge aptly illustrates his point:

> [Ge] made his "Last Supper" . . . into nothing but a genre painting. . . . Here sits Christ—but is this really Christ? It may be a very nice young man much distressed by his quarrel with Judas, who is standing there getting dressed to go denounce him, but this is not the Christ we know. . . . We ask: where, and how related to this, are the subsequent eighteen centuries of Christianity? How can it be that from this ordinary quarrel of such ordinary people . . . gathered for supper, something so colossal could ensue? . . . Everything occurring here is completely out of scale and disproportionate with the future. (21:76–77)

Dostoevsky compares Ge unfavorably with Titian, who would at least "have given this Teacher the face with which he depicted him in his famous picture 'Render unto Caesar'; then much would have become understandable immediately." Ge's picture is "false" and therefore "not realism at all" (21:77).

For Dostoevsky such an orientation toward the future, moreover, is not limited to the depiction of historical realities. It applies also to contemporary realities, as he makes clear in a number of other texts. He regards all genuinely realist art is essentially projective, for it discerns the seeds of future developments in the reality, past or present, that it depicts. Jackson once observed that for Dostoevsky art is "prophecy,"[28] and that description certainly applies to the portrayal of "immediate" as opposed to "historical" reality, to use Dostoevsky's expressions. If, in dealing with past events, truly realist art is projective historically, because the future of those events is already partly realized, in dealing with the present it is projective prophetically: it points to a yet-unrealized future by identifying the potentialities of the present.

Dostoevsky's prophetic realism draws upon his view of earthly human beings as dynamic, developmental creatures with ideals, aspirations, and capacities that are central to their identity. This is what the naturalistic "realists" miss in looking exclusively at the present, he believed, and thereby they miss a large part of their subject's integral nature: "The realists are wrong," he wrote in a notebook of the mid-1870s, "for man is a whole only in the future, and is far from entirely exhausted by the present" (24:247). The same is true of the depiction of a society or an age. A great work of art, he wrote in a discussion of

---

28. Jackson, *Dialogues with Dostoevsky* (Stanford, Calif.: Stanford University Press, 1993), 176. On Grigoryev's view of art as prophecy, see also Dowler, *Dostoevsky*, 48.

Victor Hugo, expresses not only the static character but the "aspirations" of its time (20:29). In his persistent search for "new types" in literature, noted in chapter 2 above, Dostoevsky was seeking discernment of the directions and trends in which society was moving, the fertile seeds of the future in the real nature of the present. Writing to his brother of the need to revise and reissue his novel *The Double*, he asked, "Why should I lose a splendid idea, a type with the greatest social importance, which I was the first to discover and of which I was the herald?" (28/1:340). His reference in another place to the writer's responsibility to "study life and extract laws from life itself" also suggests his attention to aspects of reality that entail extrapolation into the future (20:115).

Oddly enough, Dostoevsky's interest in the temporal aspect of depicting reality in art reappeared later in Russia as an element of Soviet "Socialist Realism," which otherwise descended directly from the aesthetic thinking of his nineteenth-century opponents. His assertion that "man is a whole only in the future" could well have been uttered by Russian Marxists after him, as could the statement just quoted about extracting "laws" from life. Such convictions led in Soviet Russia to the idea that human and social reality are inherently vectored; as applied to art, this meant that to portray reality accurately it was necessary to describe not only its present state but the direction of its movement. In the notorious definition of Socialist Realism adopted by the Soviet Union of Writers in 1934, what is demanded of the artist is "the truthful, historically concrete portrayal of reality *in its revolutionary development*."[29] Dostoevsky and the Socialist Realists, however much they differed about the "revolutionary" aspect of human development, were in agreement that successful realism requires the gift of prophecy.

Dostoevsky, moreover, was no less supremely confident of his own ability to discern the laws and prospects of human development than the Socialist Realists were of theirs. The narrow-minded "realists," he reportedly told a contemporary, "understand only what takes place before their eyes, but they themselves are not only unable, because of nearsightedness, to look ahead, they do not even understand how for someone else the *future results of present events* can be crystal clear."[30] Such confidence on his part may seem inconsistent with his critique of the utilitarian reasoning of Dobrolyubov and company, but his point there was that the likelihood of specific consequences in the future could never outweigh the immediate certainty of aesthetic value in the present. Here, on the other hand, he is arguing that his grasp of future

---

29. *Pravda*, 6 May 1934 (emphasis added).
30. Quoted in V. V. Vinogradov, *Problema avtorstva i teoriia stilei* (Moscow: Gos. izd. khudozhestvennoi literatury, 1961), 535 (emphasis in original).

probabilities is better than theirs, to the point of making possible the prediction of actual occurrences: "With their realism," he said of his opponents, "for the moment granting them the use of the term, "you won't explain a hundredth part of the real facts that have actually taken place. But we with our idealism have even prophesied facts. It has happened" (28/2:329). Still, Dostoevsky's assurance (like that of the Socialist Realists) seems excessive; he never entertained the possibility of erring in his predictions. His confidence in his own prophetic vision played a large role in the development of his philosophy of history, as we shall see in chapter 6.

In sum, Dostoevsky's reflections on realism "in the highest sense" effected several extensions, well beyond the radicals' aesthetic thinking, of the notion of faithfulness to reality in art. The result of each extension was to require of the artist a better *understanding* of reality—a greater, deeper harmony between the artwork and the essential identity of the real.

Dostoevsky's view of the cognitive role of art was thus distinguished by the far greater importance he attributed to art as a source of knowledge. For all the materialists, science was the model of cognition; for them, what contributions art could make to knowledge were essentially auxiliary and inspirational. "The moral sciences," Chernyshevsky wrote in his principal philosophical work, *The Anthropological Principle in Philosophy*, "have a theoretical answer to nearly every problem that is important for life,"[31] so that the "explanations" of reality that art can provide are essentially not new knowledge but the application to particular cases of truths known by the sciences. For Dostoevsky, art makes discoveries and provides grounds for predictions independently of the sciences. Discernment is the beginning: the artist, he wrote in "Mr. ——bov," is a person with a special talent for noticing and pointing out salient features of reality (18:89–90). The artist observes and displays elements of reality not manifest to others; he is one who, as Jackson puts it, "*sees* into life, perceives all its richness and complexity in depth."[32] And beyond discernment of facts and relations, the good artist has the ability to explain and predict, rivaling the scientist in those respects.

Yet Dostoevsky emphatically rejected the notion that artists, however perceptive, have a *duty* to convey knowledge of a useful sort, such as Dobrolyubov maintained when he insisted that the Russian artists of his day had an obligation to inform people about the realities of serfdom. One may *hope* that the artist will serve as a teacher, Dostoevsky affirms, but in the long run allowing free scope to creativity is the best guarantee that art will be useful: "If

---

31. Chernyshevskii, *Polnoe*, 7:265.
32. Jackson, *Dostoevsky's Quest*, 72 (Jackson's emphasis).

we desire the greatest freedom for art, it is precisely in the belief that the freer it is in its development, the more useful it will be to human interests" (18:102). For Dostoevsky, knowledge in the aesthetic realm is a by-product of artistry, for it results from the artistic creation of the particular harmony (beauty) that is true realism. Artistry produces knowledge, though that is not its aesthetic justification; its justification is that the knowledge it provides is in harmony with the reality it portrays, thus making it one source of the beauty needed by humanity. Cognitively, the failure to achieve realism is a failure to discern and convey truth; aesthetically, it is a failure of artistry.

The Moral and Social Value of Art

When Chernyshevsky wrote in 1855 that a good artist not only reproduces and explains reality but passes judgment on it, he had in mind the artist's role in condemning injustices in the social and economic life of Tsarist Russia. Dostoevsky vigorously opposed the radicals' revolutionary program, but he found quite congenial the general principle that art fulfills a normative role in society; it is the third such principle he shared with some, at least, of his ideological opponents in the realm of aesthetics. A major element in his case against the extreme antiaestheticism of Pisarev and others was his attempt to show the redemptive moral and social value of art. It is in this context that we must approach his tantalizing statement that "Beauty will save the world."[33]

By the "idea" that the good artist will always bring to his work, Dostoevsky was not thinking of a purely descriptive notion. He had in mind a notion of how things *ought* to be, as indicated by his frequent use of the word 'ideal' as virtually interchangeable with 'idea' in these contexts; a hard fact-value distinction was not part of his conceptual apparatus. What governs the selection of events and details to portray is the artist's "vision," which is both normative and descriptive: it not only perceives facts, patterns, and potential developments but passes moral judgment on them in a fully Chernyshevskian sense.

33. In the novel, Ippolit attributes the statement to Prince Myshkin: " 'Is it true, Prince, that you once said that "beauty" will save the world?' 'Gentlemen,' he [Ippolit] cried out loudly to everyone, 'the Prince maintains that beauty will save the world!' " (8:317). In Dostoevsky's notes for the novel, the thought is expressed in a line reading simply "The world will be saved by beauty," followed by a still more enigmatic line reading "Two patterns [*obrazchiki*] of beauty" (9:222). Jackson translates *obrazchiki* as "kinds" of beauty, and he goes on to argue that Dostoevsky distinguished between an objectively good, redemptive, ideal beauty and a "wholly subjective" beauty that is its antithesis (*Dostoevsky's Quest*, 40–41). What Jackson calls "subjective" beauty, it seems to me, is best conceived not as a *kind* of beauty but as a mistaken idea of it.

Consider Dostoevsky's description of the "idea" of Victor Hugo, a writer he greatly admired:

> His idea is the basic idea of all the art of the nineteenth century; Victor Hugo was virtually the first to proclaim this idea as an artist. It is a Christian and highly moral idea. Its formula is the renewal of the fallen man, unjustly oppressed by the yoke of circumstances, age-old stagnation, and social prejudices. It is the idea of the justification of the humiliated and the pariahs of society rejected by every-one. . . . Perhaps even by the end of the century it will finally be embodied wholly, fully, clearly, and powerfully in some great work of art that will express the aspirations and character of its time. (20:28–29)

Dostoevsky's profound moral approval of the "aspirations" expressed by Hugo is evident in this passage, as is his conviction that depicting such aspira-tions is not only realistic and informative, for they are in truth part of the "character" of the time, but contributes to their furthering, which means pro-moting the moral and social betterment of humanity. Good art, then, is in-evitably "tendentious" in the sense of asserting and promoting extra-aesthetic values. That is why in "Mr. ——bov" Dostoevsky is at pains to make clear that he is not criticizing Marko Vovchok's work for being tendentious: her fault is that she did her work inartistically and thereby harmed her cause rather than helping it (18:92).

What might occasion some surprise in this connection, however, is that Dostoevsky, rather than simply accepting the compatibility of tendentiousness and artistry, argues that the latter *requires* the former. He did not, of course, deny that tendentiousness could exist without artistry, as in the case of Marko Vovchok; even in his own case, while writing *Demons* he feared that his anti-revolutionary zeal might interfere with his artistry: he had great hopes for the novel, he wrote in a letter, "not from the artistic but from the tendentious side. I want to express some ideas, even if my artistry should perish in the process" (29/1:111–12). But in "Mr. ——bov" he suggested that a product of true artistry will *inevitably* be tendentious in the best sense: it will serve the artist's idea in an effective, unconstrained, convincing manner; one need only concentrate on artistry and tendentiousness will follow.

This was, in fact, one of Dostoevsky's oldest convictions on the subject of art in society; as early as 1849 he stated that "an author should concern himself only with the artistic quality of his work and the idea will come of itself, for it is a necessary condition of artistry" (18:128–29). The thesis that tendentious-ness is a requirement (though of course not the only requirement) for true artistry remained a set conviction throughout his professional life, and it completed a remarkable broadening of the concept of artistry, comparable to his ambitious extension of the concept of realism. "Artistry," as he understands it, extends beyond matters of style to comprehend the artist's abilities as teacher, prophet, and moralist; it includes the ability to perceive patterns of development and the ideals and hopes of the time. It is incompatible not with tendentiousness but only with the external effort to assign or mandate a tendency—or with the fanatical inner devotion to a tendency that blinds one to the other demands of artistry.

But why exactly is tendentiousness a necessary condition of artistic quality? The germ of an answer is present in a much-quoted notebook entry of 1876 or 1877:

> In poetry you need passion, you need *your idea*, and without fail the pointing finger, passionately raised. Indifference and the actual reproduction of reality are worth absolutely nothing and, most importantly, mean nothing at all. Such artistry is absurd; a simple glance that is the least bit observant notices far more in reality. (24:308; Dostoevsky's emphasis)

The implication is that a judgmental approach to reality is a necessary condition of capturing it perceptively, of even noticing what is important in it: an ardent normative commitment serves to energize the artist's powers of discrimination. Thus art cannot meet artistry's demand for realism without issuing from a normative judgment.

Another implication of the passage just quoted, however, might seem to be that *any* such judgment will suffice, whatever its content. But we know that Dostoevsky's own moral commitment was to the Christian law of love, which assigns the highest value to the loving, harmonious interrelation of all human beings. His overarching moral commitment, in other words, was to a form of harmony and thus a form of *beauty*—let us call it moral beauty. In this sense the natural human need for beauty becomes a *moral* need for Dostoevsky, and the significance of art is broadened beyond the kinds of harmonies considered in examining the strictly aesthetic value of art and beyond its cognitive value. To the extent that art also serves *moral* beauty, it comes to have ethical and social significance. Art informed by such an "idea" will depict and promote moral value and beauty at the same time. The "pointing finger, passionately raised" will not only generate a truer realism but will point to the morality and beauty in the reality portrayed—or else to obstacles to their realization.

The bond between moral and aesthetic value in Dostoevsky's thought is so close that some commentators have considered them identical. No less an authority than his friend, the philosopher Vladimir Solovyov, claimed the writer for his own view that beauty is an aspect or expression of absolute goodness. "In his artistic work," Solovyov wrote, Dostoevsky "never set beauty apart from goodness and truth. . . . Truth is the good as thought by the human mind; beauty is the same good and the same truth as physically embodied in living, concrete form."[34]

There is an important kernel of truth in Solovyov's statement, but if it is taken to mean that for Dostoevsky everything with positive aesthetic value also has positive moral value, it goes too far. Although Dostoevsky does not often expatiate on the beauties of material nature, he does acknowledge them; yet he restricts morality to the spiritual world, as we saw in earlier chapters. In "Mr. ———bov" he ascribes aesthetic merit to some works of literature and visual art with no apparent consideration of their moral merit; we can readily associate harmony and tranquillity with the examples of beautiful art he cites in the essay, such as the Apollo Belvedere and the "artistically excellent" poem about nightingales and sunsets, but there is no suggestion that moral value is an element in these examples. Indeed there is nothing in the essay to suggest that moral goodness is in any way relevant to the ideal of the beautiful.

In Dostoevsky's fictional world, physical beauty is correlated with moral virtue as much negatively as positively: the saintly Sonya of *Crime and Punishment* has irregular, angular features,[35] whereas others far from moral perfection are described as markedly beautiful or handsome, including the ax-murderer Raskolnikov, the amoralist Svidrigaylov, and, in *The Insulted and Injured*, Prince Valkovsky's debauched lover. Furthermore, in Dostoevsky's description, quoted earlier, of the supreme beauty experienced in Prince Myshkin's epileptic aura, there is no evident moral dimension, no reference to standards of human behavior or relationships.[36] For all these reasons, the undoubted connection that does exist in Dostoevsky's thinking between moral and aesthetic value cannot simply be understood as a dependence of the latter upon the former. It can only be illuminated by distinguishing between the ways in which the two are joined and the ways in which they are distinct.

Prince Myshkin's aura is a mystical experience, having to do with the harmonious metaphysical integration of the self with the higher spiritual reality, and beauty at that high level of abstraction is something purely contemplative, offering nothing like a behavioral norm, much less a program for saving the world. Beauty in that generic sense, which we may call *metaphysical* beauty,

34. Vladimir Solov'ev, *Sochineniia v dvukh tomakh* (Moscow: Mysl', 1988), 2:305–6. See also Jackson, *Dostoevsky's Quest*, 44–46.

35. See the comments of Victor Terras in *Reading Dostoevsky*, 72.

36. For another view, see Jackson, *Dostoevsky's Quest*, 50–51.

consists in the harmony and tranquillity of union with the divine and all reality. Thus contrary to Solovyov's pronouncement that for Dostoevsky beauty is "the good . . . as physically embodied in living, concrete form," the evidence of both "Mr. ———bov" and Dostoevsky's account of Prince Myshkin's mystical experience suggests that beauty as a metaphysical reality is not an expression of the good and has no need of physical embodiment. Of course, physical forms in both nature and art can "embody" beauty in the sense of partaking of, or hinting at, the harmony of the "higher synthesis," just as moral action can. When Zosima in *The Brothers Karamazov* speaks of "the mystery and beauty of God's world," he is marveling at the harmonious mutual adaptation of natural beings that is the core of the teleological argument for the existence of God. But the essence of beauty for Dostoevsky consists not in its embodiment in nature, art, or human moral conduct but in its ideal status as a metaphysical value.

But if there is little justification for considering beauty an expression of the good in Dostoevsky's universe of values, there is far more reason to consider the good an expression of beauty. It cannot be denied that he frequently associates beauty with moral goodness, and I believe that the bulk, at least, of what he says about the relation between the two makes sense if we postulate something like the following conceptual picture: The abstract cosmic harmony that is the essence of metaphysical beauty is particularized in the human realm as the moral harmony of altruism, the human summum bonum. On the most general, metaphysical level, beauty is conformity with the ideal of the harmonious unity of reality in the "highest synthesis"; within the specifically human sphere of that synthesis, beauty is represented by the *moral* conformity to the ideal of the unity and harmony of mankind, the ideal expressed in the Christian law of love. Thus morality enters the orbit of the beautiful exclusively on the human level, where "the highest synthesis" requires the loving unity of all. Generically, beauty is a metaphysical feature of the cosmic order; moral beauty is a feature of human relationships within that order. Put more briefly, for Dostoevsky beauty is cosmic, morality is human; harmony in the human sphere is moral beauty.[37] The essential disagreement, then, between Solovyov and Dostoevsky is that Solovyov's metaphysical absolute is fundamentally ethical in nature, whereas Dostoevsky's is fundamentally aesthetic.

---

37. Dostoevsky might be thought to have asserted the identity of the good and the beautiful when he wrote in a notebook: "Only that is *moral* which coincides with your feeling of beauty and with the ideal in which you embody it" (27:57; Dostoevsky's emphasis). The statement means that everything moral is beautiful, but it does not entail that everything beautiful is moral. Hence it is quite compatible with the conception of the beautiful as a broader category that includes but is not exhausted by the moral.

Of course, given Dostoevsky's characteristic preoccupation with the human realm, *moral* beauty is a major concern even in the aesthetic sphere, and it is that species of beauty he often has in mind when he uses the terms 'beauty' and 'beautiful' without qualification. His subsumption of moral goodness under the general heading of beauty first became evident in notes he wrote on the topic "Socialism and Christianity" in 1864, apparently in connection with the ideas about altruism that he expressed in such other texts as *Winter Notes on Summer Impressions*, his notebook reflections on the death of his first wife, and (indirectly, as I have argued in chapter 2) *Notes from Underground*. The notebook entries make obvious the link with beauty in a way the other texts do not. Here he is speaking of Christlike self-sacrifice as the highest expression of an individual's will:

> It is clear that this supreme self-will is at the same time the supreme renunciation of one's own will. My will consists in not having a will, for the ideal is beautiful.
> What does the ideal consist in?
> To attain the full power of consciousness and development, to be fully aware of one's *self*—and to give up *all* of this voluntarily *for everyone*. . . .
> There is something far higher than the belly-god [of the socialists]. It is to be the ruler and master even of yourself, of your own *self*, and to sacrifice this *self*, to give it up—for everyone. In this idea there is something irresistibly beautiful, sweet, inescapable, and even inexplicable. (20:192–93; Dostoevsky's emphasis)

Dostoevsky had, of course, proclaimed as early as 1854 that "there is nothing more beautiful [*prekrasnee*] . . . than Christ" (28/1:176),[38] but it was only after these reflections of 1864 that he repeatedly classified, not only the supreme moral state that Christ uniquely possessed, but good moral states, acts, and agents generally under the rubric 'beautiful', in both his fiction and his nonfiction. Perhaps the best-known instance is his remarks to correspondents about his work on *The Idiot*. To his friend Maykov, he wrote at the end of 1867 that the novel's idea was "to depict a thoroughly beautiful person" (28/2:241). In a letter of early 1868 to his beloved niece Sofya, he expanded on this notion, turning once again to the model of Christ:

> The chief idea of the novel is to depict a positively beautiful person. Nothing in the world is more difficult, especially now. . . . The beautiful is an ideal, but the

---

38. This passage casts doubt on Dowler's assertion that, although Grigoryev had associated beauty with Christ in the 1850s, Dostoevsky had still not made such a connection by 1863 (Dowler, *Dostoevsky*, 123).

ideal—both ours and that of civilized Europe—is still far from being worked out. There is only one positively beautiful figure in the world—Christ, and so the appearance of this measurelessly, infinitely beautiful figure is of course an infinite miracle. (The whole Gospel of St. John has this meaning: he sees the whole miracle solely in the incarnation, solely in the appearance of the beautiful.) (28/2:251)

A part of Christ's beauty, for Dostoevsky, was just that as God incarnate He personified the metaphysical synthesis of the divine and the human. But that Dostoevsky also had in mind the moral nature of the God-man Christ is made clear when in the same context he lists other major literary efforts to create "beautiful figures": the three "strong attempts" he mentions are Don Quixote ("the most finished" in Christian literature), Mr. Pickwick, and Jean Valjean. We may assume that Dostoevsky was drawn to these figures because all of them were benevolent idealists, devoid of malice, who strove to bring benefit to others—paragons, in fact, of the law of love. He attributes the special success of the first two to their respective creators' "compassion for the beautiful that is mocked and is unaware of its own value" (28/2:251).[39]

Dostoevsky's persistent limitation of (moral) beauty to altruism is also evident in contexts where he explicitly withholds the designations 'beauty' and 'beautiful' from manifestations of egoism, so that the latter is as much the antipode of (moral) beauty as it is of moral virtue. Consider, for example, this outburst against Chernyshevsky and other liberal-minded writers in 1867: "And what have they . . . presented to us? Instead of the loftiest divine beauty, which they spit upon, they are all so full of the foulest self-love, so full of the most shameless prickliness and of the most thoughtless pride that it is simply incomprehensible" (28/2:210).

Dostoevsky's Ridiculous Man also sees in egoism the loss of moral beauty. When he first encounters the people of the idyllic twin earth, he is struck by their beauty, which in this parable is made an emblem of their inner character: "Oh, how beautiful they were! Never have I seen on our earth such beauty in people. Perhaps only in our children in their very first years could you find a distant, albeit weak reflection of this beauty." He immediately divines its source: "With my first glance at their faces I understood everything, every-

---

39. Such compassion, Dostoevsky observed, has the effect of exciting sympathy in the reader, and he goes on to lament that *The Idiot* may be unsuccessful because he has not been able to arouse such sympathy for his own hero, Prince Myshkin. Among critics who would agree, Mochulsky contends that Dostoevsky achieved his "perfectly beautiful individual" not in Myshkin but years later in the virtuous Makar Dolgoruky in *The Adolescent;* see Konstantin Mochulsky, *Dostoevsky: His Life and Work,* trans. Michael A. Minihan (Princeton, N.J.: Princeton University Press, 1967), 531.

thing! This was an earth undefiled by the Fall; on it lived people who had not trespassed, who lived in just such a paradise . . . in which our fallen ancestors once lived." The moral beauty of these "children of the sun" is inseparable from their limitless mutual devotion, their "complete, all-embracing love of one another" (25:112, 114). But then, corrupted by his presence, they sink from altruism to unbridled egoism; "each began to love himself more than all the others." That is the end of their beauty, and he bitterly laments the loss of their former state, when "they were guiltless and so beautiful" (25:116–17).

If the good is metaphysically related to beauty as species to genus for Dostoevsky, we might expect it to be epistemologically related as well, such that our moral conscience could be interpreted as a variety of our sense of beauty. Without addressing this point directly, he does speak of our perception of beauty in terms remarkably parallel to the terms he uses for conscience and entirely consistent with a genus-species relation between them.

To begin with, he contends that beauty is known innately because its ideal was implanted in people by their creator. In a letter of 1876 he left no doubt that he regarded knowledge of the beautiful as a structural endowment, just as he speaks of conscience. Responding to a reader of his *Writer's Diary* who asked about his references to the biblical tale of the Devil's challenge to Christ to turn stones into bread, Dostoevsky explained his point as follows: "To that Christ answered: 'Man does not live by bread alone,' that is, he stated an axiom about man's spiritual origin, too. . . . And since Christ bore in Himself and in His Word the ideal of Beauty, He also decided that it was better to implant in souls the ideal of Beauty; having it in their souls, all will become brothers to one another" (29/2:85). We recognize beauty, then—and presumably here he had in mind generic beauty, not simply moral but metaphysical—when what we see or contemplate, whether in art or in any aspect of human experience, matches that inherent conception of the beautiful lodged in our souls at birth. But the presence of that conception has (ideally) a moral and social consequence: "All will become brothers to one another." It may have been this thought of the moral implications of the perception of beauty that led Dostoevsky to jot in a notebook of the early 1870s the closest thing to an explicit definition of 'aesthetics' to be found in all his writings: "Aesthetics," he wrote, "is the discovery of beautiful moments in the human soul, by man himself, for self-perfection" (21:256).

The second parallel between conscience and the sense of beauty has to do with possible disagreement among people as to the existence or character of those "beautiful moments." In regard to actual judgments of beauty, Dostoevsky faces an epistemological problem identical to the problem he faced in the case of conscience. If the ideal of true beauty was implanted in all of us by our creator, everyone should recognize it; but manifestly some do not. Dosto-evsky dramatized such failure of aesthetic judgment in the incredulous ques-tion his alter ego Shatov puts to the amoralist Stavrogin in *Demons*: "Is it true," Shatov asks, "that you declared you knew no difference in beauty between some lascivious, bestial thing and any kind of heroic deed, even giving up one's life for humanity?" (10:201). True beauty resides in "the ideal of the Madonna," Dmitry implies in *The Brothers Karamazov*, but the majority of people find it in "the ideal of Sodom" instead—or, inconsistently, in both at once. It is in connection with such internal conflicts over beauty that Dmitry makes his much-quoted remark that "here the devil is fighting with God, and the field of battle is the human heart" (14:100).

Dostoevsky's resolution of the epistemological problem, not surprisingly, is also identical to the way he handles ethical disagreements: our perception of beauty (including, of course, *moral* beauty, or our perception of the good) can be corrupted by various influences both internal and external, as a result of which our aesthetic discriminations become confused and disrupted, even to the point of complete reversal. Indeed he considered such aesthetic disruption to be characteristic of Western (and Western-inspired) thinking throughout his century. Writing to his friend Strakhov in the aftermath of the Paris Com-mune, he spoke bitterly of the impact of the revolutionary mentality on the perception of beauty:

> In essence it's all the same old Rousseau and the dream of recreating the world anew through reason and experience (positivism). . . . They desire the happiness of man and remain at Rousseau's definitions of the word 'happiness', that is, at a fantasy that is not justified even by experience. The burning of Paris is a mon-strosity. . . . But indeed to them (as to many) that madness seems not a monstros-ity but, on the contrary, *beauty*. And so, in modern humanity the aesthetic idea has been muddled. (29/1:214; Dostoevsky's emphasis)

Just as in the case of moral conscience, Dostoevsky presents our general sense of beauty as "muddled" through the impact of affective, volitional, and intellectual factors that draw our attention away from the innate ideal we know intuitively.

Prominent among these factors is what he considered the monomaniacal in-tellectualism of the modern age—its blindness toward the moral-aesthetic di-mension of human life and its worship of "science" and "reason" as offering the only hope of human salvation. Accordingly a central element in Dosto-evsky's own biblically inspired program of salvation was the reversal of this mentality. A notebook entry written in 1876, just a year before "The Dream of a Ridiculous Man," is related thematically to that parable, and it well illustrates both the dominance of the moral-aesthetic ideal and the close union of its two dimensions in his thinking:

> In our time the questions are raised: Is the good really good? For example, are Christ's patience and humility good? How should human equality be established? Through universal love and utopia or through the law of necessity, self-preservation, and the experiments of science? But in the Gospel it is already foretold that laws of self-preservation and experiments of science will show nothing and will set no one's mind at rest. What reassures people is not the progress of intellect and necessity but *the moral recognition of the supreme beauty that serves as an ideal for all*, before which all would prostrate themselves and rest content. There, you would say—that is the truth, in the name of which all would embrace and set about acting to achieve it (beauty). (24:159; emphasis added)

By the "moral recognition" of supreme beauty Dostoevsky is singling out what I have called moral beauty as the species of harmony and tranquillity to be achieved in humankind by following the Christian law of love.

It is in this sense, I believe, that Dostoevsky can proclaim that "beauty will save the world." The very real, historical corruption portrayed through parable in "The Dream of a Ridiculous Man" must be reversed, and that can be accomplished only by reinvigorating mankind's inherent sense of moral beauty. The recognition of cosmic or *metaphysical* beauty in the abstract also has the greatest value to man, but as essentially contemplative it indicates no direction of action. But the recognition of *moral* beauty discloses an ideal of human action, a norm of conduct and program for the future.

Thus in its moral, human application the aesthetic sense has in a generalized way the same features as the moral conscience: it is innate in man, it has Christ as its paradigm, it can suffer corruption, and it can be reanimated. In fact, from the spiritual standpoint the sense of moral beauty and the moral conscience are simply the same capacity, in that the beauty and good they discern are not different realities but different words for the same ideal of universal love. Thus if Dostoevsky had *moral* beauty in mind when he wrote that beauty will save the world, as I believe he did, he could have written, with no shift in fundamental meaning, that *the good* will save the world. This is the kernel of truth in Solovyov's statement.

Dostoevsky's assurance of that truth should not be confused, however, with the discursive justification of art and artistic freedom that, in answer to the arguments of his ideological opponents, he was eager to advance in "Mr. —— bov" and other writings. In "Mr. ——bov" he did not raise the metaphysical and religious points on which his view of art as redemptive depended, perhaps at least in part because he knew they would be ineffective against his adversaries. He *was* convinced that art brings great utility to man and society, but his principal arguments against the utilitarians were that they fail to recognize the urgent human needs for beauty and creativity and that the value of art in satisfying those needs directly is far more assured that the merely possible value of satisfying other needs indirectly and eventually.

Dostoevsky's remarks in "Mr. ———bov" about the possible long-term benefits of "pure" art in particular cases are meant not to establish its utility but to show that easy assumptions about its lack of utility cannot be justified: it is just as plausible that a particular work will prove useful in the future as that it will not. Yet even "pure" art can be justified quite rationally, he argues, and in terms a consistent follower of Chernyshevsky should accept, on the grounds that it fulfills a natural human need. If one wishes to consider this a form of "utility," Dostoevsky implies in "Mr. ———bov," so be it; but it is an immediate utility, dependent on no calculations of consequences, and thus immune to the problems of predictability.

This is another way of saying that the strictly *aesthetic* value of art should be the primary criterion for evaluating it, despite the undoubted cognitive and socio-moral value art also has. Kashina is wrong in asserting that for Dostoevsky cognition is "the meaning and mission of art," as are those who see art's chief value as redemptive. The paramount virtue of art for Dostoevsky resides in its artistry. It does give knowledge and it will save the world, but as art it should be judged on the basis of its artistry, not its intellectual, moral, or social impact. The utilitarians, he claimed, ignored artistry and saw only the social value of the artist's "idea." But such an approach is self-defeating because without artistry the work will neither create beauty nor serve the idea effectively.

Admittedly, the breadth that Dostoevsky gives to the concept of "artistry" enriches it beyond any limited notion of "pure" aesthetic value. For him it means not only the agreement or harmony of the work's style with its genre but with the reality it portrays and with an "idea" to which the artist is, moreover, passionately committed. Nonetheless it is the artistry, thus defined as the creation of many harmonies, that makes the work beautiful and thus worthy as *art*, and on the basis of which it deserves specifically aesthetic praise. In the end, then, despite his abstract agreement with some of the utilitarians' basic premises, Dostoevsky was closer to the proponents of "art for art's sake." Aesthetically, increasing our knowledge and saving the world are simply incidental blessings.

CHAPTER 5

A Christian Utopia

In previous chapters there was little need to consider alterations in Dostoevsky's thinking over time, for in metaphysics and epistemology, philosophical anthropology, ethics, and aesthetics his outlook remained remarkably stable. With regard to the sociopolitical dimension of human existence, however, the reverse appears to be true, and commentators examining his ideas in that area have typically focused on evidence of change. Stephen K. Carter, for one, has found no less than six distinct stages in the evolution of Dostoevsky's social thought.[1]

Without question there were changes in some of Dostoevsky's political attitudes over the course of his creative life. An ardent opponent of serfdom, in the 1840s he played an active role in the dissident Petrashevsky circle, a role that cost him ten years in Siberia. Yet subsequently his orientation shifted to the conservative and even reactionary side, as he became a virulent critic of socialism and a staunch defender of the Russian autocracy. In the 1840s, he sounded like a typical St. Petersburg Westernist, ridiculing the Moscow Slavophiles for their national chauvinism; in a letter of 1845, for example, he cited with manifest approval a satirical piece that "triumphantly proves that Adam was a Slav and lived in Russia" (28/1:114). Yet by 1861 Dostoevsky was a spokesman for the conservative, nationalistic "native soil" movement

---

1. Stephen K. Carter, *The Political and Social Thought of F. M. Dostoevsky* (New York: Garland, 1991), 215–27. An approach of a different kind to the evidence of change in Dostoevsky's sociopolitical thinking is taken by Aileen Kelly, who argues that the writer, because of "unresolvable dilemmas" in his personal moral life, was never able to enunciate a settled view but was "forced by events constantly to reassess his position"; see her article "Dostoevskii and the Divided Conscience," *Slavic Review* 47 (1988): 242.

(*pochvennichestvo*) in Russia; by 1877, he was hailing the Tsarist advance on Constantinople in the Russo-Turkish War (24:271–72, 288), and he wrote, in a section of *A Writer's Diary* entitled "Confessions of a Slavophile," "I have many purely Slavophile convictions" (25:195). Dostoevsky, it would seem, having earlier approached society as a liberal-minded, humanistic universalist, ended his career as a religious and ethnic nationalist and an apologist for Russian imperialism.

From a philosophical perspective, however, the significant question is whether these undoubted changes in policy stance reflected a fundamental modification in his understanding of the social and political nature of man and the ideals and institutions appropriate to that nature. Students of Russian *pochvennichestvo* have described it as a product of just such a paradigm shift, reflecting the European romantic reaction, heralded by Johann Gottfried von Herder, against Enlightenment beliefs in a universal human nature and a common social ideal. Apollon Grigoryev, Herder's principal Russian disciple and an influential member of the editorial board of the Dostoevsky brothers' journal *Vremya* (Time) in the early 1860s, shared Herder's convictions that the concept 'man' is a mere abstraction with no real content, that every individual is an organic product of a particular culture at a particular time, and that all national cultures are equally valid historically.[2] But if those propositions are accepted, some age-old philosophical issues are foreclosed. As Isaiah Berlin argued in his essay on the German writer, Herder's position can be interpreted as a rejection of absolute values and hence a refusal even to entertain such questions as "What is the best life for human beings?" and "What is the most perfect society?"[3] Did Dostoevsky go that far?

Wayne Dowler has demonstrated the influence of Herder's, and more directly Grigoryev's, thinking on Dostoevsky in the early 1860s, and there is evidence that Dostoevsky was sometimes drawn to the organicist, antiuniversalist point of view, as in this characteristic passage from 1862:

> "Our ideal [the Westernists say] is marked by panhuman features. . . ." Thus the theoreticians wish to make of all mankind, of all nations, something completely impersonal, which would be the same in all the countries of the globe, in all the various climatic and historical circumstances. . . . But we would very much like someone from this clan of theoreticians to answer the following questions: Would humanity really gain much by turning each nation into some sort of effaced coin, and what exactly would the benefit be? Let any of the theoreticians show us the

2. Wayne Dowler, *Dostoevsky, Grigor'ev, and Native Soil Conservatism* (Toronto: University of Toronto Press, 1982), 16, 20, 54.
3. Isaiah Berlin, *Vico and Herder: Two Studies in the History of Ideas* (New York: Vintage, 1977), 206.

panhuman ideal that every individual must make of himself. . . . No, humanity will live a full life only when each nation develops on its own principles and brings from itself to the common sum of life some particularly developed aspect. (20:6–7)

Yet it would be a mistake to accept a relativistic interpretation of such texts. Dowler admits that Dostoevsky, even after proclaiming himself a *pochvennik*, nonetheless "clung to some form of universalism" and never really abandoned the notion of a panhuman ideal.[4] Looked at in its full context, even the passage quoted above bears out that judgment: in it Dostoevsky is rejecting not the reality of a panhuman ideal but the Westernists' abstract *conception* of the ideal, which to him overlooks the contribution of the separate nations to its historical elaboration. It is only after such contributions are taken into account, he goes on to say immediately following the passage quoted, that we can "dream of a full panhuman ideal" (20:7).

Dostoevsky's own dream was constant and clear, as I have argued in previous chapters: it was the dream of a community of perfect Christian brotherhood and love, which he insistently advanced as an ultimate, absolute value for all peoples, whatever the "native soil" from which they sprang. "There are no sharp distinctions among national tasks," he wrote in the same essay quoted above, "because at the basis of every nationality lies one common human ideal, simply with a local coloration" (20:19). In the mid-1870s, looking back at the history of his own convictions, he claimed stubborn allegiance to the ideal of universal brotherhood from his days of radical dalliance in the 1840s to the present: "You will say," he addressed an imagined critic in one of his notebooks, "that Dostoevsky now and Dostoevsky then are not the same. . . . But I have not altered my ideals in the least, and I do believe—but in the Kingdom of God, not the commune" (24:106). He had, of course, added to his understanding of humanity the conviction that specifically *national* characteristics have a significance far beyond anything he contemplated in the 1840s, and that conviction had fateful consequences for his later sociopolitical outlook, as we shall see in the next chapter. But on the crucial point of a common human ideal, Dostoevsky remained an Enlightenment universalist all his life. "We are by no means such *pochvenniki* that we deny a panhuman ideal," he wrote in a notebook in the mid-1860s; "we . . . are Christians, fully Christians. And the first dogma of Christianity is the commonness of the law for all, the commonness of the ideal, all are brothers" (20:202).

Over the period 1863 to 1877, Dostoevsky on three separate occasions sketched his vision of the ideal Christian community based on the law of love.

---

4. Dowler, *Dostoevsky*, 66.

Although the three sketches differ strikingly in approach, they agree on the contours of the ideal and on the opposition it faces from human weakness. An examination of these utopian texts will set the stage for an exploration of his forays into the particular sociopolitical questions that concerned him in the Russia of his day.

Utopian Sketches

Dostoevsky's earliest mention of ideal social relations, occurring in the section entitled "An Essay on the Bourgeoisie" in his *Winter Notes on Summer Impressions* (1863), is couched unexpectedly in the quintessential Enlightenment language of a "social contract." His use of this idiom is explained by the fact that, in setting out the complaints about Western Europe that resulted from his first trip abroad, he was addressing a Russian audience not only familiar with Western conceptions of society but sympathetic (dangerously so, in his opinion) to the socialist version of the social contract theory.

His procedure was to contrast the idea of a social contract based on socialist principles with the societal model he considered superior. He notes that the socialist model (like, he might have added, all of the traditional social contract theories advanced in the eighteenth century) is based on the principle of rational self-interest: each individual is supposedly willing to enter into the contract because it is to his or her personal advantage. To recommend the contract, then, the socialist theorist

> undertakes to produce, to define the future fraternity, calculating its weight and size, tempting you with its advantages, explaining, teaching, relating how much profit each will gain from this fraternity, how much each will win; he determines what each person will look like and how much he will be burdened; he determines in advance the division of earthly goods, how much of these goods each deserves and how much each in return must voluntarily contribute to the community at the cost of his individuality. (5:81)

Despite Dostoevsky's obvious distaste for this notion of building fraternity on a foundation of self-interest, he does acknowledge that there is "great allure" in the idea of "living purely if not on a fraternal then on a rational basis—that is, in living well, with everyone protecting you and demanding of you only work and consent" (5:81). But he identifies two significant shortcomings of the plan to create a utopia out of selfish intentions. The first, not so much stated as repeatedly implied, is that such an ideal looks only to quantifiable, material goods, with no consideration of the spiritual nature of man: that is surely the point of his arch references to calculating "the weight and size" of the proposed fraternity and determining "how much . . . each deserves and how much each in return must voluntarily contribute."

The second shortcoming of the socialists' utopia is the one on which Dostoevsky dwells, and his treatment of it in *Winter Notes* anticipates his later arguments against rational utopias in both *Notes from Underground* and the Legend of the Grand Inquisitor: it is that the utopia cannot be achieved without an unacceptable constriction of individual liberty. He suggests this in his initial description when he refers to the socialist organizer's task of determining "what each person will look like." But he makes his point abundantly clear through irony when he imagines the reaction of a member of the proposed community to the terms of the contract he is being asked to enter:

> The man, it seems, is completely secure; they promise to give him food and drink and to provide work for him, and in return they ask of him only the smallest drop of his personal freedom for the common good, the smallest, smallest drop. But no, the man does not wish to live even on these terms, for even the little drop is difficult for him. It still seems to him, stupidly, that this is a prison and that it is better to be on his own, because then he is fully free. . . . Of course the socialist can only desist and tell him that he is a fool, is immature, has not developed, and does not understand his own personal advantage. (5:81)

The socialist, Dostoevsky goes on, believes that human needs can truly be met only in a human anthill. But because people will not willingly live in an anthill, the unspoken implication of Dostoevsky's analysis is that the socialist "utopia" can be sustained only by force. The supposedly voluntary contract based on rational self-interest is both a sham, because it cannot satisfy an all-important human need—the need for freedom—and a delusion, because it seduces people into believing that it provides a genuine transfiguration of egoism into brotherhood.

The fraternal utopia that Dostoevsky offers in *Winter Notes* as an ideal alternative is one based not on rational calculations of self-interest but on each individual's inherent devotion to the well-being of the others. It is, in fact, not the result of a deliberate contractual arrangement at all; but, to make his point in the context of a critique of Western contract theory, Dostoevsky is willing to describe his utopia, as he says, in "rational, conscious language" (5:80). Even then, the perspective of the belletrist is evident when he chooses to present his case as a dialogue between the individual and society.

The individual begins by making voluntary concessions to the community that are so sweeping that, if the relationship were viewed in modern Western contractual terms, it would be disqualified as giving oneself into slavery. The individual, "of his own accord, without any external pressure or thought of profit," says to the community:

"Only all together are we strong; take me wholly, if you need me. Think not of me in issuing your laws; do not be concerned in the least. I cede to you all my rights; please consider me at your disposal. My supreme happiness is to sacrifice everything to you so that in return you will suffer no harm. I shall annihilate my-self, I shall blend in without reservation if only your brotherhood will flourish and endure." (5:80)

But of course Dostoevsky's individual is not stating terms of consent to a con-tract; he is, rather, expressing his unqualified devotion to his fellows—a devo-tion that, in Dostoevsky's model, is thoroughly reciprocated by them. Accord-ingly, the community's answer to the individual is equally self-denying:

"You give us so much. We have no right to refuse what you give us, for you yourself say that all your happiness lies in this, and what else can we do when our heart ceaselessly aches for your happiness. So take everything from us, too. With all our strength we shall strive at every moment so that you have as much personal freedom as possible, as much self-expression as possible. . . . We are all behind you; we all guarantee your security; we work vigilantly on your behalf. For we are brothers; we are all your brothers, and we are many and strong." (5:80)

Dostoevsky is quick to point out that for such a community of mutual devo-tion to be viable, its members must of course be marked by complete and gen-uine love for one another. If they are, then the giving of oneself to the others will be entirely voluntary and free. The ineradicable human desire for freedom is not a threat to the stability of the social structure as it was for the socialists, be-cause no coercion is exercised over the individual. All are genuinely free be-cause each individual wishes the well-being of others and willingly accepts whatever limitations on his activity are required to assure such well-being.

Yet Dostoevsky is not so credulous as to see no weaknesses in the concept of a utopia of mutual love. Just as even the slightest desire for freedom is a dan-ger in the socialist utopia, human nature presents a comparable threat to the utopia of love: even the slightest egoism, "the slightest calculation in favor of personal advantage," is a contaminant that, in Dostoevsky's words, "will at once smash and destroy everything." And the psychological position of the individual in such a situation is very difficult: he must give up everything, yet have no thought of a benefit in return, a situation that Dostoevsky compares to trying *not* to think of a polar bear—for all one's effort, "the damned bear will constantly come to mind" (5:79–80). Given the equivalent psychological difficulties in the two situations, Dostoevsky obviously must face sooner or later the question of whether a utopia of mutual love devoid of all self-interest is any more feasible, realistically, than a utopia of rational self-interest devoid of all urge to rebel.

The second text in which Dostoevsky expounds on the ideal of a community of mutual love, written just a year later, is the notebook passage in which he reflects on the death of his first wife, Maria Dmitrievna. As we saw in chapter 2, in that passage he presents the ideal as the result of an ethical imperative—the Christian commandment to love others as oneself—and he discusses it in the context of seeking a justification for belief in immortality. Despite the different approach to the subject, Dostoevsky's description of the ideal in the notebook is entirely consonant with the description in *Winter Notes*: the ideal is "that the person should find, should recognize, should with the full force of his nature be convinced, that the highest use someone can make of his personality, of the full development of his *self*, is to annihilate this *self*, as it were—to give it totally to each and every one, undividedly and unselfishly. . . . This indeed is the paradise of Christ" (20:172).

The striking difference in the treatment of the ideal in this second text, however, is the far greater emphasis Dostoevsky places on egoism, which becomes here a seemingly insurmountable obstacle to the realization of the ideal. Indeed, he begins by suggesting that the ideal is hopelessly unrealistic, saying that to obey the Christian commandment is "impossible" because "the law of personality is binding on earth. The *self* stands in the way." As he goes on, however, it becomes evident that it is only the *full* realization of the ideal that is impossible on earth, and that in fact progressive movement toward the ideal is characteristic of earthly life. It is an eternal ideal, "toward which man strives and must strive, by the law of nature." Man on earth is a "developing" being; his history is "nothing but development, struggle, striving, and attaining this goal" (20:172). The struggle involved is essentially a contest between two elements in human nature: his spiritual nature mandates and guides a movement toward the ideal, while his material or purely animal nature resists that movement. "Man strives on earth," Dostoevsky writes, "toward an ideal *antithetical* to his [animal] nature" (20:175).

As we saw in chapter 2, Dostoevsky is convinced that in principle the ideal *is* realizable, and one of his arguments for immortality rests on the reasoning that since it is not fully realizable in this life, there must be a future life for man in which it will be achieved completely. By definition this will be a situation in which the power of egoism has been fully vanquished, and Dostoevsky's musings on it in the notebook reflections add interesting detail to his conception of what such an ideal community must be like. We know little of the next life, he admits—"what it is, where it is, on what planet, in what center"—but we do know one "profoundly significant" thing. Surprisingly, this is that the institution of marriage will no longer exist; he quotes the Gospel according to St. Matthew: "[For in the resurrection] they neither marry, nor are given in marriage, but are as the angels [of God] in heaven" (20:173 [Matt. 22:30]). Dostoevsky's point, somewhat less surprising when we remember that these reflections were prompted by the death of his wife, is that the earthly institution of marriage is in one sense an egocentric, socially divisive institution, for it creates attachments that privilege some individuals (one's own family members) to the exclusion of others. Dostoevsky labels it "the greatest departure from humanism, the complete separation of the couple from *everyone* (little remains for all)"; thus the situation of a family as set apart from the rest of humanity is "egoistic in the full sense" (20:173; Dostoevsky's emphasis).

Yet the institution of marriage as Dostoevsky understands it has another side, so that it provides him with an example of the burdensome spiritual dialectic he finds in earthly human life. The procreation and nurturing that the family makes possible is essential for "the succession of generations" over which individuals move closer to the ideal goal, and thus it is a requisite for progress; it is a "law of nature," he contends, that man achieves development by means of the family (20:173). Dostoevsky is here suggesting something like the "cunning of reason" that is so critical an element in the Hegelian dialectic: a force opposed to the goal is an essential element in working toward it. In the transitional state in which man exists on earth, development is achieved through the very institutions that prevent its full success. Once the ideal has been achieved in the future life, there will be no need for progress and hence no need for the "succession of generations" that marriage produces.

Dostoevsky's third picture of an ideal community, some thirteen years after his wife's death, appeared in the section of his *Writer's Diary* for 1877 entitled "The Dream of a Ridiculous Man," which we examined above in the context of aesthetic theory. In this text he sketched an idyllic social order entirely comparable to the community of mutual love described in the earlier works, but with additional details concerning its structure. The parable form of the later text gave him the latitude to describe the features of his idyllic community in greater detail than before.

The Ridiculous Man's "twin earth" is materially equivalent to our own, but with a huge difference in social relations: its inhabitants live in perfect peace and harmony because of their limitless love and respect for one another. Theirs was a community reminiscent of our earth's prelapsarian condition. There was no crime, and hence no need for jails or guillotines. There was no political system, no courts or legal rights or duties; when joint action by these "children of the sun" was needed, it flowed from spontaneous good will and a talent for cooperation. Similarly, there were no property relations, no "mine" and "thine." The people had no organized religion, but they did have "a kind of urgent, vital, and unbroken unity with the Totality of the universe" (25:114). The spirit of mutual devotion extended even to their relations with the natural environment: they loved their trees with uncommon intensity, and the trees responded in kind; wild animals, too, lived peaceably with them, "conquered by their love" (25:113–14).

But, as we saw earlier, this idyll is gradually destroyed by the contamination introduced by the visitor from the fallen earth. The "slightest calculation in favor of personal advantage" that Dostoevsky had feared as early as *Winter Notes* made its appearance, and as he predicted then it did "destroy everything." People learned to lie, perhaps innocently at first, but once the "atom of falsehood" penetrated their hearts it led to sensuality, jealousy, and cruelty. Blood was shed, and "each began to love himself more than all the others." There followed with tragic inevitability the whole panoply of coercive and dissociating institutions known in the fallen world—private property, a system of justice, codes of law and the guillotine, slavery. "Wise" men appeared who argued that for self-preservation people must create a rational, harmonious society; "and so in the meantime, to hasten matters," Dostoevsky adds sardonically, "the 'wise' strove to exterminate as quickly as possible all those who were 'unwise' and did not understand their idea, so that they would not interfere with its triumph" (25:115–17). The Ridiculous Man, who had been so inspired by the social ideal in action, is bitterly disappointed at this second loss of paradise and is distraught at the unwitting role he played in it.

Considered as an exercise in political philosophy, Dostoevsky's parable makes novel use of a conceptual device popularized by Hobbes, Locke, and Rousseau before him: he posits a "state of nature" or original condition in which people live together in the absence of political relations. As with those thinkers, too, the point of the exercise is not so much historical as theoretical. It matters little whether the original condition ever actually existed; what is important is the relative desirability of the two contrasted states—one with and one without political relations and the institutions that sustain them.

But there is a fundamental difference in the way in which Dostoevsky uses the concept of a state of nature. For the earlier thinkers, in that state the individual's existence and well-being are either so radically threatened (Hobbes) or so insufficiently secure (Locke and Rousseau) that each is willing to accept political rule and its attendant limitations in return for a guarantee of personal security; this is the "contract" mandated by rational self-interest. For these thinkers, then, the original condition was a device used to justify the political authority of some people over others: authority is justified because in effect it expresses the very will of the individuals who are subordinated. The original condition imagined by the Ridiculous Man, on the other hand, is a state of perfect security and harmony. It is used not to justify political rule but to demonstrate its superfluity and irrelevance to true human well-being. In Dostoevsky's parable, political institutions are a consequence of moral degeneracy: it is a failure of morality—a departure from the law of love—that ushers in political relations, which exacerbate rather than correct the moral collapse. For the earlier thinkers, the institutions of political authority are a progressive development over the unsatisfying original condition; for Dostoevsky, they represent a decline, which can be overcome not by any "contract" but only by moral regeneration. Progress must consist not in moving away from the "original" condition but in acknowledging it as actually a *terminal* condition—the social ideal toward which one must strive. "Paradise" is produced not by some institutional structure but by a moral law, and the function of the "dream" is to display what the Ridiculous Man calls the "truth" of the ideal.

Ideal and Reality: The Social Issues of the Day

Dostoevsky's conception of the fundamentally moral character of the social ideal, as displayed in all three of his utopian sketches, profoundly influenced his approach to specific questions of economic, social, and political philosophy. With a few notable exceptions, such as particular criminal cases before the Russian courts, he showed little interest in the practical intricacies of such questions, so convinced was he that the institutional ways and means of social improvement paled into insignificance before the question of moral values.[5] The Ridiculous Man ends his reflections on his dream by repeating what he calls an "old truth": in order to build paradise, "the main thing is to love others as yourself. That is the main thing, and it is everything; absolutely nothing more is needed: you'll at once find how to build it" (25:119).

---

5. See Gary Saul Morson's discussion of this aspect of Dostoevsky's journalistic writing in his "Introductory Study" in Fyodor Dostoevsky, *A Writer's Diary*, trans. Kenneth Lantz (Evanston, Ill.: Northwestern University Press, 1993–94), 1:40–48.

This is not to say that Dostoevsky was silent on issues of the day or presented his fellow citizens with no definite political profile. On the contrary, not only his great novels but his nonfiction works of every description touched on such issues; the long series of essays written from 1873 to 1881 that made up *A Writer's Diary*, for example, were self-conscious expressions of his strongly conservative viewpoint on social topics of a wide variety, from child abuse to international politics. Yet in all these essays the ethical dimension was uppermost: his attention to other aspects of the issues he considered was never as broad or as sustained. His treatment of four major topics in particular displays his profoundly moralistic approach to social and political questions: they are serfdom, autocracy, revolution, and socialism.

Serfdom

A constant in Dostoevsky's social outlook, from his radical youth until his death, was his abhorrence of serfdom. His biographers have made much of the fact that, when his father was murdered on the family's modest country estate in 1839, young Fyodor (then an eighteen–year-old student in St. Petersburg) was convinced that the act had been committed by their own serfs. Whatever the truth about that still murky event, there is no doubt that he early conceived a hatred for the institution of serfdom that biographers have described as "obsessive," "visceral," and "burning" and that endured long after the emancipation of 1861.[6]

Opposition to serfdom was at the heart of Dostoevsky's association with the Petrashevsky circle. Although in his deposition before the Investigating Commission after his arrest in 1849 he insistently denied advocating revolution and stated that the "whole basis" of his political thought was to wait for improvements from the autocracy (18:123, 161), to others his revolutionary sympathies at the time were clear, and they centered on the need to abolish serfdom. He is said to have told his friend Apollon Maykov that the purpose of the Petrashevsky circle was to foment a revolution in Russia, and a police spy reported that at a meeting of the group Dostoevsky had sided with a young man who spoke in favor of an immediate peasant uprising.[7] All this came after Nicholas I had given some indications in the course of the 1840s that he considered serfdom an evil. But with the onset of the European revolutions of 1848 there was no action by the Russian government to eliminate the institution, and this led

---

6. Carter, *Political and Social Thought*, 216; Joseph Frank, *Dostoevsky: The Seeds of Revolt, 1821–1849* (Princeton, N.J.: Princeton University Press, 1976), 256–57.

7. Carter, *Political and Social Thought*, 53.

some, apparently including Dostoevsky, to conclude that the liberation of the peasantry could come only from below.[8]

When Alexander II ascended the throne after the death of Nicholas I in 1855, Dostoevsky was serving his term of Siberian exile (following five years in prison) as a private in the Russian army. News of the young Tsar's liberal sympathies reached him there, including, of course, a report of Alexander's famous speech of March 30, 1856, in which he advised the Moscow gentry that "it is better to begin the abolition of serfdom from above, than wait until it begins to abolish itself from below."[9] Joseph Frank has well sketched the importance of this pronouncement to Dostoevsky:

> [He] had become a revolutionary *only* to abolish serfdom and *only* after the seeming dissolution of all hope that it would be ended, to quote Pushkin, "by the hand of the Tsar." But now the glorious day had dawned of which Pushkin could only dream, and the Tsar whom Dostoevsky was to support so fervently for the rest of his life was the Tsar-Liberator who had finally decided to eradicate this intolerable moral blight from the Russian conscience.[10]

And it was precisely as a *moral* blight that Dostoevsky always condemned serfdom. Its economic costs were seemingly of no concern to him, and even in the turbulent discussions leading up to the actual emancipation proclamation on February 19, 1861 (O.S.) he gave little attention to the terms under which the emancipation was to take place—terms that were heavily criticized by many. He did hope that the peasants would be freed with land rather than as landless workers, and he was happy that in the end they were so freed, although the need to "redeem" the land specified by the Emancipation Act laid on them onerous financial obligations. Years later he lamented that the freed peasants were falling into "a far worse slavery, and to far worse landlords" (23:42), but he blamed this on the greediness of the new landowners, especially Jews, who were buying up estates in western Russia. Serfdom is an evil for Dostoevsky because it bestializes one group of people for the benefit of another group, makes some human beings "material and means" for the use of others (22:31). If particular inhumanities persist even after the institution of serfdom has been legally abolished, those are separate evils that must also be combated morally.

---

8. Frank, *Dostoevsky: The Seeds of Revolt*, 247–49.

9. Quoted in Joseph Frank, *Dostoevsky: The Years of Ordeal, 1850–1859* (Princeton, N.J.: Princeton University Press, 1983), 208.

10. Ibid. (Frank's emphasis).

Just a year before his death, Dostoevsky returned to the subject of serfdom in *A Writer's Diary* as part of his response to the critique of his Pushkin speech by the liberal law professor A. D. Gradovsky, already noted in chapter 3 of this book. Upbraiding Dostoevsky for relying on moral reform as the road to progress, Gradovsky had insisted that social betterment can never be realized solely by improving the personal qualities of individuals; to prove his case, he had argued that although both the masters and the slaves to whom the Apostle Paul preached may have become good Christians, the immoral institution of slavery remained in force among them.[11] Dostoevsky in turn defended his thesis of the primacy of the moral factor by countering that since slavery persisted in Paul's time, people could not yet have become perfect Christians. And the same is true of serfdom, he insisted. Drawing a portrait of a hypothetical gentry woman who *had* become a perfect Christian, Dostoevsky pictured her relations with her serfs in these words: "She is a 'mother,' to them, a real mother, and the 'mother' would immediately have eliminated the former 'mistress.' This would have happened of itself. The former mistress and the former slave would have vanished like fog before the sun, and completely new people would have appeared, with completely new, unprecedented relations between them" (26:163).

Dostoevsky's discussion of slavery and serfdom here recalls his description of the "original condition" in "The Dream of a Ridiculous Man," and it shows that he did equate that condition with an ideal future state of perfect Christianity. His discussion also adds new and perhaps surprising content to the Dream, for it indicates that he did not consider the ideal inconsistent with social stratification based on a hierarchy of talents and on the resulting differential value of the contributions of various individuals. His response to Gradovsky continues as follows:

> In Christianity, genuine Christianity, there are and will be masters and servants, but it is impossible even to think of a slave. . . . The masters will no longer be masters, and the servants will not be slaves. Imagine that Kepler, Kant, and Shakespeare live in the future society: they are engaged in great work for all, and everyone acknowledges and reveres them. But Shakespeare has no time to break off work, tidy up around him, clean his room, and carry out the trash. I assure you that without fail some other citizen will come to serve him; he will want to do it, will come of his own free will, and will carry out Shakespeare's trash. Will he

11. Gradovsky's article, entitled "Dreams and Reality" (*Mechty i deistvitel'nost'*) appeared in the newspaper *Golos* (The Voice) for 25 June 1880. Dostoevsky quotes lengthy passages from it in the course of his response (26:149–74).

then be humiliated, a slave? Far from it. He knows that Shakespeare is infinitely more useful than he: . . . "Acknowledging that you are superior to me in genius, Shakespeare, and coming to serve you," he would say, "by that very acknowledgment I have shown that I am by no means inferior to you in moral human worth and that, *as a person*, I am your equal." . . . For in truth all will be new people, children of Christ, and the erstwhile animal will be conquered. (26:163–64; Dostoevsky's emphasis)

Dostoevsky's opposition to serfdom, then, is based entirely on what he considered its evil nature as an institution that degrades and humiliates individuals and compels them to serve others arbitrarily and unwillingly; it makes a person created in the image and likeness of God slavishly dependent on the will of another (22:25). It is inconsistent with the Christian ideal of a society of loving, voluntary cooperators, however patriarchal and socially stratified such a society may otherwise be. Dostoevsky reaffirms the primacy of the moral element by insisting to Gradovsky that the social ideal is "solely, exclusively a product of the moral perfection of individuals" (26:165). Speaking of the French bourgeoisie, he writes: "If there were brothers, there would also be brotherhood. If there are no brothers, you will not achieve brotherhood by any sort of 'institution'" (26:167). The Tsar's heroic elimination of the institution of serfdom was a supremely moral action on the part of an individual, which removed a major obstacle to brotherhood; the *pochvenniki* generally, as Wayne Dowler has pointed out, valued the emancipation more highly than the Petrine reforms, placing it on a par with the conversion of Russians to Christianity.[12] But serfdom would have vanished without government action, "like fog before the sun," if the moral attitudes of the masters had been different.

Autocracy

Whether or not Dostoevsky was being entirely candid when he told the Investigating Commission in 1849 that he had "always believed in the government and in autocracy" (18:161), with respect to the latter, at least, there is no evidence that he ever preferred another form of government for his native Russia. His biographers write of the great influence on him of the patriotic historian Nikolay Karamzin, who saw the unlimited power of Russia's monarchs as the root of the country's greatness.[13] While still in Siberian exile in the

12. Dowler, *Dostoevsky*, 97.
13. Frank, *Dostoevsky: The Seeds of Revolt*, 55–58.

1850s Dostoevsky composed verses affirming that greatness (2:403–10)—verses that under the circumstances might be considered merely self-serving were they not entirely in keeping with the political sentiments he expressed consistently from that point forward. In letters and notebooks as well as journalistic essays he associated autocracy with the strength of the Russian state and at the same time considered it, paradoxically, not a limitation on the citizenry but the source of their liberty: it is "the cause of all the *freedoms* of Russia" (24:278; Dostoevsky's emphasis).

As Joseph Frank and others have pointed out, Dostoevsky's praise of autocracy was by no means inconsistent with his moral opposition to serfdom. His subversive activity in the 1840s was prompted by dissatisfaction not with the institution of autocracy but with the quondam occupant of the Russian throne. Dostoevsky surely would have been just as willing in 1849 to sing the praises of an autocrat who seriously proposed to end serfdom as he was in 1861 when he described Alexander II as "blessed of the blessed eternally for what he is doing for us" (18:50).

What is most important from the standpoint of Dostoevsky's political philosophy is that autocracy, in the rarefied interpretation he gave it, was entirely compatible with his social ideal as we have sketched it above, for it was not really a governmental "institution" at all. That autocracy entails the absence of a constitution and of every other institutional limitation on the authority of the monarch is quite in keeping with the ideal, which assumes among community members a spontaneous, entirely voluntary mutuality that is defined by no rules other than the Christian law of love and that requires no specification of rights or duties, no delimitation of spheres of authority. Furthermore, as we have seen, the ideal is consistent with a patriarchal hierarchy of social strata within society, and it was precisely as a benevolent father that Dostoevsky pictured the Tsar. Writing approvingly, in the last year of his life, of the Russian people's attitude toward their ruler, he stated: "They are the Tsar's children, his own real, genuine children, and the Tsar is their father" (27:21). The mutual, familial love between the ruler and his subjects, each recognizing the human dignity but also the particular talents and services of the other, are for Dostoevsky simply a special case of the mutual love among all members of the community.

The condition, inherent in his ideal model of society, that all the actions of its member be voluntary—including, of course, voluntary submission to the autocrat's will—shows that the model in fact accepts one of the fundamental principles of democracy—namely, that rule be exercised with the consent of the governed. In Dostoevsky's case, however, although consent is essential, there is no requirement that it be anything but tacit, for there is no formal mechanism to allow the public registration of consent to either rulers or matters of policy. His assumption—breathtakingly visionary from the standpoint of Western democratic thought, but common among Russian conservatives of the day—is that the rulers will always be persons of good will who will do what is best for the community despite the absence of controls on their selection and their actions.

As for policy matters, Dostoevsky assumes with equally visionary assurance that the community will always arrive at a decision that every member can freely accept. "If all were actively Christians," he wrote in a late notebook, "not a single social question would be raised. . . . If there were Christians, they would settle everything" (24:291). He never directly faces the question of what is to be done if different individuals, even with the best of intentions and the greatest mutual love, arrive at different conclusions about what is good for society, though he does suggest that such disputes would be submitted to a higher authority, whose decision would willingly be accepted. That would seem, at least, to be the implication of his statement, when speaking of Russians as "the Tsar's children," that "children will not be unfaithful to their own father and, as children, will lovingly accept from him any correction of all their errors and mistakes" (27:22–24).

In the few cases in which Dostoevsky uses the terms 'democracy' and 'democratic' in a favorable sense, it is always with reference to the ideals of consent, equality, or the common interests of the Russian people, never as an institutionalized form of government. Thus he refers, for example, to "the universal democratic mood and universal consensus . . . among all Russians, starting with the very top"; unlike the revolutionary pressures for democratic change in Europe, he adds, "our upper stratum itself became democratic or, more accurately, populist" (23:28; emphasis omitted). It was apparently in this spirit that he welcomed the revitalization of local self-government which was the object of the zemstvo reforms of 1864: he approved of the zemstvo assemblies as arenas of cooperative action among landowners, urbanites, and the rural communes, without regard to such questions as the democratic or undemocratic character of their makeup and functioning.

In Dostoevsky's more typical, pejorative uses of the terms 'democracy' and 'democratic', he appears to have been influenced by Aristotle's negative appraisal of democracy as meaning rule by the poor in their own interest.[14] In a notebook entry of the mid-1870s, drawing on an article in Russkii vestnik (The

14. Aristotle, Politics, bk. 3, ch. 7.

Russian Messenger) that quoted Aristotle, Dostoevsky paraphrased the Greek philosopher's conceptions of the three "perverted" forms of government— tyranny, oligarchy, and democracy—accurately characterizing the latter as "government that has in mind only the good of the indigent"; he adds the comment, still paraphrasing Aristotle, that none of these forms is concerned with the *social* good (24:85). These ideas made their way into the March 1876 installment of *A Writer's Diary*, where he expanded on the idea that democracy destroys the unity of society because it serves one class only (22:85). All the great powers of Europe, he predicted, would be "weakened and undermined by the unsatisfied democratic aspirations of a huge portion of their lower-class subjects, their proletarians and paupers"; but he was confident that such a thing could not happen in Russia, because the Russian masses were content (22:122).

Dostoevsky's final argument for autocracy is that, properly conceived, it does not diminish personal liberty. On the contrary, he claims repeatedly that autocratic Russia is the freest land on earth, freer certainly than the European republics that trumpet their liberties as superior to those of any monarchy. His reasoning here is based on his conception of the extent to which Russia, in contrast to the Western European nations, approaches the social ideal. We shall examine Dostoevsky's distinction between Russia and the West in this regard in the following chapter, but his paradoxical argument has broad application to the general concept of a society grounded on thoroughgoing mutual love and respect. The basis of the argument is again the assumption that every party in such an ideal society wishes only the best for the other parties. That being the case, the talented and paternalistic citizens who serve as rulers have nothing to fear from their devoted children, who would never wish to harm them. The Russian autocracy, like presumably any other autocracy in so harmonious a state, can allow "all freedoms, for they are *not afraid* (as in the West) of the people and their subjects" (24:272–73; Dostoevsky's emphasis). It is for this reason that autocracy can be "the cause of all the *freedoms* of Russia." Dostoevsky's antiformalist, anticontractual, anti-Western ideal of a paternalistic, libertarian autocracy is summed up in these words in *A Writer's Diary*:

> With us everything is grounded as nowhere in Europe. . . . Civil liberty can be established in Russia most fully, more fully than anywhere else in the world. . . . It will not be established by a written piece of paper but will be built simply on the childlike love of the people for the Tsar as a father, because children may be permitted much that is unthinkable among others, among the contractual nations. (27:22)

Revolution

As a champion of human freedom and a prophet of radical moral renewal, Dostoevsky strikes many as a consummate revolutionary; to his admiring biographer Konstantin Mochulsky, he was "one of the greatest spiritual rebels in world history."[15] With respect to *political* revolution in the sense of using violence to overthrow an existing order, however, Dostoevsky was no rebel. Except for a few years as a young man, when he had a part in clandestine discussions about eliminating the scourge of serfdom in Russia, he was one of history's most confirmed antirevolutionaries. His novel *Demons* is a passionate indictment of the revolutionary mentality and its ruinous impact on society and individuals alike, including the revolutionaries themselves. The novel's purpose, Dostoevsky wrote Alexander Romanov, the future Alexander III, was to depict in artistic form "one of the most dangerous ulcers of our present civilization" (29/1:260–61).

At first glance it may seem odd that the mature Dostoevsky should have condemned political revolution so vehemently. Unlike Leo Tolstoy, he was not a pacifist opposed in principle to violence of every kind; although he spoke out against capital punishment, he did not believe that society, short of its ideal Christian future, could dispense with all institutions of force and coercion, and he accepted without complaint the likelihood and even the desirability of war under certain circumstances. Nor was he opposed in principle to radical change in the institutional structure of society. The elimination of serfdom was just such a change, for which he himself once contemplated revolutionary action, and he valued the emancipation just as highly after his attitude toward political revolution had shifted from qualified acceptance (in the 1840s) to hostility. What was it in Dostoevsky's thinking that accounted for this shift?

For Dostoevsky the emancipation, motivated by the Tsar's love of the people, demonstrated that fundamental social change could be peacefully effected in Russia "from above." That the peasants were freed without bloodshed, whereas in Western Europe armed uprisings were required, gratified Dostoevsky immensely (24:130). It signified to him the presence of a social consensus: Russian society was ready for the radical institutional alteration, which thus could be accomplished in a harmonious manner, with love rather than hatred. The emancipation—a patriarchal, nonviolent, universally accepted step in the direction of perfect brotherhood—was thenceforth his model of desir-

---

15. Konstantin Mochulsky, *Dostoevsky: His Life and Work*, trans. Michael A. Minihan (Princeton, N.J.: Princeton University Press, 1971), 217.

able social change, and he came to regard both the thinking and the tactics of political revolutionaries with the greatest suspicion.

With regard specifically to the Russian revolutionaries of his day, Dostoevsky was of course opposed to their socialist program (to be discussed in the next section). But in his arguments against them he made a number of points that are applicable to the assessment of violent revolution everywhere, whatever its proposed alternative to the existing order, and that may be considered general expressions of a conservative opposition to the use of force to effect fundamental sociopolitical change. He concentrated on two broad arguments against revolutionary action: first, that it is immoral, and second, that it is counterproductive.

Dostoevsky's condemnation of revolution as a violation of morality is rooted in his deontological ethics, according to which (as we saw in chapter 3) the morality of any action is determined not by its future consequences but by its present, inherent character. The revolutionary, accepting the notorious maxim that the end justifies the means, argues that his action will bring great future benefit to society, benefit more than sufficient to outweigh any present harm. But Dostoevsky rejects the revolutionary's principle and considers his reasoning irrelevant to the ethical situation. The revolutionary is willing to harm others today, to terrorize, maim, and kill them if necessary, in order to achieve a supposed benefit tomorrow. For Dostoevsky, this is to sanction actions that violate the law of love and hence are directly and immediately unethical.

Dostoevsky typically depicted the revolutionary as having repudiated moral constraints. In *Demons*, although Kirillov's behavior is not always consistent with his expressed sentiments, Dostoevsky presents him as the author of an article rejecting morality and affirming "the latest principle of universal destruction for good ultimate ends" (10:77). The very title of the novel is indicative of Dostoevsky's ethical assessment of the book's protagonists, whom he likens in its famous epigraph to individuals possessed by devils, after the biblical story in Luke 8:32–37 (hence Constance Garnett's familiar rendition of the title as *The Possessed*). The diabolical character of their attitude was ever before Dostoevsky's mind as he depicted them in the novel. The fundamental motive he attributes to them is the exact opposite of love—that is, hatred. He portrays the arch-revolutionary Pyotr Stepanovich Verkhovensky as detesting even his own countrymen: "The Russians ought to be extirpated for the good of humanity," Verkhovensky remarks (10:172). And Dostoevsky's alter-ego Shatov attributes to the Russian radicals "an animal, boundless hatred of Russia"; they would be the first to be disappointed if Russia were transformed as they wished, Shatov states, for then they would have no one to hate (10:110–11).

Dostoevsky did not always describe a revolutionary situation as morally black and white, however. Although he portrayed the leading figures in *Demons* as espousing an immoral nihilism, he did recognize the possibility of a disjunction between their desperate theories and their personal impulses, as in the case of Kirillov, and he did at times acknowledge (perhaps with his own past in mind) that proponents of revolution could be genuinely interested in the greater good. Still, in Dostoevsky's eyes, worthy intentions by no means exonerated such individuals of immorality, for the evil of their immediate actions could never be justified by subsequent consequences. But he does not lay all the blame on the revolutionaries. Recognizing that popular unrest may be an understandable response to injustices perpetrated by those who control society's resources, he acknowledges that the absence of a community of loving brotherhood may be as much the moral fault of the defenders of the status quo as of the rebels. His ethical analysis of revolution as representing a bilateral departure from the social ideal of perfect brotherhood is pithily summarized in this notebook description of "communism" as a perversion of Christianity: "Instead of *voluntary love*, the unloved resort to sticks and wish to take for themselves what the unloving did not give them" (24:164; Dostoevsky's emphasis). That the rebels are "unloved" does not exonerate them, but neither are the "unloving" excused; both sides are violating the demands of morality.

Nonetheless it is the revolutionaries who are the targets of Dostoevsky's special scorn, and this may be connected with what he perceived as their unparalleled egoism. In Dostoevsky's ethical universe, if hatred is the opposite of love as a moral feeling, egoism is the immoral misdirection of love from its proper object—one's neighbor—to oneself, one's own benefit, will, and power. The revolutionaries in *Demons* are notorious for their vanity and arrogance, which Dostoevsky depicts with memorable penetration. Each is convinced that all must bow to him because he knows the truth. Shigalov proclaims: "There can be no resolution of the social equation but mine" (10:311); Pyotr Verkhovensky counters with the boast: "One person, one person alone in Russia has devised the first step and knows how to take it. I am that person!" (10:324). Each is interested in gaining power over society, in demonstrating the force of his will by imposing it on others. Kirillov declares that he worships his own will as the attribute of his "divinity" (10:472). Verkhovensky's harangue to the members of his revolutionary cell after they have murdered the potential traitor Shatov is suffused with the arrogance of intellect and will that Dostoevsky despised in the revolutionary mentality:

Your whole task now is to see that everything is overthrown—both the government and its morality. We alone shall remain, having ordained ourselves in advance to assume power. The intelligent we shall recruit; the stupid we shall saddle and ride. You must not shy from that. We must reeducate a generation to make them worthy of freedom. Many thousands of Shatovs still lie ahead. We shall organize to seize the initiative; it is shameful not to take control of everything that simply stands there gaping at us. (10:463)

It was on the basis of his insight into the revolutionary mentality that Dostoevsky was able to anticipate so startlingly in this brief passage not only the Bolsheviks' seizure of power in Russia, but also their preparations for doing so, the censorship and other elements of a totalitarian state they introduced, the Great Terror they instituted to contend with "many thousands of Shatovs" (not to mention imagined Shatovs), and the very rationalizations they employed to justify their actions.

In both *Demons* and the Legend of the Grand Inquisitor, Dostoevsky considers the view of those who justify the imposition of their own will on others by arguing that in assuming responsibility for others they are sacrificing themselves. For Dostoevsky, true self-sacrifice is, of course, the height of virtue, and hence one might think he would be sympathetic to such an argument. But in fact he gives no moral credit for the particular "self-sacrifice" or "martyrdom" of the revolutionary, for he sees it as purely a result of vanity, a response to a desire for personal glorification rather than a product of love. The need for self-glorification, he believed, can lead to the most immoral actions under the guise of doing something to benefit others at one's own expense. Shatov accuses Stavrogin of a "passion for martyrdom," shown even in his marrying the cripple Maria Lebyadkina, and argues that Stavrogin's inability to distinguish good from evil is a consequence of that passion (10:201–2). The monk Tikhon, speaking with Stavrogin in the suppressed chapter "At Tikhon's," gives him this counsel: "You are wrestling with a desire for martyrdom and self-sacrifice; subdue this desire also . . . and then you will conquer everything. You will discredit all your pride and your demon! You will end a victor and will gain freedom" (11:29).

Dostoevsky's second major charge against the proponents of violent revolution is that their actions, questions of morality aside, are unlikely to produce the socially beneficial results expected of them. In this context, in other words, he borrows the radicals' utilitarian perspective for the purpose of arguing that their forecasts of consequences are at best unsupported and at worst mistaken: violent revolutions are at least as likely to produce harm as to produce good.

The radicals' lack of evidence to support their fiery claims of utopian benefits to result from their activity was a recurring theme in Dostoevsky's antirevolutionary rhetoric. It is evident, for example, in his disgust at the speeches of the revolutionaries—Garibaldi and Bakunin among them—whom he happened to hear in Geneva at the Congress of the League of Peace and Freedom in 1867. He ridiculed their program as consisting in "fire and sword—and after everything has been destroyed, then, in their opinion, there will be peace." "All this," he commented, "without the slightest proof, all this already memorized twenty years ago" (28/2:224–25). The absence of anything resembling factual grounding for the revolutionaries' hopes is also behind his frequent complaints of the merely theoretical character of their proposals, their separation from "life."

At the same time, Dostoevsky holds that there is good reason to believe that revolutionary action is typically counterproductive—that its actual consequences are on balance socially harmful rather than beneficial. He himself marshals no particular historical evidence for this conclusion; rather, the thinking behind it appears to be based on the premise, shared with the mainstream of European conservative thought, that the only assured aspect of violent revolutionary action is its destructiveness. When he has Pyotr Verkhovensky proclaim that "we shall make such an upheaval that everything will be gone from its foundation" (10:322), Dostoevsky is saying that violent revolutionary action is aimed primarily and in the first instance at destruction. Destructive consequences from the action are thus virtually guaranteed; constructive consequences, in contrast, are consigned to the future, in which the causal connection between destruction and the supposed eventual construction may be uncertain to the point of mystery. When Verkhovensky seeks to justify the hypothetical revolutionary program of "cutting off a hundred million heads" on the grounds that the future benign order will save *five* hundred million from destruction, he is overlooking the fact that the immediate loss is assured whereas the future gain is no more than a matter of speculation. It was apparently on such grounds that Dostoevsky felt justified in stating in the mid-1860s that "the revolutionary party . . . will spill far more blood than all the benefit received is worth" (20:175). Certainly the revolutionaries depicted in *Demons* create nothing but terror, destruction, and death.

Much has been made of Dostoevsky's preference for gradualism over revolutionary action in the attempt to effect social reform—that is, for slow, step-by-step progress toward the social ideal.[16] He did go on record more than once in favor of a gradualist approach, most famously in his praise in *A Writer's Diary* of a minor government official who quietly used whatever funds he could accumulate, through great sacrifice on the part of himself and his family,

16. See Morson, "Introductory Study," 1:65, 98–99. Expressions of Dostoevsky's gradualism are found as early as 1861 (see, for example, 18:66–70).

to buy the freedom of individual serfs—three or four altogether over his life-time. To Dostoevsky this was the height of self-sacrificing love and social responsibility: "This is the kind of people we need! I am terribly fond of this funny type of little people who seriously imagine that they, with their microscopic deeds and doggedness, are able to help the common cause without waiting for a general campaign and initiative" (22:25).

Still, it would be wrong to conclude that the operative distinction here for Dostoevsky is the distinction between minor, gradual changes and radical, sudden changes. The emancipation he so ardently sought was in his eyes not a small but a giant step, and it was accomplished by the stroke of a pen. The important thing for Dostoevsky is not the scope or rapidity of a change but its consensual character. If it is universally acceptable, it will be voluntarily honored by all; if there is serious objection, force will be required to carry it out. The proponent of violent revolution is in favor of imposing ideas and institutions on a society unprepared to receive them; the society's hostile reaction necessitates the use of still greater force, ultimately causing the revolution either to fail altogether or become counterproductive. Dostoevsky suggests this response in a notebook entry of the mid-1860s: "A society can accommodate only the level of progress to which it has developed and has begun to understand. Why reach further, for the stars in the sky? That can ruin everything, because it can frighten everyone." Here in fact he does provide a bit of historical evidence, taken from the unsuccessful Western European uprisings of 1848: "In forty-eight even the bourgeois agreed to the demand for rights, but when they drove him further, to the point where he couldn't understand anything (where in fact things were stupid), then he began to defend himself and was victorious" (20:175). For Dostoevsky small steps are ordinarily better because they are more likely to find general agreement and thus to avoid violence; they are more likely to avoid the vicious cycle of hostility, countered by force, leading to greater hostility, thus moving away from the society of mutual brotherhood rather than toward it. Just such a cycle was produced by the Petrine reforms, Dostoevsky believed: Peter's innovations, far from being consensual, "tore one part of the people from the other, leading part" (20:14).

Socialism

From the 1840s until the end of his life, the problem of socialism was never far from Dostoevsky's mind. As a *Petrashevets* he had been sympathetic to the thinking of Fourier and his French and Russian followers, though he denied to the authorities in 1849 that he was a socialist himself. And he never thereafter considered himself a follower of the doctrine except in a highly extended, specifically Christian sense. But socialism as preached by his radical Russian opponents remained a preoccupation because he came to regard it as the foremost ideological threat to his country's well-being; he returned to it again and again with a kind of obsessive horror, damning it morally, economically, and politically. Calling it "French socialism," he described it with repugnance in 1877 as "the height of egoism, the height of inhumanity, the height of economic incoherence and confusion, the height of calumny against human nature, the height of the destruction of every human liberty" (25:21).

His criticism of socialism in the 1849 deposition was remarkably temperate by comparison, especially considering his need to defend himself against the charge of being a socialist sympathizer. He explained that he had read the books of socialist thinkers because they were written "intelligently, passionately, and often with sincere love of humanity." He seems at the time to have regarded socialism as a kind of fledgling social science, chaotic but promising, "a science in ferment." "Out of the present chaos," he went so far as to say, "there will develop subsequently something orderly and favorable to the public good, just as chemistry developed out of alchemy and astronomy out of astrology." But he did express the firm conviction that, because there are "mistakes" in all the socialist systems offered by the theorists, the application of any of them would bring inevitable ruin, not simply to Russia but to France (18:162). Still, the implication was that there could be good socialist systems.

In later years, too, Dostoevsky occasionally suggested that benign forms of socialism could exist. Belinsky, he commented in *A Writer's Diary*, preached socialism on *moral* grounds and was convinced that a socialist system would not destroy personal freedom (21:10). George Sand, too, "based her socialism . . . on the moral sense of man, on humanity's spiritual thirst, on its striving for perfection and for purity, and not on ant-like necessity" (23:37). Generalizing in a notebook entry, he contended that the highest moral idea developed by Western European culture consisted precisely in "the future socialism and its ideals" (24:185). But it was only by interpreting the term 'socialism' as standing for a moral system of mutual love and brotherhood that he could ever consider himself a socialist or speak favorably of socialism as a principle of community.[17] It is in this sense, too, that he used the expression 'Russian socialism' to describe a superior form of community, distinct from the Western varieties:

17. Aileen Kelly interprets Dostoevsky's favorable references to the *ideals* of some socialists as indications that a significant change took place in his attitude toward socialism in the 1870s; see Kelly, "Dostoevsky," 251.

the Russian people, he wrote, "believe that in the end they will be saved only by *worldwide unification in the name of Christ*. This is our Russian socialism!" (27:19; Dostoevsky's emphasis).

Ordinarily, Dostoevsky applied the term to something quite different—to a socioeconomic system that to him was totally repugnant. What, then, did socialism typically mean to him and why was he so adamantly opposed to it?

Dostoevsky never explicitly defined 'socialism' in the pejorative sense, though a few general features of his conception of it are made clear by the contexts in which he used the term. He invariably looked at socialist programs as deliberate efforts, inspired by Western European theoreticians, to recast the existing, historically created social and economic relations of a community in accordance with a blueprint that included the abolition of property ownership, the equalization of economic rewards, and the elimination of poverty. As to the differences among the various socialist proposals, he had little to say; he did not discuss particular institutional arrangements in any detail. He used the terms 'socialism' and 'communism' essentially interchangeably, though he employed the latter sparingly and often with greater scorn, as in a reference to "the vile ravings of the ridiculous communist tramps" (5:91). He never identified the particular "mistakes" he found in the socialist systems mentioned in his 1849 deposition, and he dismissed the debates among various factions at the 1867 Geneva Congress as "four days of shouting and swearing" (28/2:217). The name of Karl Marx appears only once, in passing, in a published work by Dostoevsky (21:203), despite the facts that the *Communist Manifesto* was discussed in the Russian legal press in the 1860s and that the first volume of *Das Kapital* appeared in Russian translation as early as 1872; his only other mention of the name is in a personal letter in which he speaks of Jews as ardent supporters of socialism in both Russia and Western Europe (30/1:43). Dostoevsky's picture of socialism as a socioeconomic concept was painted with a very broad brush, and he appeared confident that his objections were so fundamental that they could be applied to all its variants.

In the last three decades of his life, Dostoevsky leveled a barrage of remarkably diverse charges against socialism. Some of them, such as its inappropriateness to the Russian character and its damning association (in his opinion) with both Jewry and Catholicism, are related to his nationalistic theory of history and thus are better left for the following chapter. His other charges, though not unconnected to his conception of socialism's non-Russian origins, have a broader application to the concept as a socioeconomic system. They have to do, first, with what Dostoevsky considered, paradoxically, to be the "egoistic" character of socialism; second, with its emphasis on material satisfaction at the expense of spiritual well-being; third, with his conception of the importance of property ownership; and, fourth, with his conviction that socialism is incompatible with individual freedom.

In calling socialism "the height of egoism" Dostoevsky was placing it at the opposite pole, morally, from the conception of the ideal society. Although he had already spoken of a connection between socialism and egoism in *Winter Notes on Summer Impressions* in 1863, he gave his closest attention to the subject in a series of notes he made in 1864–65, apparently intended for an article, never completed, to be titled "Socialism and Christianity" (20:191–94). In the notes he contrasts Christian society with socialist society: the former is a true, organic community of individuals based on mutual giving without the reservation of individual "rights," whereas the latter is essentially composed of separate individuals joined together only by their mutual demands on each other. Socialism is a state of "fragmentation . . . into persons," where each person has in mind only his own development and his own will (20:192). Socialism is thus the logical extreme of individualism, with each person thinking only of his or her own good: "A socialist cannot even imagine how one might voluntarily give oneself up for everyone. . . . The whole infinity of Christianity over socialism consists in the fact that the (ideal) Christian, in giving up everything, demands nothing for himself" (20:193). Because the socialist does not believe in the possibility of voluntary giving, he wants a coercive structure that protects him by imposing restrictions on others. A decade later, Dostoevsky wrote that the message of socialism, unlike the message of Christianity, is "for oneself, one's own rights" (24:92). For him the egoistic character of socialism is closely tied to its origin in the egocentric West, as we shall see later.

A second charge that Dostoevsky persistently brought against socialism is that it overlooks the spiritual dimension of humanity and reduces individuals to their material capacities, or, in one of his favorite uses of synecdoche, to "the belly." Dostoevsky's notes for "Socialism and Christianity" suggest that he associated this criticism with the previous one, postulating a causal connection between the lack of true community and a focus on physical needs; that would seem to be the implication of his statement in the notebook that if you leave people in the state of "fragmentation into persons," you will get nothing more than "the *belly*" (20:192; Dostoevsky's emphasis). The notes provide no explanation of how this connection is understood to work—that is, of why a focus on individual rights, even an extreme focus, must end in reducing those individuals to physical capacities alone. Dostoevsky does offer an empirical argument of a sort, however, by appealing to the statements of contemporary socialists themselves:

The socialists do not go beyond the belly. As for our "Young Russia"—all they have been doing now for several years is bending every effort to prove that there is nothing more than what the belly contains. Let them dare to deny these things. . . . They admit it *proudly*: boots are better than Shakespeare, it is shameful to talk about the immortality of the soul, etc., etc. (20:192–93; Dostoevsky's emphasis)

Actually this passage offers no evidence that the attitudes Dostoevsky decries are connected specifically with the *socialism* of these antagonists. On the contrary, it prompts the suspicion that when he writes of socialism's fixation on "the belly" he is confusing his opponents' socialism with their materialism and atheism. This is an understandable confusion, given the coincidence of the doctrines in their thinking, but it is not a relevant argument against socialism per se, much less against the varieties of *Christian* socialism extant in Europe in Dostoevsky's day.

The closest thing to a specifically economic argument against socialism to be found in Dostoevsky's writings is his defense of the institution of property ownership. Although he never discusses socialism as an economic system in any detail, he does associate it with the abolition of ownership relations: through the "destruction" and "confiscation" of property, he writes caustically, "the communists" wish to "limit the errant will of the people" (21:256). The prospect fills him with horror, but not because he favored a capitalistic, industrial economic system. Rather, it was because he believed *land* ownership in particular to be the pillar of social order, morality, and even religious faith. Here we see his *pochvennichestvo* in full flower: his belief in the importance of people's rootedness in their "native soil" led him to extravagant claims about the benefits of land ownership:

Morality, social moorings, the peacefulness and maturity of the land, and order in the state (industry and likewise every kind of economic well-being) depend upon the level and the progress of land ownership. If land ownership and management are weak, diffuse, and disorderly, then there is neither a state nor citizenship nor morality nor love of God. To the extent that land ownership and management grow stronger, everything else can be established. (21:270)

"All must have the right to land," he adds, and when this right is even slightly violated, "there is unrest and the disintegration of society" (21:270).

For a proper understanding of such sweeping claims, however, two qualifications are essential. The first is that the type of land ownership Dostoevsky favored was not individual ownership by persons who may or may not live on it but the common ownership by its inhabitants that was characteristic of the Russian *obshchina*, the peasant village commune. Like the Slavophiles, the Populists, and his fellow *pochvenniki*, Dostoevsky revered this institution and feared that in the unsettled conditions following the emancipation it might not survive—that is, that the peasant communities which now had in principle a legal right to own their land would in fact be broken up. Reacting to a government proposal in 1876 to replace communal ownership by personal land ownership in the countryside, he penned the following notes:

> Destroy our commune, and our people will straightaway be corrupted in a single generation, and in a single generation they will provide themselves with the material for advocating socialism and communism. . . . In the most thoughtless manner we preach the destruction of the commune, one of the strongest, most original and most important distinctions of the essence of the people. (24:299–300)

> The commune keeps a person on the land. . . . Disperse each to his own plot and he will mortgage everything and sell it to a Yid. . . . It is better to keep him in check, in the commune. (25:227)

The second needed qualification is that, although Dostoevsky was willing to tolerate the existence of personal and even absentee land ownership alongside the group ownership of the *obshchina* ("Everyone must have a right to land, even if others cultivate it" [24:234]), he did not regard the right of personal ownership as unlimited. The personal right to own land, he wrote, is valid "up to a certain point." He made no effort to define the point, but while acknowledging that "complete abolition of ownership is terrible," he added that "unlimited ownership may be compared with a barony" and "is not right" (24:231). Thus when Dostoevsky in the passage quoted earlier spoke of the inadmissibility of even the slightest abridgment of the right to own land, he was not rejecting limitation to a reasonable amount of *personal* ownership.

Although the foregoing objections to socialism are prominent in Dostoevsky's writings, his most repeated and most impassioned argument against it is that a socialist system would destroy human freedom. The socialists, he contended, seek to attain their goal by forcibly changing people's economic life (20:171); French socialism is "the *compulsory* union of humanity" (25:7; Dostoevsky's emphasis). He never accepted the revolutionaries' argument that their objective was to set people free and that the compulsion required to establish socialism would give way to a reign of liberty. For, as he analyzed it, enslavement was required not only to initiate but to perpetuate the socialist program: "They establish its despotism and say that precisely that is freedom!" he said of the socialists in his notes for *Crime and Punishment* (7:161). Even if by some miracle a noncoercive transition to socialism were possible, the resulting social order would rest on coercion.

What is his justification for equating socialism with despotism? His reasoning is closely connected with the second argument considered above—namely, with the materialistic character of socialism as he understands it. The radicals, he contends, unanimously regard "universal material wealth" as the social ideal. But it was a tenet of Dostoevsky's view of society that general material prosperity cannot be guaranteed without regimentation: in order for it to exist, he argued, all have to "submit and consent to live in a society very much like an anthill."[18] He does not contend that universal material wealth cannot be achieved, only that it cannot be guaranteed in a free society. The choice, be believes, is between freedom and "the belly"; the socialists bring man "the law of shackles and enslavement through bread" (30/1:68).

In the absence of socioeconomic analysis to back up these contentions, Dostoevsky was left to his literary resources to lend credence to them. The effort produced two of the most memorable scenes in his fiction—the doomed "crystal palace" imagined by the Underground Man and the supposedly secure and happy but unfree society described by the Grand Inquisitor. The two scenes provide different perspectives on the problem of combining prosperity with liberty.

In part 1 of *Notes from Underground*, the narrator imagines an idyllic future in which "new economic relations" make it possible for people to live both in perfect harmony and with material abundance for all. An ideal situation, it would seem—until human dissatisfaction with merely material benefits bursts on the scene:

> Shower him [the individual] with every earthly blessing; submerge him, head and all, in a sea of happiness so that nothing but bubbles appear on the surface; give him such economic contentment that nothing whatever remains for him to do but sleep, eat gingerbread, and busy himself with assuring that world history does not cease—and even then, yes, even then, out of sheer ingratitude, out of sheer abusiveness, this very person will do something vile to you. He will risk even his gingerbread and will purposely desire the most ruinous nonsense, the most uneconomical absurdity, solely in order to inject into all this positive sensibleness his own ruinous, fantastic element. (5:116)

18. *Neizdannyi Dostoevskii. Zapisnye knizhki i tetrady, 1860–1881 gg.*, ed. V.R. Shcherbina et al. (Moscow: Nauka, 1971), 210.

"One's own voluntary, free wanting," as we saw earlier in chapter 2, would come into play, and the implication of this, unspoken in *Notes from Underground*, is that thenceforth the crystal palace could remain intact only through the imposition of coercive restraints on individuals. People are not willing to submit merely for bread (24:160), and hence bread cannot be guaranteed without tyranny. In a notebook of the early 1870s, Dostoevsky sketched the application of these points specifically to socialism in an imaginary reply to its champions:

> A part of my own free will is demanded from me, and I do not wish to give it up.
> Thus in essence socialism arouses the protest of personality and will never be realized . . .
> Your rationality is completely irrational, for it does not indicate what to do with individual protest other than treating it despotically.[19]

Recourse to despotism in the face of recalcitrance is perhaps what Dostoevsky had in mind when he wrote in a notebook for *Crime and Punishment* that "socialism is the despair of ever getting man organized" (7:161).

In the Legend of the Grand Inquisitor—Dostoevsky's powerful assault in *The Brothers Karamazov* on both Roman Catholicism and the radical socialist movement in Russia as he viewed them—the relation between liberty and material well-being is explored more deeply and darkly. Jesus has returned to earth in Spain at the height of the Inquisition, "when, for the glory of God, fires blazed in the land every day" (14:226). Recognized in Seville by the Grand Inquisitor himself, He is taken into custody, and the aged cardinal confronts the prophet of universal love with a stunning charge—inhumanity. Because Jesus insisted that people must have freedom of choice, the cardinal argues, He "rejected the only way to make people happy" (14:229).

Specifically, the cardinal argues that Jesus condemned humanity to a life of misery on two counts. First, a society of genuinely free individuals can never satisfy the material needs of all. "No science," he states, "will give them bread as long as they remain free"; "freedom and an abundance of earthly bread for all are unthinkable together, for never, never, will they be able to share among themselves" (14:231). The last clause reflects the Grand Inquisitor's egoistic assumptions—assumptions that Dostoevsky thought endemic in socialist theory: it is because of the selfishness of individuals, their unwillingness to share, that

---

19. Ibid., 294 (Dostoevsky's ellipses).

universal material security cannot be achieved without the abrogation of freedom.

But the Grand Inquisitor has a second, more subtle argument for the need to deprive people of freedom in order to make them happy. For he contends that freedom is not merely an obstacle to material security but a psychic burden that men yearn to escape. Abandoned by Christ to face alone all his cares and problems, man wants nothing more than to be relieved of the heavy responsibility for his own actions and is willing to pay virtually any price: "Nothing has ever been more unendurable for man and for human society than freedom" (14:230). Because "peace and even death are dearer to a person than free choice in the knowledge of good and evil," man is only too willing to hand over his freedom to someone else; he can be happy only when he has done so (14:232). Submission to the will of others, then, is a blessing; it is not only voluntary but is eagerly sought by the creatures whom Christ forsook when he burdened them with the torments of freedom.

In this way, it appears at first glance that the Grand Inquisitor has resolved the problem of protest and has managed to combine material well-being with contentment in the form of willing consent to be regimented. His answer to the Underground Man is that the latter's hypothetical rebel, who wishes to smash the crystal palace for no better reason than his own whim, is a purely fictitious construct based on an erroneous view of human nature. Provided that these so-called "rebels" are approached skillfully and caringly, with appropriate appeal to the "miracle," "mystery," and "authority" they crave (14:232), they will cede their freedom to resist, not only willingly but with a great sigh of relief. They will not be free, but there will be no protest because freedom is the last thing they want.

What are we to make of this seeming shift in Dostoevsky's thinking from the Underground Man's eternal rebel to the Grand Inquisitor's willing slave? Actually a problem arises here only for the interpreter who tries, unaccountably, to ascribe to Dostoevsky the Grand Inquisitor's slavish view of humanity—unaccountably because the novelist himself embedded a clear corrective to such an interpretation in the structure of his narrative. On one level, we have what the cardinal *claims* to be the case: the only speaker in this encounter with a silent Christ, he boasts of having created a crystal palace that combines material well-being with contented, willing acquiescence in slavery: "We corrected your work. . . . And people rejoiced that they were again led like a herd and that finally so terrible a gift, which had brought them so much suffering, had been lifted from their hearts" (14:234). But on another level, we have who the cardinal is and what he is doing. He is, after all, the Grand Inquisitor, charged with finding and prosecuting those who will not accept the benign mandates of the authorities; and what he is doing is burning them at the stake—almost a hundred in Seville alone on the very day before Christ came (14:226). The cardinal has *not* in fact succeeded in establishing peace and avoiding protest, not even in a community as equally devoted to providing "every earthly blessing" as the Underground Man's imagined community had been. By his person and his behavior, the Grand Inquisitor gives the lie to his own theories of peace and prosperity through willing slavery—theories thus shown to be nothing more than rationalizations of his own arrogant willfulness. Once again, then, Dostoevsky has brought home his conviction that the universal material prosperity sought by socialists cannot be achieved without protest and suppression. On this point, the Underground Man was right and the Grand Inquisitor wrong, as the latter's own activity revealed.

But in relentlessly showing the failure of the socialists' ideal—the impossibility of achieving it without unacceptable regimentation—is not Dostoevsky also casting doubt on the attainability of his own social ideal, which surely must be hostage to the same human egoism and rebelliousness that create a problem for the socialists? It is time to confront a sore point in the interpretation of Dostoevsky's social thought: the question of the realizability of his ideal.

Is the Kingdom of God Possible on Earth?

In his 1864 reflections on the death of his first wife, as we saw above, Dostoevsky insisted that a community of universal mutual love could exist *only* in a future life, because in this life egoism is inescapable: "the law of personality is binding on earth." This conception of an ontological gulf separating worldly existence, marked by inevitable moral imperfection, from the otherworldly, morally perfect existence of a transfigured humanity was never explicitly disavowed by Dostoevsky, for whom the distinction was enshrined in Christian scripture. In sketching an outline of human history in his notes on "Socialism and Christianity" in 1864–65, he referred to the Christian period as the third and last stage of human progress, adding that "here development stops, the ideal is attained . . . there is a *future life*" (20:194; Dostoevsky's emphasis). In the mid-1870s, as war with the Ottoman Empire loomed, he commented frequently on the persistence of "the doctrine of the sword" as a mark of man's earthly failure to live up to the Christian ideal. Noting that wars have recurred every quarter century or so in Europe throughout recorded history, he concluded that war is a "normal condition" in this world; it will not end until the Second Coming, when, it is foretold, "the world will be reborn *suddenly* by a miracle" (24:270, 276; Dostoevsky's emphasis).

In the context of such remarks it would appear that for Dostoevsky the actual transition from imperfect to perfect realization of the ideal is marked by a sudden, essentially apocalyptic and mystical transfiguration of man into another being of largely unknown nature who exists not on the earth as we know it but in a realm of perfect mutual love, following the scriptural model of death, resurrection, and ascension into another world. This was certainly the interpretation of his ideal put forward after his death by Solovyov, who contested Konstantin Leontyev's claim that Dostoevsky's ideal of universal harmony was intended to be realized on earth. Solovyov wrote:

> The universal harmony Dostoevsky prophesied by no means signifies a utilitarian flourishing of people on the present-day earth but is precisely the principle of that new earth on which truth and justice [*pravda*] abide. And the coming of this universal harmony or Church Triumphant will take place not at all by means of peaceful progress but in the torments and agonies of a new birth as described in the Apocalypse—Dostoevsky's favorite book in his last years.[20]

This interpretation is, of course, consistent with Dostoevsky's enduring religious belief in the bodily resurrection of mankind at the time of the Second Coming—that is, in the physical resurrection of people into "different bodies, not the present ones—that is, perhaps like Christ's body at the time of His resurrection, before the ascension," as he expressed it in an 1878 letter in which he commented favorably on the theories of resurrection put forward by the eccentric Russian religious thinker Nikolay Fyodorov. "Solovyov and I," Dostoevsky continued, "believe in real, literal, personal resurrection, and believe that it will take place on earth" (30/1:14–15). The resurrection of Christ on earth was extended to the general resurrection of earthly mankind, resulting in a radical transformation that is both bodily and spiritual.

For all the apparent definiteness of Dostoevsky's conviction of the unattainability of the social ideal in earthly life as we now know it, however, there was in his thinking another strain, evident already in the 1864 reflections, that worked against the postulation of an ontological gulf between present-day humanity and resurrected humanity and that pushed him in the direction of expecting a recognizably earthly Kingdom of God. For if he called the ideal otherworldly as a terminal state, and hence unattainable in this life, he also believed that movement toward it was not only possible in this world but constituted the very meaning and purpose of earthly life: "All history," as he wrote in the 1864 reflections on his wife's death, "both of humanity and in

---

20. V. S. Solov'ev, *Sochineniia v dvukh tomakh* (Moscow: Mysl', 1988), 2:322.

some degree of each person separately, is nothing but development, struggle, striving, and attaining this goal" (20:172). The very need for the natural law of the "succession of generations," made possible by marriage and the family, is that "by means of this law of nature man achieves the development . . . of the goal" (20:173). In the 1864 reflections, Dostoevsky repeatedly refers to present-day man as "developing" and "transitional"—transitional to the transfigured, selfless creature of the paradise of Christ. Thus although in earthly life man does not reach the ideal, he makes progress toward it, coming closer to the ideal over the course of time. The whole meaning of progress, Dostoevsky had written as early as 1861, comes down to "self-enlightenment in the name of love of one another" (19:126).

But how is it even possible for progress to be made by individuals who are ruled by the "law of personality," as Dostoevsky stressed so strongly in the 1864 reflections? He insisted there that to make progress the individual must strive toward an ideal that is "opposed" to his nature and which he must continually "negate"; significantly but cryptically, however, Dostoevsky also stated that the individual does this "in accordance with the same law of nature, in the name of the ultimate ideal of his goal." What he did not make entirely clear in the 1864 text was his view of human "nature" as a composite: even untransfigured, earthly humans have not only an animal but a spiritual nature, making them responsive not only to the law of personality but to the law of love, which counter each other in a moral dialectic as enduring as earthly life. In an essay on women's rights written in 1861, three years before his wife's death, Dostoevsky had addressed the other, more positive side of the "egoistic" phenomenon of marriage, the side that relates to the embedding of the law of love in man's spiritual nature:

> Marriage was created by nature; marriage is nature's law, and if there remains in you one drop of faith in progress, then you must not think that the natural, mutual duty of people to one another, such as the duty of man to woman and vice versa, would ever be destroyed. . . .
>
> Man, because he is man, would feel the need to love his neighbor, the need to sacrifice himself to benefit his neighbor, because love is unthinkable without self-sacrifice, and love, we repeat, can never be destroyed. For that, man would have to hate his own nature. (19:130–32)

This is, of course, entirely consistent with Dostoevsky's view, examined in chapter 3, of the inherent knowledge of the law of love that is part of people's spiritual nature, thanks to the gift of their creator, and that normally makes itself known to them through conscience (though, as we saw, conscience can be dimmed to the point of extinction in some human beings). In any event, marriage for Dostoevsky appears to have the interesting dual character of serving as both a force for progress, by manifesting and encouraging the expression of love, and an obstacle to progress, by channeling that love in exclusive directions, toward some individuals and away from others. Thus there is at least a basis in the spiritual side of "nature" for selflessness, making possible the progressive movement toward the ideal.

In his notes on "Socialism and Christianity," Dostoevsky presented in broad outline his conception of the course of this progressive movement in human history (20:191–94). He imagined a three-stage development conforming to the thesis-antithesis-synthesis pattern associated with the Hegelian dialectic, in which a second stage negates the first but is in turn negated by the third, thereby in effect returning to the first, but on a higher plane. In Dostoevsky's scheme the first is the stage of primitive patriarchal communities, in which people live "in masses" and "spontaneously"—that is, instinctively and unreflectively. In the second stage, which he calls "civilization," personal consciousness develops, negating the accepted patriarchal laws of the masses. This fragmentation into persons, however necessary for still further development, is in itself a "diseased" condition, according to Dostoevsky, for it leads to the loss of faith in God and a general malaise resulting from losing the "spontaneous sensations" that are "the source of living life." The final stage, Christianity, is a return to spontaneity and the mass, but now with full understanding of the ideal, "in the full power of consciousness and development": "Man returns to the mass, to spontaneous life, consequently to a natural condition, but how? Not by obeying authority but, on the contrary, in the highest degree voluntarily and consciously. It is clear that this highest voluntariness is at the same time the highest renunciation of one's will. My will consists in not having a will, for the ideal is beautiful" (20:192). Thus history for Dostoevsky is a process leading up to and culminating in the establishment of the ideal community of mutual love.

The logic of Dostoevsky's belief in the possibility, indeed apparently the inevitability, of progress toward the ideal on earth pushed him relentlessly toward the vision of a paradise that was evolutionary rather than apocalyptic, and earthly rather than celestial. To say, as he did even in the 1864 reflections, that there are different degrees of approach to the ideal, is to say that there are different degrees to which the "law of personality" is overcome in the course of history. "The more correctly society develops . . . the closer it will come to the ideal of humaneness," he wrote as early as 1861 (19:126–27). That human beings are able to make such progress, that they have in them the traits needed to combat and overcome selfishness—specifically, a knowledge of the moral law, with conscience on its side, and the power of will to observe it—made it increasingly difficult for him to resist the conclusion that a closer and closer approach could be made until the ideal itself was reached.

It was, after all, such a simple matter, as Dostoevsky suggested more than once, spurning the imagery of apocalyptic transformation. If, in the course of history, altruism can increasingly get the better of egoism, why could not a determined moral resolve bring total victory? "If you love one another," he wrote in a notebook of 1875–76, "you will immediately achieve [your goal]" (24:164). The same thought appears in "The Dream of a Ridiculous Man," published in 1877, where the dreamer exclaims that a simple change of heart on the part of individuals could create paradise: "In a single day, *in a single hour*—everything could be worked out instantly! The main thing is to love others as yourself"; if you do, "you'll at once find a way to work it out" (25:119; Dostoevsky's emphasis). The dreamer's epiphany transforms his own moral attitudes, but at the end of the dream he returns thus spiritually altered to the same life of time and matter he had left, with no suggestion of a transition to eternity or an ontological transfiguration into another kind of human being with a different kind of body.

Of course, in *Winter Notes* Dostoevsky wrote that "even the slightest calculation" in favor of self-interest could ruin everything (5:79–80), but he never offered a compelling reason for thinking that the progressive temporal reduction of the power of egoism on earth that was implicit in his theory of history cannot of necessity ever be complete—that it must be asymptotic rather than linear. That he was struggling with this point just at the time of writing "The Dream of a Ridiculous Man" is evident both in the text itself and in notebooks of the period. In one notebook, for example, he wrote, "It is *impossible* now for everyone to be a Christian; only individual cases are possible," adding that "perhaps these individual cases *secretly* lead and preserve the people" (24:291; Dostoevsky's emphasis). But, we may ask, if *some* can become true Christians, why not others, such as those they "lead and preserve"? Furthermore the Ridiculous Man, in concluding his fantasy, states significantly that, having seen "the truth," he now knows that "people can be beautiful and happy without losing the ability to live on earth" (25:118). The implications of Dostoevsky's progressivist position were driving him in the direction of an earthly utopia, in which self-interest is either eliminated altogether or rendered powerless and negligible.

And there was still another consideration that inclined Dostoevsky toward the possibility of an earthly paradise, and this was perhaps the consideration that turned the balance in his late and most intensely patriotic years. Over and above the inherent logic of his view of the progressive moral improvement of human beings and their societies, Dostoevsky was convinced that there was striking empirical evidence that some nations were closer to the ideal than others and had a greater chance of implementing it. Closest of all—indeed, the one "God-bearing" nation—was Russia.[21]

In the broad terms in which we sketched Dostoevsky's theory of history above, it may seem to suggest a single, uniform, worldwide sequence of advance. But in fact he found within the third stage—"Christianity"—a pattern of uneven development among nations, placing some distant from the social ideal and others so close as to be on the threshold of attaining it. Already in *Winter Notes* he had claimed that the nations of Western Europe were, in their present condition, constitutionally incapable of supporting a fraternal union. By contrast, he implied that in the Russian nation the "law of personality" is far weaker, even to the point of disappearance. It was on the basis of his belief in the unique moral character of his countrymen that by the mid-1870s he was willing, at least at times, to suspend all skepticism concerning the earthly achievement of his desired paradise and declare himself a confirmed utopian.

The mutation of desire into belief in Dostoevsky's thinking about the ideal society is documented in a revealing passage in a notebook of 1875–76. Having initially written "I want [*khochu*] the full kingdom of Christ," he crossed out "I want" and replaced it with "I believe in [*veryu*]":

> I believe in the full kingdom of Christ. . . . I believe that this kingdom will be accomplished. Though it is hard to divine, one can observe, if only mentally, signs in the dark night of conjecture, and I believe in these signs. . . . And the universal kingdom of thought and light will come to pass, and *it will be with us in Russia*, perhaps sooner than anywhere else. (24:127; emphasis added)

Here, signs of progress toward the ideal are explicitly turned into grounds for faith in its full realization on earth, in Russia first of all.

In the late 1870s, Dostoevsky's confidence in the earthly feasibility of his Christian utopia increased in tandem with his interest in the theocratic ideas of Vladimir Solovyov. Dostoevsky's acceptance of the theocratic ideal, and his conviction that Orthodox Russia was the arena in which it was destined to be realized, were signaled in book 2 of *The Brothers Karamazov* in the discussion of Ivan Karamazov's article on church-state relations.[22] Ivan, opposing the sepa-

---

21. The expression "a God-bearing nation" (*narod-"bogonosets"*) was applied exclusively to the Russian people by Shatov in *Demons* (10:196).

22. On the content and significance of this discussion and its relation to the ideas of Solovyov, see Marina Kostalevsky, *Dostoevsky and Soloviev: The Art of Integral Vision* (New Haven, Conn.: Yale University Press, 1997), 121–29.

ration of church and state, had argued that the former should wholly absorb the latter, with ecclesiastical institutions replacing state institutions. Father Paisy enthusiastically seconded the notion: "The church is indeed a kingdom, ordained to rule, and in the end it must undoubtedly come forth as a kingdom over all the earth" (14:57). Zosima, concurring, remarks that the transformation of society into "a single universal, sovereign church" is "destined to come about!" Father Paisy also makes clear that it is specifically the *Orthodox* church that will assume the functions of the state: to become a church ruling over the world "is simply the great destiny of Orthodoxy on earth. This star will shine forth from the East" (14:61–62).

None of the participants in the discussion assumes that ecclesiastical rule would ipso facto usher in the full Christian utopia in which all egoism is vanquished. But they agree that it would be a giant step in that direction. The crux of Ivan's argument, strongly seconded by Zosima, is that the assumption of state functions by the church would work to strengthen the individual moral conscience, which is, as Zosima insists, the only effective deterrent to sin. Between them they identify two ways in which this would happen. First, because there would no longer be a distinction between what is legally right and what is right from a moral and religious point of view, the criminal would no longer be able to rationalize his law-breaking by appealing to a higher, spiritual standard. By avoiding this source of a divided conscience, it is possible that crimes would be "decreased by an unbelievable amount," in Zosima's words (14:61). Second, those who do commit crimes would be treated in such a way as to correct and invigorate their moral conscience. The mechanical and barbarous forms of punishment that prevail in the nontheocratic state serve only to isolate the criminal from society and engender bitterness and hatred; they are not effective deterrents. A ruling church, on the other hand, would address itself to the reformation and regeneration of the criminal, leading him "as a son of a Christian society" to recognize his wrongdoing. Thus both crime and attitudes toward it would inevitably change, Ivan contends, "not suddenly, not immediately, but rather quickly." As for the establishment of the theocracy that will have such transforming consequences, Zosima is patiently confident: although to humans it may still seem very distant, in accordance with divine predestination we may already have reached "the eve of its appearance" (14:59–61).

The idea of an earthly kingdom of God, with which Dostoevsky had flirted for much of his adult life, beginning with his radical period of the 1840s, obviously had great appeal to him, and in his last years he virtually yielded his better judgment to it, all but convinced that his own country would be the New Jerusalem. No longer, it seems, must there be an indefinitely protracted "succession of generations"; no longer was there need of an apocalypse and a mystical metamorphosis into a different type of bodily reality; no longer must "the law of personality" remain binding on earth. "With us in Russia," at least, the ideal society was within reach.

For a full grasp of Dostoevsky's faith in the superior qualities and the special historical role of the Russian people that make this transformation feasible, it is necessary to proceed to the final dimension of his understanding of man—man as a *national* creature.

CHAPTER 6

"The Russian Idea"

In his last two decades, Dostoevsky's musings on "the mystery of man" turned increasingly to what was for him a crucial piece of the puzzle—the question of national identity and its role in human life. He became convinced that, over and above such traditional epithets for the human animal as "political" and "rational," it is important to recognize that man is also a *national* animal, in the sense that every individual is born into a particular ethnic community and develops by assimilating the distinctive features nurtured by that community. Thus nationality is a common trait of human beings, but it is one that divides them into groups and hence has great importance for an understanding of their systematic differences.[1]

In acknowledging the significance of nationality, as in so many areas of his thought, Dostoevsky was following the lead of the Russian romantics before him, especially as their views were refracted through the thinking of his early idol, Vissarion Belinsky. In 1846 Belinsky had written: "What *personality* is in relation to the *idea* of man *nationality* is in relation to the *idea* of humanity. In other words, nationalities are the personalities of humanity. Without nationalities humanity would be a dead logical abstraction, a word without meaning, a sound without tenor. . . . A nation without nationality is like a man without

---

1. The Russian terms ordinarily translated 'national' (*narodnyi*) and 'nationality' (*narodnost'*) in this chapter harbor ambiguities that Dostoevsky often does not clarify; both are derived from the Russian *narod*, usually translated either 'nation' or 'people'. Typically the terms refer to ethnic identity, but they can also refer to the geographic or political identity of a state (in which case Dostoevsky occasionally uses *natsiia* instead of *narod* and *natsional'nyi* instead of *narodnyi*), and in addition they can refer to the people in the sense of the folk or common people—in Russia primarily the peasantry. I shall add Dostoevsky's Russian term parenthetically where it seems needed for clarity.

personality."[2] Dostoevsky was intimately familiar with the essay in which these lines are found, and his own comments on the importance of nationality read like a gloss on them, as we shall see below.

Dostoevsky also joined many of his predecessors in going beyond the simple recognition of national differences to make judgments of relative national worth: he affirmed the superiority of his own nation and disparaged others, with particular, sometimes venomous scorn directed at Poles, Jews, and Western Europeans. Furthermore, the assertion of Russian superiority served him as ground for a more specific chauvinistic claim—namely, that it is the mission of the Russian nation to implement "the Russian idea," which he defined, on the most abstract level, as "universal panhuman unification" (25:20). He fervently believed that the matchless qualities of the Russian people gave it the capacity to deliver other peoples from evil and lead the world to the kind of harmony and unity envisaged in his social ideal. If his theistic providentialism inclined him to expect world salvation, he found its instrument in the Russian people and its formula in "the Russian idea." The formula survived not only its originator and the generation after him but the entire Soviet period of Russian history, reemerging with renewed vigor as a rallying cry of Russian nationalists in the last years of the twentieth century and into the twenty-first.[3]

Understandably, Dostoevsky's messianic nationalism is the most controversial feature of his intellectual outlook. Critics have long charged that the devaluation of other peoples inherent in his view was starkly at odds with his Christian message of universal love and brotherhood. Some commentators dismiss his chauvinistic pronouncements as nothing more than the ideological efflux of a regrettable xenophobia, and therefore not to be taken seriously as an element of his thought.[4] Xenophobia there surely was in Dostoevsky's makeup;

2. V.G. Belinsky, *Selected Philosophical Works* (Moscow: Foreign Languages Publishing House, 1956), 395, 397 (Belinsky's emphasis).

3. Dostoevsky apparently first used the expression 'the Russian idea' (*russkaia ideia*) in a letter to Apollon Maykov in January 1856 (28/1:208) and then used it repeatedly in his post-Siberian career, beginning with his earliest writings for *Vremya* in 1860 and 1861. Concerning the notion of "the Russian idea" in general see M.A. Maslin, ed., *Russkaia ideia* (Moscow: Respublika, 1992)—an anthology of nineteenth- and twentieth-century Russian writings; Arsenii Gulyga, *Russkaia ideia i ee tvortsy* (Moscow: Soratnik, 1995)—a sympathetic discussion of Dostoevsky, Solovyov, and other exponents of the concept; and Tim McDaniel, *The Agony of the Russian Idea* (Princeton, N.J.: Princeton University Press, 1996)—a study of the history and contemporary significance of the concept by an American sociologist. McDaniel, like some other commentators, credits Vladimir Solovyov with having "first introduced [the expression 'the Russian idea'] in a systematic way" (24), on the strength of a talk bearing that title that Solovyov gave in Paris in 1889. But Russian readers were familiar with the expression long before that, through its frequent use by Dostoevsky in the 1860s and later. Solovyov's talk, moreover, was not published in Russia until 1909.

4. For a discussion of critical approaches to xenophobia and other explanations of Dostoevsky's attitude toward the Jews, see P. Torop, "Dostoevskii: Logika evreiskogo voprosa," in *Sbornik statei k*

but whatever the psychic roots of his nationalism, it was conceptually more complex than is often acknowledged. He himself regarded it as a defensible element of his worldview, and it is logically connected with his understanding of human history, of the relation between society and the individual, and of the realizability of the Christian ideal on earth. For those reasons it is worth examining with an eye to its conceptual structure. His nationalism was undeniably flawed; yet, as I shall try to show, it was not inconsistent with his understanding of the ideal of Christian love and brotherhood.

Lively discussion of Russia's national identity was not new in the country's intellectual life in Dostoevsky's day. Russian historians for decades had debated their nation's place in world history and the relative importance of common versus national factors in the evolution of a people's character. In the late eighteenth and early nineteenth centuries Nikolay Karamzin, whose historical writings figured prominently in Dostoevsky's early education, traversed a path from a kind of universalist humanism, which had led him to proclaim that "the national is as nothing compared to the human,"[5] to a strongly patriotic defense of Russia's distinctiveness and preeminence among nations. The sobering voice of Peter Chaadayev, whose "Philosophical Letters" of 1829 (first published in 1836) relegated Russia to insignificance on the world stage, only served to intensify the debate, for Chaadayev accepted the premise that national differences in history and culture between Russia and the West were fundamental and determining. The Slavophiles of the 1830s and 1840s used the same premise to ground their opposing view of the inappropriateness of Western institutions and values for a Slavic culture that was not only unique but inherently superior. In the mid-1840s, just what (if anything) constituted the national uniqueness of Russia was hotly debated on the pages of the journals *Moskvitianin* (The Muscovite) and *Sovremennik* (The Contemporary) by Belinsky, Mikhail Pogodin, Ivan Kireevsky, Aleksey Khomyakov, and others. By the 1850s, Slavophile conceptions had penetrated Russian educated society to the extent that even the Westernist Alexander Herzen began to stress the national differences between Russia and the West.[6]

Attention to nationality was also stimulated in Russia by international events during the first half of the nineteenth century. The campaign against

---

70–letiiu Professora Iu. M. Lotmana (Tartu: Tartuskii Universitet, 1992), 281–319, especially 284–87. Observers reported xenophobic outbursts from Dostoevsky as early as the 1840s; see James L. Rice, *Dostoevsky and the Healing Art: An Essay in Literary and Medical History* (Ann Arbor: Ardis, 1985), 57.

5. Quoted in Andrzej Walicki, *The Slavophile Controversy: History of a Conservative Utopia in Nineteenth-Century Russian Thought*, trans. Hilda Andrews-Rusiecka (Oxford: Clarendon Press, 1975), 33.

6. Joseph Frank, *Dostoevsky: The Years of Ordeal, 1850–1859* (Princeton, N.J.: Princeton University Press, 1983), 230–33.

Napoleon brought Russia's armies triumphantly into the heart of Western Europe, prompting a surge of national patriotism. When after the Decembrist revolt of 1825 Nicholas I came to power, convinced that noxious revolutionary ideas from the West were responsible for the uprising, he sought as far as possible to isolate Russia from the rest of Europe and to promote distinctively Russian virtues, under the slogan "Orthodoxy, Autocracy, Nationality"; the isolation was increasingly rationalized as needed to protect Russia from the intensifying class struggles in Western Europe, which culminated in widespread revolutionary agitation in 1848. Just a few years later, the Crimean War (1853–1856) generated another wave of patriotism, and its troubling conclusion provided one more occasion for reflection on Russia's place in the world.

By the mid-1850s Dostoevsky, far from having been immunized against excesses of patriotism by either his Westernist leanings of the 1840s or his personal mistreatment at the hands of the Russian state as a prisoner and exile in Siberia, was as ardent a believer in Russia's uniqueness and greatness as any Slavophile, and he remained so until his death. Most important for our purposes, however, was his philosophical interest in national identity and its historical role—always, of course, with special reference to his native country; with the resumption of his literary career in St. Petersburg in 1860, he began to spell out his ideas on these subjects in the journal *Vremya* (Time), which he founded with his brother Mikhail. The quasi-Slavophile doctrine of the importance of national as opposed to universal human traits, preached in the journal by the Dostoevsky brothers, Apollon Grigoryev, and other contributors, came to be called *pochvennichestvo*—the "native soil" movement, after *pochva*, the Russian word for soil.[7]

Never a tightly defined program theoretically, *pochvennichestvo* comprised elements that could be construed in different ways. At its root was a broad empirical theory about the impact of a nation's history and culture on not only the attitudes but the capacities and other traits of the individual—a theory that in itself was neutral with respect to the relative merits of nations. As thus indeterminate, however, the theory was open to elaboration in both chauvinistic and nonchauvinistic directions, and tendencies toward both sometimes coexisted in its supporters simultaneously. Dostoevsky himself exhibited symptoms of this ambivalence early in his post-Siberian career; subsequently he came to believe that there was in fact no conflict between humane universalism and his own affirmations of Russian superiority.

7. For an excellent study of this movement see Wayne Dowler, *Dostoevsky, Grigor'ev, and Native Soil Conservatism* (Toronto: University of Toronto Press, 1982).

Let us begin with an examination of basic or neutral *pochvennichestvo* as Dostoevsky himself presented it in the early 1860s.

Pochvennichestvo without Chauvinism

Dostoevsky's fullest statement of the theoretical basis of his "native soil" outlook came in his critique of Westernism in an 1862 essay entitled "Two Camps of Theoreticians"—the other camp being, of course, the Slavophiles, who also received their share of criticism in the essay. The Westernists, he contended, ignored the diversity of human development and sought to impose on all peoples a "panhuman ideal" that abstracts from national distinctions and reduces individuals to commonly shared traits. In an earlier work he had accused the Westernists of wishing "to turn man into a worn fifteen-kopek piece" (19:149), and in "Two Camps" he returned to this apt image of an old, effaced coin—a national symbol whose distinguishing features have been worn away—to protest the denationalization of individuals (20:6).[8]

As early as 1849 Dostoevsky had commented on the "profound malleability" he had discovered in man (28/1:158), and in "Two Camps" he stresses the extent to which that malleability is expressed in the national diversity produced by different backgrounds and environments. Every people [*narod*], he writes, "developing under the particular circumstances that exclusively characterize the country it inhabits, inevitably forms its own perception of the world, its own cast of mind, its own customs, its own rules of social life" (20:7). The botanical analogy behind *pochvennichestvo* is evident: different soils produce different plants bearing different fruits.

But Dostoevsky does not use the analogy solely to highlight malleability and differences. His further argument is that institutions and ideals, being products of a particular soil, may not be exportable to other soils; as he had written in *Vremya* a few months earlier, "every fruit needs *its own* soil, *its own* climate, *its own* cultivation" (19:148; Dostoevsky's emphasis). In "Two Camps" this point becomes the basis of his attack on what he perceives as the Westernists' misguided and destructive attempt to impose an alien culture on Russia in the name of "panhumanism":

> Sometimes what is recommended as panhuman proves somehow to be no good at all in a particular country and can only retard the development of the people to

8. For still another use of this image, see 20:207.

whom it is applied. . . . We believe that every plant is threatened by degeneration in a country that lacks many of the conditions for its life. It even seems to us sometimes that this desire to level every people in accordance with a single ideal defined once and for all is at bottom too despotic. It denies to peoples all right of *self-development*, all intellectual *autonomy*. (20:7; Dostoevsky's ellipses and emphasis)

In other writings of the period as well, he stressed both the difficulty and the undesirability of transferring cultural forms from one soil to another. In *Winter Notes on Summer Impressions* he suggests the existence of "a kind of chemical bond between the human spirit and its native land"; "the soul," he comments, "is not a *tabula rasa*, not a lump of wax from which universal man can be molded." Because a national character is the work of centuries, it is "not easily refashioned" (5:52, 61, 78). In another of his *Vremya* essays, the Russian soil takes on a mystical character as the nurturer and defender of the Russian nation; he is convinced "that there is in our earth something of our own, something native; that it is embedded in the natural, ancestral foundations of the Russian character and customs; that salvation lies in the soil and the people. . . . Western ideals can never wholly suit us." Others may claim a right to promote something like "panhuman" ideals, but "the right of nationality is the strongest of all the rights that peoples and societies may have" (20:209–10).

Despite the note of anti-Westernism and the evident attachment to Russian culture that are apparent even in this presentation of a general theory of national identity, the theory as such has no inherent chauvinistic bias in the sense of assigning a superior status to any one nationality. Presumably the "right of nationality" can be claimed by any nation, and in "Two Camps" Dostoevsky gives the theory a generous interpretation that explicitly grants to all peoples an equal voice in the world symphony of cultures and histories. "In speaking . . . of nationality," he writes, "we do not mean by it the national exclusiveness that most often contradicts the interests of all of humanity. No, we mean here true nationality, which always acts in the interest of all peoples" (20:19). This is a new element in the theory—the idea that there is an overarching common human interest that the "true" nationality of every people somehow serves, as opposed to the "exclusive" nationality that sacrifices the common interest to the separate interests of its own people.

But what entitles us to assume that every nation can simultaneously serve both its own interests and the general interests of mankind—for that is what this version of *pochvennichestvo* appears to require? By way of answering this question, Dostoevsky goes on in "Two Camps" to describe an elaborate, preordained harmony of national "tasks," each task apparently as legitimate as the next and each serving both national man and universal man:

Fate has distributed tasks among us—to develop one or another side of the common man. . . . Humanity will complete the full cycle of its development only when each people [*narod*], in keeping with the conditions of its material situation, will have fulfilled its own task. There are no sharp distinctions among the national tasks, because at the basis of every nationality lies one common human ideal, simply with a local coloration. Thus there can be no antagonism among peoples so long as each understands it own true interests. The trouble is that such understanding is exceedingly rare, and peoples seek their glory only in an empty priority over their neighbors. The various peoples working out their panhuman tasks can be compared with specialists in science; each is particularly occupied with his own subject, toward which, in preference to others, he feels a special inclination. But they all have in view one common science. (20:19–20; Dostoevsky's ellipses)

On the basis of this preestablished harmony, strongly reminiscent of Herder's views, Dostoevsky then argues that attention to the defense and elaboration of one's own national character is the best way to reach the full human potential desired by all: "Humanity will live a full life only when each nation [*narod*] develops on its own principles and brings from itself to the common sum of life some particularly developed aspect. Perhaps only then, too, may we dream of the full panhuman ideal" (20:7). The different national characters are inherently not hostile but complementary.

If *pochvennichestvo* had meant no more to Dostoevsky than the existence of distinct national identities, their rootedness in the national "soil," and their compatibility as equally valuable contributions to the common human project, there would be no ground for criticizing the doctrine as nationalistic in a pejorative sense. In that case Dostoevsky might be convicted of naive utopianism, but not of setting the interests of any one nation above those of others.

Because the complementarity of national contributions was not logically entailed by the basic principles of *pochvennichestvo*, however, those principles were also open to development in a chauvinistic direction. And it was this direction that most attracted Dostoevsky even before the writing of "Two Camps," but still more urgently in later years. Although he continued to invoke the importance of "panhuman ideals" and defended his very chauvinism in their name, after 1862 he never again dwelled on the thesis of the *equal* significance of all nationalities. Rather, he insistently proclaimed the preeminence of the Russian national character over all others and assigned to Russia, in virtue of that preeminence, the paramount role in world history.

He based his view of Russian superiority on two related but distinguishable traits of the Russian character: first, its fraternity, or special capacity for brotherly love; and second, the remarkable combination of talents he called its "universality."

Russian Superiority: (1) Fraternity

True to the principles of *pochvennichestvo*, Dostoevsky tied the development of the Russian character to the superior soil that had produced it. As evidence of the distinctive virtues of the Russian milieu, he offered a battery of historical arguments. Particularly important for his case were the theories of the French historian Augustin Thierry (1795–1856), whose views of the origins of the West European states gained currency in Russia beginning in the 1840s, especially after they were taken up by the conservative writer M. P. Pogodin as a basis for distinguishing Russia's history from that of Western Europe. Thierry had traced the existence and intensity of class struggles in England, France, and other states to the circumstance that those states originated in the conquest of one people by another, such as the Anglo-Saxons by the Normans and the Gauls by the Franks. The resulting class divisions in those societies, Thierry maintained, were rooted in the intractable mutual hostility of peoples alien to one another and related only as victor and vanquished. Pogodin, seconding Thierry's analysis, argued that the case of Russia was fundamentally different: the Russian state originated not in armed conquest but in voluntary agreement among people with a shared ethnic identity, and for that reason it was essentially free of class struggles and conflicts; rather, it was based on the mutual respect and affection of all the elements of the population. The Thierry-Pogodin thesis was eagerly embraced by Dostoevsky and the Slavophile philosophers, and it even found echoes among such Westernists as Turgenev and Herzen (18:235–36).[9]

Dostoevsky's uncritical acceptance of the thesis is evident as early as his 1849 deposition to the Investigating Commission. By way of countering the charges against him, he disclaimed any intention of wishing to apply the socialist ideas of the West to Russia. The West, he wrote, has been marked for many centuries by "the most stubborn struggle between society and an authority based on an alien civilization of conquest, violence, suppression"; Russia, on the other hand, is fundamentally different: "Our land was not formed in the Western way!" Fourierism and every other Western system are thus "unfit for our soil" (18:123, 134).

---

9. Walicki, *Slavophile Controversy*, 47–48; Dowler, *Dostoevsky*, 31; Joseph Frank, *Dostoevsky: The Stir of Liberation, 1860–1865* (Princeton, N.J.: Princeton University Press, 1986), 35–36.

That these thoughts were more than an ad hoc defense against the charge of sedition is shown by the fact that they survived his years in Siberia and reappeared more fully formed in the *pochvennichestvo* manifestos of the early 1860s. In an article of 1861 Dostoevsky, imagining a Western interlocutor, treats him to a harangue in which the Thierry-Pogodin legacy is obvious:

> We have long had a neutral soil, on which everything comes together in an integral, harmonious, unanimous unit, all the classes come together peacefully, concordantly, and fraternally. . . . It is just in this that we differ from you, for you have had to fight for each step forward, for each of your rights, for each of your privileges. . . . We have no class interests because we have no classes in the strict sense. We have no Gauls and Franks. (18:49–50)

Thereafter he regularly appealed to what he called in a letter of 1868 "the loving, not aggressive, basis of our state" as the principal explanation of the superior character of Russian society and a greater force for social well-being than any formal institutional arrangement. "Our constitution," he wrote, "is the mutual love of the monarch for the people and the people for the monarch" (28/2:280).

Ironically, a powerful refutation of the dreamy thesis that Russian or Slavic society is uniquely unified and loving had been laid out by Belinsky before Dostoevsky ever began to defend the idea. In his "Survey of Russian Literature for 1846" Belinsky ridiculed the thesis, commenting that it had become "a veritable monomania" among Russian writers. "We, on the contrary," he continues, referring to those who shared his view of the matter, "believe that love is inherent in human nature generally, and cannot be the exclusive attribute of any one nation or tribe, no more than can breath, sight, hunger, thirst, mind or speech." He grants that the early Slavs may have known "gentle and loving patriarchal relations," but he argues that their subsequent recorded history is marked more by hostility and violence; both patriarchal custom and with it love as the underlying principle of life have long since disappeared irretrievably:

> Even before the appanage period we find in Russian history the by no means loving traits of the crafty warrior Oleg, the stern warrior Svyatoslav, then Svyatopolk the assassin of Boris and Gleb; the children of Vladimir who had unsheathed the sword against their father, and so on and so forth. . . . The appanage period was no more a period of love than it was of humility; rather it was a period of carnage reduced to custom. The Tatar period goes without saying: hypocritical and treacherous humility was then needed more than love and genuine humility. The

criminal laws, tortures and executions of the Muscovy period and subsequent times as late as the reign of Catherine the Great compel us again to seek love in the pre-historic Slav days. Where does love come in here as a national principle? A national principle it never was.[10]

We know that Dostoevsky had read this article at the time,[11] but that did not deter him from displaying years later the very monomania that Belinsky had described and continuing to present supposed historical evidence of the unique fraternal unity of Russia. We saw in the last chapter that he regarded the Great Reforms of the 1860s, above all the emancipation, as testimony to the fundamental harmony of Russia's population under the rule of a benevolent Tsar; the reforms reaffirmed "the fusion of our educated society and its representatives with the popular [narodnyi] element" after the temporary rifts created by Peter's policies (18:35). He also took the continued existence of the peasant commune and the artel in Russia as signs of the fundamental fraternity of the Russian people (20:21).

But perhaps the historical circumstance that he invokes most often in arguing for the special virtue of the Russian soil is Russia's retention of "true" Christianity in the form of Orthodoxy. Russians, he suggests, have "preserved and reinforced" the essence of Christianity more than any other people (25:69). He fully accepted the Slavophiles' view that the schism between Eastern and Western Christianity was created by Rome's willful withdrawal from the universal communion. The Western church, on this interpretation, moved increasingly toward secularization and materialization, whereas the Eastern church continued to place first the spiritual union of humanity in Christ. In the West, "Christ has been lost" (29/1:214); Orthodoxy alone has "preserved the divine image of Christ in all its purity"—which meant, of course, the divine law of brotherly love (21:59). Dostoevsky found graphic evidence of the West's lack of devotion to Christian values at the time of the Crimean War, when the so-called "Christian" countries of Western Europe sided with the Moslem Turks. He expressed his outrage in 1854 in a patriotic poem, and from that time on, as Joseph Frank has observed, Dostoevsky could never believe that the European peoples were truly committed to Christianity.[12]

Out of this harmonious, thoroughly Christian soil, Dostoevsky argued, came a people with a fraternal character unparalleled elsewhere: a capacity for

10. Belinsky, *Selected Philosophical Works*, 390–91.

11. It was, in Joseph Frank's words, "the fateful article that certified the total shipwreck of his [Dostoevsky's] literary reputation and his public repudiation by the critic who had raised him to fame" (*Dostoevsky: The Seeds of Revolt, 1821–1849* [Princeton, N.J.: Princeton University Press, 1976], 212).

12. Frank, *Dostoevsky: The Years of Ordeal*, 183.

mutual love and respect, the ability to sympathize with others, to share with them in a spirit of brotherhood, to sacrifice oneself for them if need be. In the 1861 introduction to his "Series of Articles on Russian Literature" he greeted ecstatically the imminent emancipation of the serfs as evidence of the brotherly inclinations of the Russian people: "The Russian spirit is broader than class hostility, than class interests and privileges. . . . Our new Russia has under-stood that there is but one cement, one bond, one soil on which all come to-gether and are reconciled: this is a universal, spiritual reconciliation, the foun-dation of which lies in our upbringing" (18:50).

Dostoevsky places special stress on the uniquely ethical nature of the Russ-ian character. Because Russians, he implies in *Winter Notes on Summer Impres-sions*, are "drawn instinctively toward brotherhood," they are morally superior to other peoples (5:80). In letters he calls the Russian people "infinitely higher, more noble, more honest" than Europeans and claims that "all the moral ideas and goals of Russians are higher than [those of] the European world" (28/2:243, 260). Russian fraternity creates an atmosphere of national altru-ism—a general "desire for the common cause and the common good" that is "prior to any egoism" (22:41). In the Russian character alone, it would seem, the law of love is typically more powerful than its inescapable earthly adver-sary, the "law of personality."

When Dostoevsky asserts that Russians are fraternal "instinctively" it is tempting to attribute to him a kind of biologically based, racial theory of the difference between Russians and other peoples. Certainly the national and ethnic slurs that dot his published and unpublished writings—his references to "little Polacks" (28/2:309), "damned Yids" (30/1:93), and the "infinitely stu-pid" German people (28/2:243)—could well be interpreted as reflecting a clas-sification of human groups into essentially unalterable natural kinds. At the same time, however, he insists on the influence of the environment: the whole thrust of *pochvennichestvo* is on the shaping of a people's national character by its particular historical and cultural soil.

Dostoevsky straddles the issue of nature versus nurture here because, given his understanding of *pochvennichestvo*, the conditioning of the individual by the soil is a matter of such prolonged duration that it makes no practical difference whether a given character trait is regarded as inborn or acquired. Speaking of the bourgeois inclinations of French workers, for example, he writes: "Such is their nature. A nature is not given as a gift. All this is cultivated by centuries and nurtured by centuries. Nationality [*natsional'nost'*] is not easily reshaped; it is not easy to forsake century-old habits" (5:78). In the realm of national char-acter, "second nature," it seems, is virtually as significant as first.

Yet it is also important to note that Dostoevsky is not saying nurture is everything and is not denying that there is a "first" or "original" nature on which the soil operates, and in terms of which each soil can be assessed as more or less appropriate to the true essence of the human being. His rejection of a relativism of this sort is made abundantly clear in *Winter Notes*, as we saw in chapter 3, when he compares Western (above all French) bourgeois culture with an unnamed antipode, surely intended to be Russian.

The Westernist, he wrote there, speaks of his interest in producing a fraternal society, but does not realize that fraternity is simply "not present" in the Western character. True fraternity exists only in a society (by implication, Russia) in which individuals serve others spontaneously, with no thought of personal gain (5:79). The principles of *pochvennichestvo* might suggest that Dostoevsky is simply contrasting here the diverse working of antithetical national soils on a human material with no character of its own, producing two equally "natural" national characters, one fundamentally fraternal and the other not. But we know from his reflections on the ethical nature of man that he believed an awareness of the moral law of brotherhood—the law of love—to be inherent in the spiritual nature of all humanity, where it stands in stark contrast to the egoistic principle of man's animal, material nature. But if that is so, how can Dostoevsky deny the existence of such awareness in the Western character?

Without explicitly raising this question, in *Winter Notes* he nonetheless provides unambiguous clues to its answer. After describing the fraternal character, which gives itself unreservedly to others, he writes: "That [i.e., the fraternal character] is the law of nature: man normally tends in that direction." In Dostoevsky's vision of "normal" man, the latter's spiritual nature in the form of conscience gives him an awareness of the law that commands brotherly love. Yet the principle of egoism is also present, and where egoism prevails, the national soil comes to favor it; habits and circumstances combine to deaden the moral sense, to dim the light of the law of love in the life of individuals. That the sense of fraternity is present initially and innately, regardless of environment, is indicated when Dostoevsky asks whether in the West it could be "regenerated" (*pererodit'sia*). It could be, he indicates, but he adds that it would take thousands of years, for such ideas "must first enter into the flesh and blood in order to become reality" (5:79). The implication is that in Russia no regeneration is required, for Russia's circumstances have allowed fraternity to become part of Russian "flesh and blood" over the centuries, so that it is part of Russian "nature" not only in the original or innate sense but in the sense of the durable "second nature" produced by the soil. He appears to recognize two senses in which the "need for a brotherly community" can be said to be "in the nature of man": the sense of being "born with it" and the sense of having "assimilated such a habit from time immemorial" (5:80). It is part of all men's nature in the first sense, but only of Russians' nature in the second. Fraternity may be "the law of nature," but only one national environment has fully nurtured it, so that the character which that environment has created is the only one that does not represent a deviation from the true human norm.

The most extreme contrast to the Russian character for Dostoevsky is not the Western character as such but another that has had a pernicious influence on it—namely, the Jewish character. Although some commentators have sought to absolve Dostoevsky of antisemitism,[13] no one who has read *A Writer's Diary* or his letters and notebooks can deny that they are full of expressions of the most extreme antipathy toward the "Yids" [*zhidy*], as he typically called them. All the clichés of the antisemitic tracts that abounded in Russia in his day may be found in his writings, though less so in the novels than in the nonfiction: Jews are self-important and arrogant; they complain unjustifiably about their "suffering" and "martyrdom"; they rule Western Europe, controlling everything from the stock exchange to public morality; in Russia they mercilessly exploit the peasants where they can, and would exterminate the entire Russian population if they could; their goal is to rule the world (25:74–88).

All of these accusations are found in a section of his March 1877 *Writer's Diary* in which he thought he could clear himself of the charge of antisemitism by arguing that his attitude was a reasonable response to the regrettable facts of Jewish behavior. Claiming that he never used the term 'Yid' with a desire to offend and that neither he nor the Russian people in general harbored any racial or religious animosity toward the Jews, he explains that his antipathy is directed not at the Jews personally but at the well-known "idea" they represent, which he calls "Yid-ism [*zhidovshchina*], the Kingdom of the Yids" (25:75). In the spirit of *pochvennichestvo* he interprets this idea as a pervasive element of Jewish history and culture and hence as the foundation of a severely flawed Jewish character.

His explanation of how the Jews' "soil" has operated to produce their distinctive character is as interesting for its logical weakness as for its indebtedness to his theory of national identity. Over the millennia, he argues, the Jews, as a result of repeated conquest and persecution by other peoples, have forged a powerful, exclusive unity that makes them see themselves as a state within a state:

13. See, for example, Gulyga, *Russkaia ideia*, 75–76. On the broader question of Dostoevsky's attitude toward the Jews, see David I. Goldstein, *Dostoevsky and the Jews* (Austin: University of Texas Press, 1981); and Judith Deutsch Kornblatt and Gary Rosenshield, "Vladimir Solovyov: Confronting Dostoevsky on the Jewish and Christian Questions," *Journal of the American Academy of Religion* 68 (2000): 69–98.

In order to exist on earth for forty centuries, . . . in order to lose so many times their territory, their political independence, their laws, nearly even their faith—to lose [these things] and each time unite again, to be reborn again *in their earlier idea,* if only in another form, and to create laws and virtually their faith for themselves again—no, a people so vital, a people so extraordinarily strong and energetic, a people so unprecedented in the world cannot exist without a *status in statu,* something they have preserved always and everywhere throughout their most dreadful, millennial Diaspora and persecution. (25:81; Dostoevsky's emphasis)

Dostoevsky then goes on to describe, as characteristics of the state-within-a-state mentality, the particular beliefs and attitudes that mark the Jews:

These characteristics are: alienation and estrangement on the level of religious dogma, no intermingling, the belief that there exists in the world but one national identity [*narodnaia lichnost'*]—the Jew, and even if there are others, all the same one must consider them nonexistent, as it were. "Separate thyself from [other] peoples, form thine own identity and know that henceforth thou art *one with God;* destroy the others, or turn them into slaves, or exploit them. Believe in thy victory over the whole world; believe that all will submit to thee. Firmly shun everyone. . . . Live, shun, unite and exploit and—wait, wait . . ." That is the essential idea of this *status in statu.* (25:81–82; Dostoevsky's emphasis)

Dostoevsky, somewhat surprisingly, concludes his self-defeating attempt at an apologia with the statement that, for all the Jews' faults, he is nonetheless in favor of the "full broadening" of their civil rights in Russia. He immediately limits this "full broadening," however, by adding in the same sentence that it should extend "just as far as the Jewish people themselves show their own ability to accept and use these rights without injury to the indigenous population" (25:88). But of course he had already made it clear, both in this text and elsewhere, that the Jews as a people were incapable of being so forbearing. For to him the Jews represented the polar opposite of the Orthodox Christian Russians with their fundamentally spiritual and altruistic character: the Jews are materialistic and profoundly egoistic. Given the opportunity to accept Christ as their Messiah, he explained in a letter of 1880, they remained "in all their former narrowness and obduracy, and therefore instead of [serving] panhumanity they turned into enemies of humanity, denying everyone but themselves, and now they are actually the bearers of the anti-Christ." If they should triumph, it will be because "everything selfish, everything hostile to humanity, all the evil passions of humanity" are on their side (30/1:191–92). They are, in other words, profoundly evil, capable of any atrocity, not excluding the ritual murder of Christian children.[14]

To acknowledge openly an actual hatred of the Jews would signify a failure of Christian love on his part, but that did not prevent Dostoevsky from attributing to the Jewish character an immorality that has developed over four millennia and is now a firmly established second nature. That he did believe it to be *second* nature and not absolutely unalterable, however, is confirmed by the letter of 1880, in which he writes of how a people over several generations can degenerate into "something separate from humanity as a whole, and even . . . something hostile to humanity *as a whole.*" Such, for example, he continues, "are the Jews, beginning with Abraham and continuing to our day, when they have turned into Yids" (30/1:191; Dostoevsky's emphasis). Dostoevsky's effort is to restrict his moral condemnation to what the Jews have become rather than what they are by some inherent and unchangeable essence.

The fundamental weakness in Dostoevsky's attempt to use the principles of *pochvennichestvo* to "explain" the malevolence of the Jews is that he does not convincingly distinguish between the conditions that supposedly produce the Jewish character and those that produce its moral antipode, the benevolent Russian character. Much of what he wrote in *A Writer's Diary* about the history and culture of the Jews is entirely parallel to what he wrote there and elsewhere about the Russian people: both have been the victims of outside attack and conquest over the centuries; both have nonetheless maintained a powerful unity and sense of identity; both have preserved their distinctive religious faith, separate from others (what he called, in the case of the Jews, their religious "alienation and estrangement"); both have a sense of themselves as a special, indeed a "chosen" people; both are confident that, in the end, "all will submit to them." Yet despite these pervasive similarities, he contends that the Jews have become egoistic exploiters and a threat to mankind, whereas the Russians are altruists with only the good of humanity in mind. No doubt what Dostoevsky would have liked to say in the published apologia, as he did suggest in the letter of 1880, is that the Jews' evil character stems from their *non-Christian* culture, but that would have undermined his claim that it is not on grounds of their religion that he criticizes the Jews.

In view of the virtual monopoly on brotherly love that Dostoevsky attributed to the Russian people, it should be evident why he thought himself justi-

14. Commenting in a letter of March 28, 1879, on the trial of Jews in the Georgian town of Kutaisi who were accused of kidnapping and murdering a peasant girl, Dostoevsky wrote: "How revolting that the Kutaisi Yids were acquitted. They are unquestionably guilty" (30/1:59).

fied in asserting that if the ideal of universal brotherhood were ever to be realized on earth, it would be in Russia sooner than anywhere else. He was convinced, despite the weakness of the evidence, that the Russian soil is the most
suffused by love and harmony; and he was equally convinced that the Russian
character, a product of that soil, was Christian like no other, for in Russians
the inborn voice of conscience that preaches love of others had been reinforced for centuries. He believed, he wrote in 1862, "that in the *natural* sources
of the character and customs of the Russian land there are incomparably more
healthy and vital guarantees of progress and renewal than in the day-dreams of
the most ardent renovators from the West" (20:210; Dostoevsky's emphasis).
And with progress "guaranteed" in Russia, it seemed only a matter of time before the goal was reached.

Russian Superiority: (2) Universality

In fact, however, Dostoevsky was less concerned with the full realization of
the ideal in Russia alone than with what he saw as Russia's role in leading the
way to the salvation of the entire world. In connection with this role, a second
distinctive aspect of the Russian national character as he understood it came
into play. For he believed that the superiority that made Russians ready for a
messianic mission was not exhausted by their unique spirit of brotherly love: it
had to do also with what he called their "universality" (*vsemirnost'* or *vseobshch-
nost'*), another concept he had inherited from his romantic forebears.

An explicitly messianic note was first sounded in Dostoevsky's writings at
the time of the Crimean War, in the sycophantic verses he composed while
seeking an end to his Siberian exile. In the first verse, written in 1854, he
claimed divine predestination as the warrant of Russia's victory in the "Eastern
war" and her continuing dominion over the East thereafter. Addressing an
imagined critic, he wrote:

> It's not for you to make out Russia's fate!
> Her predestined path is unclear to you!
> The East is hers! A million generations do not
> Tire of stretching out their arms to her.
> And ruling over the depths of Asia
> She gives fresh life to everyone;
> Russia's revival of the ancient East
> (God has commanded it!) draws nigh. (2:405)

In 1856, still in the heady wartime atmosphere, Dostoevsky wrote a letter to his friend Apollon Maykov in which he first used the expression 'the Russian idea', linking it with "the national feeling of duty and honor" and the prospect of Russia's future greatness—subjects to which Maykov had apparently alluded in a letter that has not survived. Agreeing wholeheartedly with Maykov's patriotic sentiments, which were by no means exceptional in the educated Russian society of the day, Dostoevsky expressed his notion of Russia's mission in a way that included not only victory in the Eastern war but the fulfillment of Europe's aspirations: "I fully share with you the patriotic feeling of the *moral* liberation of the Slavs. That is the role of Russia, noble, great Russia, our holy mother. . . . Yes! I share with you the idea that Europe and its mission *will be completed by Russia*. For me that has long been clear" (28/1:208; Dostoevsky's emphasis). Once back in European Russia at the beginning of the 1860s, he poured out his faith in Russia's world mission in the same *Vremya* essays in which he elaborated on the special gifts of the Russian character, invoking the latter as his ground for believing that Russia was destined to save the world.

The related notions of Russian "universality" and a special national mission were commonplaces in the writings of the Russian romantics, from Karamzin through the first half of the nineteenth century.[15] Although philosophically the term 'universality' echoed the German idealist conception of history as the unfolding of a universal consciousness, the Russian writers ordinarily had a more prosaic aim in using it: they were countering critics who scorned Russians for their imitativeness in borrowing Western customs, ideas, and institutions, as in the Petrine reforms. Karamzin replied that imitativeness should not be taken as a rebuke, because it was in fact "a sign of admirable development of the soul": it signified an ability to recognize and assimilate what was of general value, in whatever nation it was found; "We looked at Europe," he wrote in 1802, "and at one glance we assimilated the fruits of her long labors."[16] V. F. Odoevsky in his *Russian Nights* (1844) defined Russian 'universality' as "a natural tendency—the all-embracing many-sidedness of the spirit" and predicted that it would amaze people of other nations when they learned of its existence.[17]

Two years later, Vissarion Belinsky claimed that "the Russian is equally capable of assimilating the sociality of the Frenchman, the practical activity of the

---

15. See Dowler, *Dostoevsky*, 24–25.
16. Nikolai Karamzin, "Love of Country and National Pride," in *Russian Intellectual History: An Anthology*, ed. Marc Raeff (New York: Harcourt, Brace, 1966), 110.
17. V. F. Odoevskii, *Russkie nochi* (Leningrad: Nauka, 1975), 182–83.

Englishman and the misty philosophy of the German." Belinsky was inclined
to find some truth in the charge of imitativeness, but he also expressed the belief that he and his countrymen were "ordained to give our message, our
thought to the world," and he suggested tentatively that the message would
have to do with Russian universality:

> We do not incontrovertibly maintain that the Russian nation is foreordained to
> express the richest and most many-sided essence in its nationality, and that it is
> this that explains its amazing ability to adopt and assimilate all alien elements; but
> we venture to believe that such a thought, expressed as an assumption without
> bluster and fanaticism, is not without foundation.[18]

Thus although Belinsky in the same essay had denied that love is a distinctive
natural gift of Russians, he was willing to entertain the idea that universality
was such a gift and was moreover the earnest of a special destiny.

Dostoevsky displayed no such tentativeness. From the early 1860s, influenced not only by his predecessors but by his friend and *Vremya* colleague
Apollon Grigoryev, he enthusiastically absolutized the "many-sided essence"
of the Russian spirit and turned the doctrine of Russian "universality" into
one of the most fulsome claims of national superiority to be found in the an-
nals of chauvinism.[19] As early as 1861 he called the trait a capacity for making
a "panhuman response" (*vsechelovecheskii otklik* or simply *vseotklik*) (18:99;
19:114); his best-known term for the capacity, ultimately popularized by his
wildly successful Pushkin speech of 1880, was "universal responsiveness"
(*vsemirnaia otzyvchivost'*, sometimes also translated as "universal sympathy" or
"sensitivity") (26:145; 30/1:188).

Like his romantic predecessors, Dostoevsky viewed the Petrine reforms as
an indication of the Russian ability to assimilate what is of universal value. For
all the flaws he found in the reforms—their narrowness, their "anti-national"
spirit and despotic implementation, their strengthening of serfdom—he
praised them in his essay "Two Camps of Theoreticians" (1862) for bringing
"panhuman Western elements" into the Russian environment at least to some
degree (20:14). Peter's recognition of the value to Russia of such elements and
their acceptance by educated society, at least, are for Dostoevsky prime evidence of the Russian capacity to welcome what is panhuman wherever it is
found. In 1880, completely ignoring the popular opposition to the reforms

---

18. Belinsky, *Selected Philosophical Works*, 386–87.
19. Grigoryev, however, did not agree that Russia had a unique mission; see Dowler, *Dostoevsky*,
52–59.

that he had acknowledged in 1862, he wrote that the Russian people "not hostilely . . . but amicably, with complete love accepted into our soul the genius of other nations, all of them together, . . . managing instinctively . . . to discern and eliminate contradictions, to excuse and reconcile differences" (26:147). Dostoevsky claimed that Russia in fact responded to the principle of universal humanity more fully than had the Europe which first proclaimed it, thereby demonstrating the greater breadth of the Russian spirit (18:99).

The phenomenon of Pushkin was the particular evidence on which Dostoevsky most relied to support the claim of "universal responsiveness." In the 1880 speech he argued, largely on the strength of the poet's sensitivity to the mores of the non-Russian peoples who figure in his verse, that not even the greatest European writer—not Shakespeare, not Cervantes or Schiller—had "such a capacity of universal responsiveness as our Pushkin had"; none of the others could "embody with such force the genius of another . . . people." But if Pushkin is its ideal examplar or personification, the talent of "universal responsiveness" is characteristic of Russian literature in general and of the Russian people as a nation; it is, in fact, "the paramount capacity of our nationality" (26:145). In the explanatory notes on the speech that he published in *A Writer's Diary*, Dostoevsky stressed this latter point:

> This capacity is entirely a Russian national capacity, and Pushkin simply shares it with our entire people; and, as a quintessential artist, he is also the quintessential exponent of this capacity, at least in his activity, the activity of an artist. Our people truly contain in their soul this aptitude for universal responsiveness and universal reconciliation, and they have already displayed it time and again throughout the two centuries since Peter's reform. (26:131)

As further support for limiting "universal responsiveness" to Russians, Dostoevsky offers what is perhaps the weakest argument in his entire brief, though he thought it exceptionally strong. That Russians alone have an "instinct for universal humanity," he contended, is shown by their unique linguistic talents, for none of the world's languages is foreign to them: "Every Russian," he claimed in 1861, "can speak in all languages." Supposedly he meant that every Russian can *learn* to speak any language, and his point was that only Russians have the potential to communicate with everyone regardless of nationality. Moreover, he was not thinking simply of the mechanical exchange of information: the capacity extends to a profound sympathy with the other language. Every Russian, he goes on, "can master the spirit of every alien tongue" as subtly as if it were his own. Dostoevsky does admit the existence of an occasional polyglot European; but only the Russian people, he asserts, possess such linguistic skills "*in the sense of a universal national capacity*" (18:55; Dostoevsky's emphasis). The "gift" of speaking foreign languages, he insisted in another place, is "exceedingly significant and promises much for the future" (21:69).[20]

Again and again, often through pointed rhetorical questions, Dostoevsky suggested that Russia's unique polyglotism is the sign of a great destiny: "Doesn't this indicate something? Is it really just an accidental, pointless phenomenon? Is it really impossible to understand and even partly to divine from such phenomena something of the future development of our people, of their aspirations and aims? . . . Why have the Russians been endowed with such rich and original abilities? Can it really be to do nothing?" (18:55–56). "It is permissible to think," he concluded not long before his death, "that nature or mysterious fate, having structured the spirit of Russians in this way, structured it with a purpose" (26:211).

Looking more closely at the concept of "universal responsiveness" as Dostoevsky develops it, we find that it goes well beyond "responding" to universal values in the sense of recognizing and appropriating them. He broadens the concept to include a whole set of "universal" abilities that Russians possess to the highest degree. Consider, for example, the following description of the Russian national character in the 1861 essay: there is in that character, he writes,

> a marked distinction from the European. Its marked peculiarity is that what prevails in it is its highly synthetic ability, its capacity for universal reconciliation, for panhumanity. . . . [The Russian] . . . sympathizes with all humanity without distinction of nationality, blood, or soil. . . . He has an instinct for panhumanity. He guesses by instinct the panhuman feature even in the most pronounced idiosyncrasies of other nations. He at once harmonizes and reconciles them within his idea, finds a place for them in his conclusions and not infrequently discovers the point of unity and reconciliation in the completely antithetical, competing ideas of two different European nations. (18:55)

Dostoevsky treats Russian universality as if it were a special faculty, a complex set of talents present in Russians alone. These talents not only give Russians an awareness of "universal humanity," permitting them to understand and sympathize with others, but also make them capable of discerning petty differences and showing others how to transcend them in the name of what is

---

20. When in *A Writer's Diary* Dostoevsky pointedly remarked that his friend-turned-nemesis Belinsky consistently mispronounced the name 'Feuerbach' and could never learn a foreign language, he was implicitly calling into question Belinsky's "Russianness" (21:11).

universally human. It is, in other words, not only a moral-emotional but an intellectual and even what might be called a political capacity, in virtue of which the Russian uniquely perceives the true and false interests of all and can unite others in universal harmony. It is on the basis of this multifarious faculty that Russia can serve other nations as teacher and guide, as Dostoevsky wrote in a notebook of 1876–77:

> We really bear in our seed a kind of essence of the universal man. . . . The more powerfully we develop in the national Russian spirit, the more powerfully we will respond to the European spirit, will take its elements into our own and become akin to it spiritually, for this is panhumanity, . . . and, perhaps, we would even be helpful to them, to the Europeans, having uttered to them our special Russian word, which they, forcibly sundered, have not yet heard. Our language ability, our understanding of all European ideas, our emotional and spiritual assimilation of her—all this so as to unite in harmony and concord the uncoordinated individual national units, and this is Russia's assignment. You will say this is a dream, ravings: *very well, permit me* these ravings and this dream. (24:309; Dostoevsky's emphasis)

Pushkin himself had suggested in 1836, a year before his death, that Russians, as "unprejudiced judges," would serve as Europe's "court of arbitration."[21] Dostoevsky not only seconded that point but grounded it in a sweeping declaration of the Solomonic virtue and wisdom of the Russian people. Russians, he claimed in 1877, "have always possessed great powers for the future clarification and resolution of the many bitter and supremely fateful misunderstandings in Western European civilization." And again: "To the Russian spirit alone is given universality, is given the future task of comprehending and unifying all the various nationalities and transcending all their contradictions" (25:195–96, 199). Consistently with his 1856 statement to Maykov about "completing" Europe's mission, in the *Vremya* essays Dostoevsky phrases Russia's world destiny in terms of carrying history onward from the European era by resolving the differences and enmities in which other nations have become mired. "We suppose," he writes, referring once more to "the Russian idea,"

> that the nature of our future activity must be in the highest degree panhuman, that the Russian idea perhaps will be the synthesis of all those ideas that Europe is developing stubbornly and steadfastly in its separate nationalities; that perhaps

---

21. Quoted in William Hubben, *Four Prophets of Our Destiny: Kierkegaard, Dostoevsky, Nietzsche, Kafka* (New York: Macmillan, 1952), 66.

everything antagonistic in those ideas will find its reconciliation and subsequent development in the Russian nationality.

The capacity for "a conciliatory view of what is alien," he continues, is "the highest and most noble gift of nature, which is bestowed on very few nationalities" (18:37).

This reference to universality as a "gift" bestowed on Russians is only one of many indications in Dostoevsky's writings that the capacity is fundamentally different from the quality of fraternity that also distinguishes the Russian character. As we saw above, it was possible to interpret Russian fraternity as a heightened instance, produced by the influence of an extraordinarily benign history and environment, of a "normal" tendency shared to some degree by all human beings. Granted, the soil that creates Russians' special fraternity may also predispose them to "universal responsiveness" by combating selfishness and promoting sympathy with others. But Russian universality as Dostoevsky understands it appears to entail much more than that, and he gives no indication of how the unique intellectual and political powers he attributes to Russians might be produced by the soil.

It is true that on one occasion he referred to Russian universality as an "acquired" (*nazhitaia*) capacity (23:47). But in that passage he did not specify *how* it was acquired, and the heavy weight of evidence suggests that he saw it as derived not from nurture but from nature, in the first or biological sense. This is certainly the implication of his statements describing universality as created by "nature or mysterious fate" (26:211) and as something that Russians "bear in our seed" (24:309). Significantly, he refers to the linguistic dimension of Russian universality as one of the "physical abilities" that differentiate Russians from Europeans (18:55), implying that it is part of the permanent, unalterable equipment of the Russian person rather than a product of the Russian soil.

The conclusion seems inescapable that with respect to universality Dostoevsky was drawn to a kind of biologically based ethnic chauvinism, in that he found in one ethnic group a fundamental superiority of the "first nature" variety. If the seeds of fraternity, on the one hand, were implanted in *all* human beings by their creator, so that only environmental differences explain Russian superiority in that respect, the faculty of universality, on the other hand, is specific to Russians; no other ethnic group possesses it "as a national capacity." Thus in regard to universality Dostoevsky abandons environmental determinism; he forsakes *pochvennichestvo* altogether for a chauvinism based on a cosmic teleology. The spirit of Russians was "structured with a purpose"—the universal purpose of uniting all the peoples of the earth.

Unlike traditional versions of a "chosen people" ideology, Dostoevsky's teleological chauvinism regards the Russian people as chosen not so much to be saved itself as to save humanity. Yet for all the generous, universalistic implications of that position, it degrades other nations, placing them in a position of inferiority and dependence as helpless objects, rather than dynamic subjects, in the grand scheme of things. Dostoevsky attributed the absence of fraternity in the Jewish character to the perverting influence of their soil; but the absence of universality is a more fundamental, innate flaw that renders all non-Russian peoples incapable of finding their own salvation.

The Russian Mission in Practice

How, concretely, did Dostoevsky expect Russia to fulfill her "universal purpose"? Although in the last decades of his life he repeatedly addressed the subject, he vacillated between different visions of Russia's mission, or in other words between different conceptions of what "the Russian idea" entailed in practice, without ever settling on a single unambiguous formulation. The least imperialistic vision limited the mission to moral example and peaceful suasion: Russia would simply bring humanity "a new word," as he frequently expressed it, in the form of Christ's teaching of brotherly love. In a second formulation, articulating not only moral but political aims, he spoke of Russia's mission to unify and lead the Slavs—something he believed all of them would accept gratefully, without coercion—at least after certain misgivings were allayed. The third and most ambitious vision extended Russia's political efforts at unification to all of humanity, beginning with the world of Orthodoxy, and did not rule out violence as a possible instrument. Given that at one time or another he explicitly identified "the Russian idea" with each of these three projects, it is not surprising that the expression has been taken subsequently to signify everything from the simple preaching of Christian love to a jingoistic call for world conquest.

Dostoevsky's most impassioned presentation of the first vision—Russia as moral guide and example—is found in his Pushkin speech of 1880. In that address he insisted that Russia's universal mission would be accomplished "not by the sword but by the force of brotherhood and of our fraternal aspiration toward the reunification of the people" (26:147). He urged his countrymen to exert this moral force by becoming "true Russians;" what this means, he explained in ringing phrases, is

to strive to reconcile the European contradictions once and for all; to show in our Russian soul, panhuman and all-embracing, the way out of European anguish; to include all our brothers in this soul with fraternal love; and, in the end, perhaps, also to utter the final word of the great universal harmony, of the final brotherly concord of all tribes in accordance with the law of Christ's gospel! (26:148)

In keeping with his conviction that of all faiths only Orthodoxy truly retained a devotion to the law of love, he often expressed Russia's moral task as a religious mission to embody and disseminate the "word" of Orthodoxy, as in *A Writer's Diary* for 1873:

Is not the divine image of Christ in all its purity preserved in Orthodoxy alone? And perhaps the paramount, preordained task of the Russian people in the destiny of all mankind consists simply in preserving within itself this divine image of Christ in all its purity and, when the time comes, revealing this image to a world that has lost its way! . . . Does not [the Russian priest] preach the unique great Truth that has the power to renew the whole world? (21:59–60)

Still another clear example of limiting Russia's mission to the moral-religious sphere is found in a letter of 1869 in which Dostoevsky comments on the emerging ideas of the Pan-Slavist writer Nikolay Danilevsky (1822–85). Although he is struck by the extent of his own agreement with Danilevsky, he has some reservations:

I'm still not sure that Danilevsky will show in *full force* the definitive essence of the Russian mission, which consists in revealing to the world the Russian Christ, whom the world does not know and whose principle is contained in our native Orthodoxy. To me, that is the whole essence of our future civilizing and resurrecting of all Europe, at least, and the whole essence of our mighty future existence. (29/1:30; Dostoevsky's emphasis)

He by no means restricted himself to such spiritual, apolitical descriptions of the mission, however. In the second formulation he went beyond moral example and suasion to the arena of Russia's relations with the other Slavic peoples—the Ukrainians, Belorussians, Poles, Czechs, and above all the Serbs, Bulgarians, and other Balkan Slavs. Russia, he wrote in *A Writer's Diary* in 1876, cannot betray "a great idea, bequeathed to her through the centuries, that she has followed unswervingly up to now. This idea is, among other things, the idea of the unification of all the Slavs" (23:45).

The intensity of Dostoevsky's Pan-Slavic fervor reflected the circumstance that virtually his entire life was passed in a period of unsettled relations be-

tween Russia and the other Slavs, highlighted by such events as the Polish revolution of 1830–31, the Crimean War of 1853–56, the second Polish revolution of 1863–64, and the Russo-Turkish War of 1877–78. During these
decades Russia was continually embroiled in one or another issue concerning
the Slavs, involving not only the Slavs themselves but the Moslem Turks, the
Orthodox Greeks, and the Christian (but non-Orthodox) Western European
countries, with much mutual distrust. In all these disputes Dostoevsky, like the
Tsarist government he loyally supported, considered Russia to be the protector of the Slavs against alien faiths and powers, and thus it was easy for him to
connect the situation of the Slavs with the grand mission of reconciling and
bringing unity to mankind.

Typically he expressed this active, Pan-Slavic mission as an initial stage in
the movement toward universal fraternity. In an 1876 essay he distinguished
between Russia's destiny "in the ideal," which he described as the ultimate
unification of all humanity, and the policy needed to implement it. The first
step of that policy, he argued, was to unite all the Slavs "under Russia's wing,
so to speak." He hastens to add that this is not for the sake of conquest or to
"reduce the individual Slavs to nothing before the Russian colossus." On the
contrary, it is for their own renewal and putting them in "an appropriate relationship" to Europe and the rest of humanity. The other Slavs, he explains, in
a condescending bow to Herder's principle of the value of all national contributions, should be able to contribute "their own mite" to the treasury of the
human spirit (23:47).

All this is possible, of course, only through political unification under Russia. Already in 1868, writing to Maykov about what he called "the great renewal through the Russian idea" that was in store for humanity, he stated that
for this renewal to come to pass, "the Great-Russian tribe's *political right* and
supremacy over the entire Slavic world must be established unquestionably
once and for all" (28/2:260; Dostoevsky's emphasis). In the 1876 essay, too, he
acknowledged that political domination by Russia is an element of the envisaged unification of the Slavs; but he also went on, in a frenzy of Pan-Slavic and
pan-Orthodox enthusiasm, to justify the union in moral-religious terms:

> It will be not only a political union, and by no means for political seizure and vi-
> olence. . . . No, it will be a real exaltation of Christ's truth, which has been pre-
> served in the East, a real, new exaltation of Christ's cross and the definitive word
> of Orthodoxy, at whose head Russia has long stood. . . . And if believing in this
> "new word," which Russia at the head of a united Orthodoxy can pronounce to
> the world, is a "utopia" worthy only of mockery, then number me among these
> utopians and leave me with the mockery. (23:50)

By disclaiming violence in this passage, he is suggesting that he sees no need for coercion directed against the other Slavs. He stresses the voluntary character of their eventual union under Russia: "She is their protector and perhaps even their leader, but not their sovereign; she is their mother, but not their mistress. Even if she should at some time become their sovereign, it would be only by their own declaration, with retention of everything by which they have defined their independence and identity" (23:49). His confidence in the amicability of a future union of all the Slavs was no doubt premised on his view of their close ethnic relationship. Although he sometimes distinguished between the "Great-Russian tribe" and the other Slavs (28/2:260), typically he glossed over the differences among them. Ukrainians and Belorussians he simply claimed as Russians by other names: "The master of the Russian land is the Russian alone (Great-Russian, White-Russian, Belorussian—it's all the same)" (23:127).[22] Other Slavic peoples he considered members, along with Russians, of a "great Slavic tribe," united by, among other things, a common history of "suffering, . . . slavery, and abasement" (30/1:20; 23:103).

The family model that Dostoevsky applies to the Pan-Slavic union is the same he used to describe the Russian political order, with its supposedly harmonious but thoroughly hierarchical relations, with its Tsar-father who is also, of course, a sovereign. And the relative positions of Russia and the other Slavs in Dostoevsky's hierarchy is shown by his reaction in 1877 to what he called Danilevsky's "astonishing" proposal that Constantinople be ruled jointly by all the Eastern nationalities, with the other Slavs being given equal status with Russia. "What kind of comparison can there be here between the Russians and the Slavs?" he asks. "How can Russia share possession of Constantinople with the Slavs on *equal* bases when Russia is in all respects unequal to them— to each little nation separately and to all of them taken together? . . . Constantinople must be *ours*, won by *us*, the Russians, from the Turks and must remain ours for all time" (26:83; Dostoevsky's emphasis).

Dostoevsky could not ignore, however, the reality that some of the Slavs were not entirely convinced of the great benefits of Russian protection and leadership. He laments the rise of nationalism among them, but hopes that reason will prevail; of the Poles and Czechs he writes: "When [they] really want to be our brothers, we shall give them autonomy, for even under autonomy our bond will not be destroyed, and they will reach out to us as to a friend, an

---

22. By the same token, Dostoevsky never considered the Russian empire of his day a multinational country in any significant sense. The "Tatars," as he called the Moslem peoples, were simply excluded as "former oppressors" and "newcomers" (23:127), and the Jews were a state within a state, in opposition to "the root of the nation [*natsiia*], the Russian tribe" (29/2:140).

older brother, a great center" (24:194). As for the Balkan Slavs, he predicts that they will come to realize that Russia has only the best of intentions: "In time even the Slavic peoples [of the Balkans] will grasp the whole truth of Russian unselfishness. . . . The irresistible charm of the great and mighty Russian spirit will act on them as a kindred principle" (23:116). For now, however, it is Russia's thankless lot to care for these quarreling kinsmen by "reconciling them, making them listen to reason, and on occasion perhaps even drawing the sword for them" (26:80).

If uniting the Slavs is the "first step" in the prosecution of Russia's grand political mission, what is the next? Dostoevsky's determination that Constantinople, the capital of Orthodox Christianity, must belong to Russia suggests that the mission extends beyond unification of the Slavic peoples alone, and his eager support of the use of military force to attain that objective shows that the mission is by no means limited to moral influence. The next step, then, is to carry unification beyond Slavdom to all of the Orthodox peoples and finally to the benighted West. This is the third idiom in which Dostoevsky presents "the Russian idea," and it is the most jingoistic.

His justification for advocating the conquest of Constantinople is that only by controlling the entire Orthodox world (including Greece and the other non-Slavic Orthodox nations) can Russia resolve the Eastern Question and then, through a purified and united Orthodoxy, bring its reconciling word to all humanity. Orthodox Russia alone, he argued in 1877, has the moral qualities and the might to mobilize "the East" to fulfill this mission. Roman Catholicism "long ago sold out Christ for earthly dominion" and thereby generated both atheism and socialism; the pure image of Christ has been preserved only in Orthodoxy. Hence it is from the East that Christ's word will be taken to the world "to meet the coming socialism—this word that once again may save European humanity" (26:85).

For Dostoevsky it is a foregone conclusion that this role requires the political conquest of the entire Eastern world; never must Russia "retreat even halfway from ultimate and primary influence on the destiny of the East" (25:73). More bluntly, as he put it in a notebook: "The whole Orthodox East must belong to the Orthodox Tsar, and we must not share it" (24:313). And that this Orthodox Tsar is entitled to enlist the force of arms in pursuing the aims of Orthodoxy is an equally foregone conclusion. In this spirit Dostoevsky writes menacingly of the Tsar's mission as protector, unifier, and "when the divine commandment thunders forth," liberator of Orthodox Christendom from "Mohammedan barbarity and Western heresy" (25:68).

Dostoevsky greeted Alexander II's declaration of war on Turkey in April 1877 with a veritable paean to war as not only an instrument of Russia's mis-

sion but a force for national regeneration. "We need war and victory," he ex-
claimed. "With war and victory a new word will come, and a living life will
begin." Conceding that war is undeniably a misfortune in some respects, he
nonetheless presents a vigorous case for the benefits of a "noble" war. A prolonged peace, he wrote, "bestializes and embitters people"; it gives rise to
cowardice, cruelty, and "gross, inflated egoism," leading almost always to an
unworthy kind of war—a war for "some wretched stock-exchange interests."
A war on behalf of "an unselfish and holy idea," on the other hand, heals and
purifies humanity spiritually; it "strengthens every soul with the consciousness
of self-sacrifice, and strengthens the spirit of the whole nation with the consciousness of the mutual solidarity and unity of all the members it comprises"
(25:96, 98–102).

To counter the objections of those who would condemn even a "noble"
war on grounds of the bloodshed and misery it entails, Dostoevsky resorts,
ironically, to a reversal of his own earlier antiutilitarian condemnation of the
principle that the end justifies the means—specifically, he now argues that war
is good because even more blood might be shed without it. Except for civil
wars, he writes, generally "war is *precisely* the process through which international tranquillity is achieved with the least bloodshed, the least misery, and
the least expenditure of effort, and in which at least some semblance of normal
relations among nations is worked out." It is just this kind of quantitative, consequentialist argument that Dostoevsky had firmly rejected on ethical grounds
when it came from the socialist revolutionaries. In his patriotic ardor he was
no doubt unaware that the very phrases he uses here to justify war morally—
he states, for example, that "it is better to draw the sword once than to suffer
indefinitely" (25:101; Dostoevsky's emphasis)—could have served as slogans
for the Westernist revolutionaries whom he reviled as immoral, egoistical
"demons." And by defending war on the ground that a victory produces
"some semblance of normal relations among nations" he comes perilously
close to affirming that might makes right.[23]

But what of the culminating phase in the advance of the great ideal of universal human unity, when a united Pan-Slavic and pan-Orthodox world,
headed by a powerful Russia, faces the alien West? Is war against Europe necessary for the completion of Russia's mission? Dostoevsky no doubt harbored
the hope that the rest of the world, like the Slavs, would succumb peaceably to

23. All these statements make it impossible to agree with Bruce K. Ward's assertion that although
Dostoevsky "was unwilling to eschew the use of the sword altogether," he accepted such use "only to
protect the innocent from the sufferings inflicted upon them by injustice"; see Ward's *Dostoyevsky's
Critique of the West: The Quest for Earthly Paradise* (Waterloo, Ont.: Wilfrid Laurier University Press,
1986), 187.

what he ingenuously called "the irresistible charm of the great and mighty Russian spirit." As we saw above, he believed that the remarkable intellectual acumen and political skills inherent in the "universal responsiveness" of Russians included not only the ability to discern what is universally human in hostile peoples but the ability to bring them into accord. On this basis he regarded the peaceful acquiescence of the world to "the Russian idea" as possible in principle, and he never openly advocated war with Europe. He insisted that Russia, at the head of a united East, "will not rush at Europe with a sword, will not seize and dispossess her of anything, as Europe would do without fail if she found the opportunity to be fully united once more against Russia" (25:99). Rather, he sketched a picture of a benevolent Russia, spiritually strengthened through her loving alliance with the other Eastern lands, as being in a position to avoid use of the sword in Europe and to work her saving mission through the moral example of her benign treatment of the European lands:

> Russia is predestined and created, perhaps, for their salvation, too. . . . We shall be the first to announce to the world that it is not by suppressing the individual identity of nationalities foreign to our own that we wish to attain our own prosperity; on the contrary, we see it only in the freest and most independent development of all other nations and in fraternal unity with them, complementing each other, grafting their organic features onto ourselves and giving them our branches for grafting, communing with them in soul and spirit, learning from them and teaching them. (25:100)

These seemingly benevolent sentiments, echoing again Herder's thesis about the unique and equally valuable contributions of different voices to the world symphony, would be more convincing if the very language of his formulation did not betray his assumption of the thoroughly dominant position of Russia in this relationship. It is Russia that is "predestined" to pronounce the word of salvation and is in a position to decide whether to advance it peacefully or by the sword. In his botanical analogy, it is Russia that selects which features of other nations to accept as "grafts" and which of its own features to "give" to others, and in that process Russia can hardly avoid suppressing the individual identity of other nationalities to some degree. It is Russia that decides what of value is to be learned from others and what to teach them. Furthermore he concludes the paragraph in which the above passage occurs with the ominous statement that "it is not in peace alone, peace at any price, that salvation lies; sometimes it also lies in war." Apparently, then, he did not rule out war with Europe as a future possibility. He added in the essay that

Russia is prepared to defend the Slavic lands "from the whole of Europe," if necessary, and he lamented that Europe is not inclined at present to recognize and accept voluntarily the dominant role of Russia (25:100).[24]

In this third formulation of "the Russian idea", Dostoevsky envisaged a crusade far broader than the Crusades of the Middle Ages. He envisaged not only wresting the East from the Mohammedans by force, but turning then to conquer (preferably by moral but not excluding military means) the Europe from which the earlier Crusaders had set forth—a Europe, he believed, that was itself desperately in need of re-Christianization.

Dostoevsky's Nationalism and the Christian Ideal

That Dostoevsky described Russia's mission at different levels of concreteness helps to account for the disparity among critical appraisals of his nationalism. Commentators who focus on the abstract goal of "panhuman unification" laud him for his humanism and deny that he preached a chauvinistic nationalism. His undoubted patriotism, defenders say, was rendered innocuous by the universalist goals he attributed to his beloved country. Dostoevsky's "Russian idea," the late Arseny Gulyga wrote, was simply "the embodiment in patriotic form of the conception of universal morality"; his friend Vladimir Solovyov once described Dostoevsky's vision for Russia as consisting in "free service to all peoples and . . . bringing about, in fraternal union with them, true panhumanity, or the universal Church."[25] Other commentators, however, looking more at the particular "service" Dostoevsky proposed, condemn him for insisting that only Russians are fit to lead the world to unity, that Russia must begin by gaining control of the Slavic and Orthodox East by force of arms, and that only Russia's power, moral or otherwise, will ever induce the inferior European peoples to accept unification. To these critics, there is a flagrant contradiction between Dostoevsky's Christian ideal of mutual love and his xenophobic nationalism.[26]

---

24. Here again Ward's interpretation of Dostoevsky's attitude toward the use of force is overly generous. Ward writes: "The charge that Dostoevsky conceived a universal Russian military conquest as the precondition for the actualization of [his ideal] cannot find support in any careful study of his writings" (ibid., 188). Dostoevsky may not have labeled military conquest an absolute precondition, but he envisaged the possible need for it.

25. Gulyga, *Russkaia ideia*, 75; Vladimir Sergeevich Solov'ev, *Sochineniia v dvukh tomakh* (Moscow: Mysl', 1988), 2:304. Solovyov was not always so uncritical, however; he later censured Dostoevsky for chauvinism (Kornblatt and Rosenshield, "Vladimir Solovyov," 91–96).

26. Kornblatt and Rosenshield, "Vladimir Solovyov," 94; Walter Laqueur, *Black Hundred: The Rise of the Extreme Right in Russia* (New York: HarperCollins, 1993), 11–12.

Long before what Walter Laqueur has called the "constant chauvinistic drumbeating" of his journalistic writings,[27] Dostoevsky had given evidence not simply of fervid patriotism but of his desire for Russian world domination. Poles who were his fellow prisoners in Siberia in the early 1850s may have exaggerated the virulence of his nationalism at the time, but their testimony that he said he "would be happy only when all the nations would fall under Russian rule" fully foreshadows the imperialistic sentiments he expressed in the patriotic verses of 1854–56, the 1868 letter to Maykov, and a multitude of other remarks in later published and unpublished writings.[28]

Joseph Frank has perceptively applied to Dostoevsky a distinction, originally developed by Reinhold Niebuhr, between two types of messianism:

> Dostoevsky's Messianism . . . in one context stresses what Reinhold Niebuhr would call its "ethical-universalistic" component—the notion that Russia was destined to install a Christian reign of goodness and justice on earth—and in another becomes "egoistic-imperialistic" and emphasizes the importance of extending Russian political power. For Dostoevsky, the two were more or less identical: he viewed the second as the precondition of the first and, unlike many later critics, refused to see any insoluble conflict between them.[29]

The reason that he found the two essentially identical, I submit, lies in the paternalistic and meritocratic character of his particular brand of nationalism. Dostoevsky astutely posed the central problem of world harmony: the panhuman ideal is universal, whereas human beings are divided by ethnic and religious distinctions. And he thought he had resolved the problem neatly by the discovery that a *national* distinction of Russians is precisely their *universality*, which gives them the capacity and the right to lead humanity to the panhuman ideal. Of course, in that way his universalist sentiments were translated into advocating the imposition of the Russian will on other peoples, all of whom lacked the universality needed for their own and the world's wellbeing, and to many this has seemed to ensnare Dostoevsky in a contradiction between universalism and the subordination of other nations to Russia. But there is no evidence that Dostoevsky was in the least disturbed by any such

27. Laqueur, *Black Hundred*, 12.

28. Quoted in Frank, *Dostoevsky: The Years of Ordeal*, 112. Only by discounting all this evidence can Ellis Sandoz maintain that "it is . . . inconceivable that [Dostoevsky] should seriously have expected Russia to gain world dominion and establish the Third Rome as the providential climax of secular history" (*Political Apocalypse: A Study of Dostoevsky's Grand Inquisitor* [Baton Rouge: Louisiana State University Press, 1971], 235).

29. Joseph Frank, *Dostoevsky: The Miraculous Years, 1865–1871* (Princeton, N.J.: Princeton University Press, 1995), 254.

conflict. Certainly there were no signs of "an unbearable inner struggle" over the issue from which he was delivered only by his death, as Solovyov's over-heated dramatic imagination has it.[30]

When Dostoevsky speaks of "reconciling" and "harmonizing" the interests of all peoples, he is granting that there are differences among them that require reconciliation—differences that reach the point of incompatibility. Referring to other European peoples, he states that the Russian spirit will "transcend all their contradictions" (25:199). That it eliminates the differences, however, implies that the Russian spirit does not simply accept each of the other interests (as its capacity for "universal responsiveness" might have led us to expect) but in some way adjudicates among them, determining which elements are "acceptable" (such as the "common elements" referred to above) and which must be abandoned in order to "transcend" the contradiction. That Dostoevsky himself recognized the need for such selectivity is evident in his preparatory notes for the Pushkin lecture, where he wrote that the Russian work of reconciliation is grounded in "our ability to distinguish, among the European genii, the good spirits from the evil spirits" (26:212). The Russian judge, like a kindly father, identifies and excludes the evil spirits and in general determines the content and structure of the needed synthesis.

Dostoevsky is stating in effect that Russians understand the requirements of every other nation better than that nation itself does—an attitude ironically reminiscent of the Grand Inquisitor, whose intellectual arrogance he skewered so memorably in *The Brothers Karamazov*. Echoing the Grand Inquisitor in the international arena, Dostoevsky regarded Russia's domination of other countries as a supreme expression of love and brotherhood, whereby an enlightened and generous Russia takes on the burden of protecting and nurturing them. He assigns to Russia a privileged intellectual and political as well as moral-emotional standpoint, and he does not balk at translating that preeminence into coercive action as the need arises, despite his opposition to the Roman Catholic and socialist authoritarianism ("evil spirits" if ever there were any) for which the Grand Inquisitor stood.

Gone is the *pochvennik* principle that you cannot force on people the values and institutions produced by an alien "soil." Having once rejected "Western ideals" on the ground that "the right of nationality is the strongest of all the rights that peoples and societies may have" (20:210), he is now prepared to impose Russian ideals on other nations.

Unquestionably, Dostoevsky's chauvinistic nationalism led him to depart from the tenets of *pochvennichestvo* and from his ethical opposition to the axiom

30. Solov'ev, *Sochineniia*, 5:382.

that the end justifies the means. But it did not, strictly speaking, contradict his Christian ideal of universal love. Rather, it further illustrates his special understanding of that ideal, which did not require that individuals (or nations) be considered equal in merit.

In his philosophy of nationality as in his social and political philosophy, Dostoevsky regarded the Christian ideal as fully compatible with the hierarchical principle that acknowledges differences of status and authority based on merit, so long as all are treated with respect and not as mere means; he construes the ideal, in other words, as an ideal of mutual love and respect *among acknowledged unequals*. In Dostoevsky's comprehensive meritocracy, some have greater talents and abilities than others, entitling them to a higher position: Shakespeare is higher than his trash collector, the father is higher than the child, the Tsar is higher than his subjects, and Russians in general are higher than other people. In every case, however, the relationship is ideally pervaded by a spirit of familial community marked by full mutual recognition of the differences in merit, and hence by full voluntary acquiescence in the hierarchical system. In practice, coercion may be required when superiority is not freely respected, but it no more signifies an absence of love than does a parent's punishment of an errant child.

Dostoevsky was well aware that his meritocracy violated the Western conception of equality. But he was convinced that the Western conception was a perverted one, stemming once again from the special hostility between superiors and inferiors, rulers and ruled, described in Thierry's account of the origin of the Western states but never present in Russia, according to Dostoevsky: "We have an ancient moral idea that perhaps will triumph. This idea is our own concept, from earliest times, of what honor and duty are and what true equality and brotherhood among people are. In the West the thirst for equality was different, because the kind of dominion was different" (24:114). For Dostoevsky, insistence on the exact, reciprocal equivalence of artificially defined "rights" and "privileges" is a Western fixation derived from the need to defend oneself against hostile, malevolent rulers. True equality, on the contrary, is an equality of mutual respect and good will that does not reject hierarchical relations based on merit.

In the early 1860s, Dostoevsky toyed briefly with the idea that there is no systematic, inherent distinction of merit between nations—that each has an equally valuable contribution to make to the human enterprise. But his intense patriotism drove him rather to extend the principle of meritocracy from domestic to international relations. To do so, he resorted to highly implausible hypotheses concerning the inborn superiority of Russians and to dubious conclusions concerning their grand mission; perhaps in no other area of his thought was his reasoning more prone to what Tim McDaniel has called the "primitive logic" he displayed in distinguishing between a fragmented, egoistic West and a fraternally united Russia.[31] Dostoevsky preserved a formal consistency with his paternalistic Christian ideal, but at the cost of bifurcating humanity into qualitatively different groups, elevating the mind and will of some above others, and embracing the instrumental value of coercion—in short, at the cost of joining forces with the Grand Inquisitor. And the Grand Inquisitor, it will be remembered, was someone who thought he loved humanity but was in fact blinded by egoistic arrogance.

31. McDaniel, *Agony*, 28.

Dostoevsky's Vision of Humanity

Dostoevsky's profile as a philosophical thinker was shaped by his opposition to the ideas of the Russian Westernists, especially the more radical, "Nihilist" Westernists whose militant atheism and revolutionary socialism goaded him into formulating and defending his own fundamental beliefs. Had he not found the ideas of Chernyshevsky, Dobrolyubov, and Pisarev so abhorrent, it is unlikely that he would have dwelled so intently on the philosophical questions he took up, or argued so vigorously for his own answers. We have the Nihilists to thank for the themes of much of his writing—not only the notebooks, letters, and essays that have loomed so large in this study but also most of his great fiction, including *Notes from Underground, Crime and Punishment, Demons,* and *The Brothers Karamazov.*

We also have them to thank for the dialectical method of his philosophizing, by which I mean its dynamic counterposing of competing views. Ever concerned with combating the ideas of others, Dostoevsky always kept his sights on the opposite of what he believed and sought to establish his own positions by demonstrating the failure of their antitheses, as in his frequent recourse to the rhetorical and logical device of reductio ad absurdum. In that way his philosophical thinking was inherently polyphonic and dialogical, to use Bakhtin's terms. The character of Dostoevsky's post-Siberian novels was no matter of accident or purely stylistic preference: the dialogical novels were a natural complement to his dialectical approach to the problems of philosophy.

This does not mean that he had no independent philosophical impulse. This study has been built on the premise that Dostoevsky's searchings were prompted by a concern to solve what in his youth he called "the mystery of man"—a concern that took him into many dimensions of human existence:

spiritual, psychological, ethical, aesthetic, social, and national. Yet in each of these areas Dostoevsky had as a foil what he considered to be the erroneous and degrading view of humanity preached by his philosophical opponents in Russia; in each area, his arguments were directed toward overcoming the limitations that he believed his opponents, and especially those he labeled "Nihilists," imposed on man. What is creative in Dostoevsky's philosophical thought arises largely in his persistent efforts to disclose the shortcomings of other Russian thinkers, rather than in a detached attempt to construct a grand synthetic picture of human nature in isolation from the issues of his time and place. Such a picture does emerge, but it is revealed progressively by reference at every moment to the contrasting views of fellow countrymen, right down to the answers to Gradovsky and Kavelin sketched in his last notebooks.

The Nihilists' errors, in his opinion, were many. Above all, they made the gross metaphysical mistake of overlooking the element of the divine in human nature, centered on man's possession of an immaterial, immortal soul. They erred in explaining human behavior as the mechanistic product of self-interest, thus failing to see the supreme importance of free will in human life and wrongly asserting the primacy of material, physical needs. In the realm of ethics, they failed to recognize the voice of conscience as issuing the categorical imperative of altruism as formulated in Christian doctrine; they adopted instead a utilitarian approach to morality that endorsed the maxim that the end justifies the means, and in so doing they constricted the scope of moral responsibility and ignored the moral significance of suffering. In their aesthetic thinking they failed to recognize that human beings have needs for beauty and creativity; they misunderstood the nature of realism, the cognitive significance of art, and its true moral and social role. In social philosophy, their revolutionary socialist posture was a threat to both morality and human freedom and represented a gross misunderstanding of the noblest social ideal of humanity—the Christian utopia of mutual love. Finally, they erred in adopting a purely universalist conception of man that ignored the role of national differences in shaping the history and the future prospects of humanity.

The positive picture undergirding Dostoevsky's critical attacks is dominated by the image of a free moral creature with two conflicting "natures"—a materialistic, selfish nature moved by what he called the "law of personality" and a spiritual, altruistic nature cognizant of the moral demand to obey the law of love. It is the struggle between these antithetical natures that forms the background for virtually all of Dostoevsky's discussions of the life of man, whatever sphere of that life is in question; that struggle sets the parameters of his resolution of particular philosophical problems. Man's spiritual nature points the way to the identification and realization of ethical, aesthetic, and social values; his material nature, expressed above all in egoism, is the obstacle to a satisfying present and a better future.

Gary Saul Morson has written insightfully about the way in which Dostoevsky's emphasis on free will commits him to an open future—a future in which what people do could always have been otherwise, because they could have chosen otherwise; in his novels, as Morson points out, there is no sense of an inexorable progression toward "a pregiven ending."[1] Yet the very importance of free choice in Dostoevsky's worldview makes it easy to exaggerate. Existentialist philosophers and other commentators who focus narrowly on *Notes from Underground* are prone to regarding freedom as virtually the sole constituent of the human essence for Dostoevsky and as virtually unlimited in scope. In other words, they absolutize freedom in a way that goes well beyond what I believe were his intentions.

Dostoevsky opposed the limitation of human freedom by external restraints on individual action. That is the basis of his objection to all forms of social regimentation: it dehumanizes the individual by taking away the expression of free choice and thus moral responsibility and aesthetic creativity. Free choice entails the ability to choose either good or evil, and Dostoevsky insists that both alternatives must be available to the individual. In a notebook entry he contrasts what he calls "the law of rational agreement" (as favored, presumably by the radical socialists) with "the law of voluntariness [*svoevolie*]", which he formulates as "let me do evil." He goes on to express doubt that regimentation will ever in fact eliminate the evil choice: "Do circumstances making it impossible to do evil really eradicate evil and evildoers? Surely there will be a voice that says, I want to have the opportunity to do evil, but . . . and so on" (24:170–73; Dostoevsky's ellipses). Still, in demanding a society in which it is possible to do evil, he was not arguing for anarchy; unlike Tolstoy, he did not reject governmental institutions or the punitive, coercive measures they employ. Because of the law of personality, not all individuals (short of the ideal Christian society of the future) will shun evil voluntarily, and for that reason some restraints are necessary to protect individuals from each other. Courts, prisons, and police are regrettable but necessary elements of historical life on

1. Gary Saul Morson, "Dostoevskii, Fëdor Mikhailovich," in *Routledge Encyclopedia of Philosophy*, ed. Edward Craig (London: Routledge, 1998), 3:118–19; see also his *Narrative and Freedom: The Shadows of Time* (New Haven, Conn.: Yale University Press, 1994), especially 117–72, and "Introductory Study: Dostoevsky's Great Experiment," in Fyodor Dostoevsky, *A Writer's Diary*, trans. Kenneth Lantz (Evanston, Ill.: Northwestern University Press, 1993–94), 1:72–97.

earth as we know it, but they must not go to the extremes of regimentation that he believed the socialists advocated.

In contrast to external limitation, Dostoevsky wants freedom to be limited inwardly, morally, by acceptance of the law of love. In another notebook entry we read the following: "The society I want is not a scientific one in which I would be unable to do evil, but precisely one in which I could do any evil but would myself not wish to do so" (24:162; Dostoevsky's emphasis omitted). Free choice is not such a paramount value for Dostoevsky that we may speak of having a "duty" to be free that is superior to the duty to obey the law of love. Freedom was unquestionably an important value for Dostoevsky, but it was not man's "most advantageous advantage"—that claim was made by the Underground Man, celebrating his will to power, which is how Dostoevsky understands true egoism as the force opposing the law of love.

In addition to the supreme moral limitation on freedom, Dostoevsky also recognizes psychological limitations of various sorts that unavoidably narrow the sphere within which individuals are able to exercise free choice. We saw in chapter 3 that he accepts, with some reluctance, the idea that there are situations in which people's actions, even conscious actions, are genuinely beyond their control. Furthermore, for all his insistence on personal responsibility and his downplaying of the role of the environment in his essay on that subject, the *pochvennichestvo* he so warmly espoused had as its central tenet the thesis that the character and attitudes of individuals are shaped by the circumstances of their ethnic background. That these circumstances affect people's moral behavior was seen in chapter 6 when we examined Dostoevsky's view that Russians are inherently more "fraternal," and thus more moral, than people of other nations, particularly the individualistic Western European nations. Nurtured by a more benign cultural environment, Russians are less susceptible to the attractions of the law of personality and have a natural predisposition toward the law of love. Finally, when he comes to the distinctive Russian virtue of "universality," Dostoevsky seems to go beyond even the influence of the environment to assert that Russians are equipped by their biological nature both to know and to choose good over evil; recall his statement about the unique Russian ability "to distinguish, among the European genii, the good spirits from the evil spirits" (26:212) and to act in such a way as to promote the good spirits for the benefit of all. All these circumstances suggest that Dostoevsky was more of a determinist than he himself may have realized, and certainly more than he has been made out to be by twentieth-century philosophers who used his works as a grab bag of ideas from which to draw selectively in support of their own theories of man and the world.

He was also more of a rationalist than he or others may have realized. Dostoevsky came of age philosophically in the wake of the Enlightenment's belated impact in Russia, at a time when the term 'reason' had been appropriated by thinkers who advanced what to him was an impoverished view of the capacity of human beings to know the world around them—impoverished because it limited the knower to sense perception and what could be inferred directly from it. Dostoevsky in response spoke harshly of "rationality," denying its prevalence and power in human life; he acquired the reputation, largely on the basis of the Underground Man's anguished outcries, of someone who strikes out emotionally and willfully against the gospel of reason. But in fact, as I have tried to show, even the Underground Man offered logically sound arguments against the Enlightenment radicals, and Dostoevsky in his own voice adopted a comparable argumentative posture throughout his mature life, in one area of philosophy after another. It could be argued that Dostoevsky was the one using reasoning in his disputes with the radicals, since their positions were for the most part simply asserted, without evidential support.

Even with regard to metaphysical questions, Dostoevsky looked for appropriate evidence and marshaled it effectively. As we saw in chapter 1, he advanced several different arguments for the immortality of the soul; although some of his premises were open to question, his reasoning employing them followed recognized logical forms. He ignored the traditional scholastic arguments for the existence of God, but at the same time he found evidence for the deity not only in the arguments supporting immortality but in an analysis of the concept of infinity, in the historical ubiquity of religious belief, and above all in personal religious experience. Even the fact that his claims for the evidence he offers are restrained in both content and modality demonstrates his respect for canons of reasonableness: he does not contend that the evidence supports anything more than what I have called a "philosophical" conception of God as an immaterial, eternal synthesis of being, and he does not contend that it can produce certainty, or absolute confidence in the truth of the conclusion. For a richer conception of the deity and for full confidence in these religious beliefs it is necessary, he believed, to transcend the ordinary operations of human reason.

Transcending them in regard to particular questions, however, does not entail denying them a role in human knowledge or countenancing an alogical, antirational approach to the truth. Dostoevsky did admit as veridical certain epistemological powers that the Nihilists, for example, would reject as nonrational; it is these expansions of the human ability to know that were at the heart of his disagreements with them. But it is instructive to look at his understanding of these disputed avenues to truth in order to determine the significance he attributed to them and their actual relationship to reason.

One is the prophetic capacity he ascribed to true artists. As we saw in chapter 4, Dostoevsky attributed cognitive value to realism in art on the ground of the artist's special perceptiveness in understanding reality, which included a gift for identifying potentialities inherent in the present. Because the artist is someone with an extraordinary ability to "study life and extract laws from life itself" (20:115), he can foretell its course of development. It is not only the scientist, in other words, who can discern the course of change and predict its future; the artist may succeed in that even where the scientist fails. As Dostoevsky discusses it, however, the epistemological advantage of the artist seems to be not so much an identifiable "faculty" or unique nonrational power as simply a particularly acute sensitivity to the richness and color of the observable world. To account for Dostoevsky's reverence for the artist's foresight we need not assume some mystical power operating independently of reason and empirical observation.

A second, seemingly extrarational voice of truth identified by Dostoevsky but not recognized by the Nihilists is the moral conscience. Whereas opponents such as Kavelin argued that conscience is a social construct that merely reflects the mores of one's place and time, for Dostoevsky conscience was innate in every human being—a universal capacity that normally reveals to individuals the ethical imperative of the Christian law of love. "Normally" is an important qualifier, however, for Dostoevsky acknowledged that the voice of conscience could be stilled or corrupted by the life experiences of individuals, and for that reason he was forced late in life to acknowledge that conscience as subjectively experienced cannot ever be the ultimate warrant of the moral acceptability of one's actions: its judgment cannot be trusted without verification by the outside standard provided by religious faith in Christ.

More to the point, the one text in which he explicitly denies "rationality" to the law of love as preached by the uncorrupted conscience is one based on an extremely narrow sense of the term 'reason', in which the term refers simply to the calculation of one's own personal advantage. He makes clear this strict delimitation of the concept of reason by quoting, with seeming approval, these words of Tolstoy's Levin in *Anna Karenina:*

> "Was it by reason that I concluded I must love my neighbor and not strangle him? They told me that in childhood, and I *gladly believed it*, because they told me something that was already in my soul. But who discovered it? Not reason. Reason discovered the struggle for existence and the law demanding that I strangle everyone who hinders the satisfaction of my desires. That is reason's conclusion. But loving another is something reason could never discover, because it is unreasonable." (25:204; Dostoevsky's emphasis)

In this context Dostoevsky is not denying the rationality of the law of love with respect to reason as most philosophers have understood it: he alludes only to the narrow means-end rationality that he identified with his ideological opponents, where the end, moreover, is egoistic. Only in that sense does he contend that the law of love is "unreasonable"—because it sets others above oneself. Earlier in the same passage, he had suggested in a paraphrase of Levin's reflections that the law of love is no logical absurdity, for it is intelligible and acceptable to the human mind: "Everyone on earth understands or can understand that we must *love our neighbor as ourselves*" (25:204; Dostoevsky's emphasis).

Immanuel Kant would certainly agree with Dostoevsky that *egoistic* considerations of what will best serve as a means to promote one's own interests would never recommend the *altruism* that conscience dictates. But that did not prevent Kant from calling conscience an expression of "practical reason" (as opposed to theoretical reason)—that is, of reason as a determinant of the human will. I am not suggesting that Dostoevsky himself would ever appeal to reason as the ultimate determinant of ethical values; his thinking was too close to that of Shatov, whose febrile declarations in *Demons* included the statement that "reason [and here *razum* is used] has never had the power to define good and evil, or even to distinguish evil from good" (10:199). But Dostoevsky's only argument for the "unreasonableness" of the voice of conscience is one that assumes a purely egoistic, instrumentalist conception of rationality that few philosophers would be willing to accept. In this regard Dostoevsky was seemingly unaware that what he was denying was not rationality per se but rationality in the constricted sense he attributed to his opponents.

A third source of knowledge for Dostoevsky that no Nihilist would countenance is the personal experience of direct contact with the supernatural world. As Dostoevsky has Prince Myshkin describe such experience in *The Idiot*, it surely qualifies as mystical. Yet the line between it and what some philosophers have called "rational intuition" is very thin. Rational intuition is typically defined as a cognitive act of the rational faculty that is noninferential—that is, a direct, unmediated apprehension of a truth, such as the truth that the whole is greater than the part. Dostoevsky was no doubt innocent of such philosophical refinements, and I am sure that he would not claim that what Zosima called the "mysterious sense of our living bond with the other world" was an act of reason in the "rationalistic" sense of *rassudok*. But the fact remains that Dostoevsky does incorporate within Myshkin's description the qualification that the experience is "full of reason," using the broader, more honorific term *razum*. Furthermore, he affirmed that the genuineness of the experience was subject to a judgment of the critical mind in order to rule out the possibility of hallucination or other misperception. Reason, if not the sole source of our mystical knowledge of a higher reality for Dostoevsky, is consistent with it and participates in establishing it.

As significant as Dostoevsky's recognition of the role of rationality in mystical experience is, we must also note that he invokes such experience infrequently and limits severely the knowledge he attributes to it. Aside from his own experiences in the epileptic aura and a few isolated instances in his fiction, he does not describe it as a common feature of human life or stress the epistemological need for it in most activities of knowing. His typical uses of the term 'mystical' aside from the perception of "the higher synthesis" are pejorative, as in his arguments against spiritualism and his dissociation of the Orthodox faith from mysticism. Furthermore, the cognitive content he attributes to mystical experience, although of the highest moment as constituting his only argument for the existence of God based on direct experience, is extremely circumscribed. The contact with "the lofty, higher world" that it provides reveals nothing about that world beyond such broad abstract characteristics as unity, immateriality, and infinity. Only once did he even call it explicitly an experience of "God," and the God that it discloses is God in the limited conception I have called "philosophical"—that is, an immaterial, infinite synthesis of being. Dostoevsky does not invoke mystical religious experience as going in any way beyond that level of awareness, and certainly not to the knowledge of an anthropomorphic God, not even the God of deism who created the universe and abandoned it to its own laws and forces. Contentions that God is a creator, a providential caretaker, or a moral authority are never linked by Dostoevsky to knowledge gained mystically. Nor does Dostoevsky claim a mystical warrant for any other knowledge of man or his world. The grand speculative flights occasioned by Solovyov's mystical experience were not Dostoevsky's philosophical stock in trade; his skeptical conviction that "much on earth is hidden from us" (14:290) applied to mystical as well as scientific knowledge.

All of which brings us to the fourth and most far-reaching cognitive capacity that separates Dostoevsky from his atheistic critics—the capacity for religious faith, which for Dostoevsky is the ultimate warrant for both metaphysical and ethical truths. Rejected as a product of gullibility and superstition by his antagonists, faith is accepted by Dostoevsky as the surest support not only for the existence of God and the immortal soul but for the moral law of love. The faith of Russians, he wrote in *A Writer's Diary*, contains all their ideals and "all the justice [*pravda*] and truth [*istina*] of life" (23:118); in a notebook he wrote that it comprises "everything humane and all the loftiest points of view" (24:253). Dostoevsky relies principally on faith for some of the most important beliefs that an individual can have.

But faith for Dostoevsky does not replace or stand in contradiction to reason, broadly conceived; it simply goes beyond it. Although the articles of Christian faith are neither grounded in direct perception of any sort or deduced from the premises of a logical argument, they are also for Dostoevsky not arbitrary or alogical commitments of the will, not leaps to some paradoxical absurdity. He calls "irrefutable" Ivan Karamazov's point about the senselessness of the suffering of children, meaning that such suffering cannot be justified rationally; but he never admits that Ivan's point is rationally conclusive as an argument against the existence of God, such that to accept such existence would be simply "irrational." Dostoevsky sees Christian faith not as an irrational refuge from rationally necessitated conclusions but as a nonrational mode of cognition that is supervenient upon a correct metaphysical relationship between the individual and the whole.

In language the Nihilists should be able to understand, he often speaks of faith as a fundamental human need, comparable to the needs for beauty, creativity, and material sustenance. Even atheists, he wrote in *A Writer's Diary*, thirst for God and for faith; he attributed the spiritualism craze in the Russian society of his day to an "urge to believe" in something transempirical (22:97, 101). We remember his reference to his own "thirst for faith" in the early letter to Fonvizina and his distress at the censor's excision of his reference to "the need for faith and Christ" from *Notes from Underground* (28/2:73).

That this need is a genuine, defensible, objective human requirement is supported by the broad-brush theory of the development of human civilization that he sketched in a notebook of 1864–65 for a proposed work on "Socialism and Christianity." There he presented faith in God as an integral element of a healthy relationship of the individual to his fellows, and the lack of that faith as a diseased condition, a destructive incompleteness:

> When people live in masses (in primitive patriarchal communities, tales of which have survived)—then they live *spontaneously*.
> Then comes a time of transition, that is, further development, that is, civilization. . . . In this further development a phenomenon arises, a new fact, which no one can escape: this is the development of personal consciousness and the negation of spontaneous ideas and laws . . . In this phase of his universal genetic growth, man as an individual person has always taken a hostile, negative attitude toward the authoritative law of the mass and *the all*. For this reason he has *always* lost his faith in God, too. . . . This condition, that is, the fragmentation of the mass into persons, or civilization, is a diseased condition. The loss of a living idea of God testifies to this. The second testimony that this is a disease is that a man in this condition feels bad, is depressed, loses the source of living life. (20:191–92; Dostoevsky's emphasis)

Let us compare this description of the diseased condition of civilized, individualized humanity with Zosima's advice to Madame Khokhlakova in *The Brothers Karamazov* concerning how to achieve certainty in her religious faith through the experience of active love:

> "Strive to love your neighbors actively and tirelessly. To the extent that you succeed in loving, you will become convinced both of the existence of God and of the immortality of your soul. If you attain complete selflessness in loving your neighbor, then you will indubitably be persuaded, and no doubt will even be able to enter your soul. This has been tested, this is certain." (14:52)

The connection between love and faith as Zosima expresses it, making love a sufficient condition for the consolidation of faith, is somewhat puzzling. Why, psychologically, should loving other human beings make us more disposed to believe in God? Dostoevsky does not explain the connection in so many words, but in the light of his notes for "Socialism and Christianity" we can conjecture that he identified the need for faith as a need for connectedness, for the completion lost with the individualization of society, and that he saw love as constituting precisely such selflessness—as giving oneself to others, preferring others over oneself. In this sense, to love is to place oneself within the eternal, spiritual "higher synthesis" of being that constitutes what I have called Dostoevsky's philosophical conception of the deity.

If this interpretation of the nexus between love and faith makes sense, it applies also to Dostoevsky's assertion of a nexus between faith and rootedness in one's national soil. As a *pochvennik* Dostoevsky tended to connect all cultural phenomena with such rootedness, but he was particularly insistent in the case of faith: the whole idea behind *Demons*, he told a correspondent, is that "he who loses his people and his nationality loses the ancestral faith and God"; the novel depicts the person "who has lost the connection with everything native and, most importantly, lost faith" (29/1:145, 232). At times he seems to be speaking only of Russia, and making the point that connectedness with the people generates faith because the Russian people are stalwart repositories of faith themselves: "The first mark of indissoluble community with the people is respect and love for what the people . . . respect more and above anything in the world—that is, their God and their faith" (30/1:236). But even in that text he generalizes that "a person who denies nationality also denies faith," which strongly suggests that the very fact of national rootedness, as an element of connectedness, of contact with the "higher synthesis" of being, produces a stable faith.

At this point, however, we reach the outer limit of any "justification" of religious faith for Dostoevsky. The problem with the foregoing paragraphs as an effort to sketch the epistemology of faith as Dostoevsky understands it is that it still takes faith no further than the minimal, abstract God of Dostoevsky the philosopher. If human beings have a natural need for connectedness with a "higher synthesis," and if "active love" as Zosima calls it is a way of establishing that connectedness, the "faith" that we arrive at in that way would appear to be nothing more than belief in an immaterial, eternal synthesis of being. But religious experience can tell us that much without the need for faith. What more Dostoevsky requires of faith is *confident*, unquestioning belief not only in immortality but in the existence of an anthropomorphic God who is creator, provider, and moral authority—convictions that seemingly go beyond any product of "active love or need for connectedness."

In effect the epistemology of a specifically *religious* faith remained uncharted territory for Dostoevsky. He provided no explanation or warrant for it other than the free acceptance of Holy Scripture as an ultimate authority. We can only conclude that although he believed that religious faith was an appropriate response to a critical natural need of human beings and was not inconsistent with reason in the broad sense, it could by its nature have no epistemological justification beyond itself. Faith is the only truly nonrational capacity in Dostoevsky's epistemology.

Nonetheless, Dostoevsky was utterly convinced that if there is love there will *be* such faith, and that without it we human beings are doomed to abide in darkness: as he wrote in a notebook, "if we do not have the authority of faith and of Christ, then we shall go astray in everything" (27:85). And of course if love produces faith, then he who is without faith must also be without love, which helps to explain why Dostoevsky could never credit any of his atheistic adversaries, from the moderate Kavelin to the fanatical Grand Inquisitor, with a true and enduring love of humanity.

Finally, no aspect of Dostoevsky's conception of humanity has been so much discussed or is so intimately bound up with his opposition to the Westernists as his view of the place of evil in human nature. When he writes, as we saw in chapter 3, that "evil is more deeply rooted in humanity" than the socialists believe (25:201), the seductive oversimplification is to interpret him as saying that human beings are not fundamentally good but fundamentally evil. It is true that the socialists traced evil to the impact of flawed social arrangements, thereby absolving "human nature" from complicity in sin. And it is also true that Dostoevsky located the source of evil in the nature of earthly individuals, who could not entirely escape the impact of the "law of personality." But to say that Dostoevsky found human beings to be "fundamentally evil" is to go beyond that, to suggest that the good is either absent from human nature or is consistently no match for the power of evil. And neither of these alternatives was acceptable to him.

From the standpoint of natural "rootedness," neither good nor evil has the advantage in Dostoevsky's philosophical anthropology. Endemic in man's material nature is the preference of self over others; but endemic in his spiritual nature is the law of love: people are born with a moral conscience giving them not only an innate knowledge of the good but a recognition of its binding character. Thus altruism is as much a part of the human essence as egoism is, and the contest between the two for supremacy is the leitmotif of the great bulk of his writing, fiction and nonfiction alike. Far from holding that the evil in man necessarily overpowers the good, he suggests that in mankind's historical march there is progress toward the ideal of universal altruism, and in that sense he shares the Westernists' faith in the possibility of a triumph of good over evil.

Dostoevsky's critique of the superficiality of his opponents' conception of human evil stemmed not from a conviction that man is "fundamentally evil" but from what he considered their failure to see that the source of evil is man's inherent egoism. He found the reason for this failure in the very nature of "civilization" as it evolved in Western Europe—that is, in the emergence of individuals from the anonymous, spontaneous mass and their isolation as separate entities confronting each other in a fragmented, anomic society. The Western cult of the person transformed the individual will from being a morally suspect phenomenon to being a prime value, held up as the ideal of human development. The curse of the West was that it not only misunderstood good and evil but created a culture that systematically produced evil people. Western culture was in itself a prime source of immorality, of the affirmation of the will of every individual against all others, and at the same time a prime source of blindness to its own defects.

That Dostoevsky's antipathy toward the West became expressed in distinctions of moral worth among nations of people was unavoidable given his view that individualism was both characteristic of the West and the source of immorality. On the basis of that view, what in abstract terms began as a universalistic analysis of the existence of evil in all human beings, simply because of their dual nature, became transmuted into an analysis of the confrontation between a West inclined toward evil and a Russia inclined toward good. What appeared to be a generic human weakness became the *national* weakness of a culture founded on and nourishing an atomistic society of self-interest. In Russia, not only is goodness more prevalent, but some people are very close to being perfect—to having overcome the pull of egoism fully, for all practical purposes, thanks to the influence of a harmonious society and the loving faith of Orthodoxy. Understandably, the conviction that some groups of people are systematically far closer to the ideal than others encourages thoughts about the possibility of finally implementing the ideal on earth, under the benign leadership of the morally advantaged.

Dostoevsky was in all things a moralist who often, as in his famous Pushkin speech, preached a universalistic gospel of mutual love and respect. But, because of his definition of evil as consisting in egoism and his description of the West as the land of self-regarding individuals, his practical moral message was not humanitarian but nationalistic and divisive. His jingoism, whatever its emotional roots, was conceptually integrated with his understanding of egoism, evil, and Western culture. Of course, he had no good grounds for the moral distinction he drew between Russia and the West: as we saw in chapter 6, his case for Russian superiority was the feeblest in his intellectual arsenal.

Fortunately, Dostoevsky's "Russian idea," however integral to his thinking and however regrettably influential to this day, was not the living core or culmination of his philosophy. Conceptually, his nationalism is less fundamental than the universal values that he believed it served, less fundamental than his enduring dream of a community of perfect Christian brotherhood. If he mistakenly saw in Russia the salvation of humanity, he was mistaken about a means, not an end. Nationalism was one element in his lifelong quest to plumb the human mystery—a quest the finer moments of which will endure far longer than "the Russian idea."

It is the fate of the unsystematic thinker to leave loose ends: many problems are not thought through, some are never even touched. What is remarkable about the case of Dostoevsky is that, for all his intellectual untidiness, not only did he think things through more fully, productively, and reasonably than did the supposedly systematic "rationalists" who were his ideological adversaries, but his treatment of the problems he discussed is rich and provocative enough to warrant continuing attention more than a century after his death.

Index

Abaza, Yulia, 105, 133–34
Abraham, 211
Adam, 158
Adolescent, The, 25, 35, 51, 84, 153
Aesthetic Relation of Art to Reality, The (Cherny-
    shevsky), 120–22
Aesthetics, 11–12, 118–57
    Dostoevsky's definition of, 154
Affekt. See Insanity, temporary
Alexander II, 13, 169, 172, 223
Alexander III, 175
Alogism, 16, 54, 56
Altruism, 60, 75, 81–117, 151–54, 232, 237, 242.
    See also Love: law of
Anglo-Saxons, 204
Anna Karenina (Tolstoy), 86–91, 98, 236
Anthropocentrism, 9
Anthropology, philosophical, 9, 242
Antisemitism, 209–11
Apocalypse, the, 24, 190, 193, 196
Apollo Belvedere, 128, 136
Aristotle, 173–74
Art, 9, 120–57
    cognitive value of, 137–47, 232
    and human needs, 126–37, 157
    moral and social value of, 147–57
    play theory of, 131–32
    utility of, 119–27, 134–37, 157
    See also Beauty; Creativity; Realism
Artel, 206
Artistry, 123, 132–37, 149, 157
Atheism, 42, 49, 51–53, 55, 85, 223, 231
Aura, epileptic. *See* Epilepsy
Autocracy, 158, 168, 171–74, 200

Bakhtin, Mikhail, 2–4, 118, 231
Bakunin, Mikhail, 179
Barrett, William, 5
Beauty, 11–12, 118, 123, 147, 150
    and art, 120
    and harmony, 128–29
    human need for, 127–37, 232
    metaphysical, 150–51, 156
    moral, 151–53, 156
Belinsky, Vissarion, 35, 37, 82, 119, 138, 181,
    216
    and Russian national identity, 197–99, 205–6,
    213–14
Belov, Sergey, 87
Berdyaev, Nikolay, 2, 13, 99, 113
Berlin, Isaiah, 159
Bolsheviks, 2, 178
Brentano, Franz, 32
Brothers Karamazov, The, 9, 33–38, 41, 84, 88,
    105–10, 231
    Alyosha, 33, 53, 85, 92, 142
    Dmitry, 88, 92, 106, 109, 115, 129, 155
    Grand Inquisitor, the, 55, 73, 111–12, 116–17,
        186–89, 228–30, 241
    Ivan: and church-state relations, 194–95; and
        conscience, 92, 98; and the Grand Inquisi-
        tor, 117; and immortality, 33–37, 44–45;
        and moral responsibility, 109; and the
        problem of evil, 51–53, 110, 117, 239
    Khokhlakova, Madame, 18–19, 29, 44, 240
    Kolya Krasotkin, 85, 116, 131
    Liza, 111
    Miusov, Pyotr, 33–34
    Paisy, Father, 195

245

Brothers Karamazov, The (continued)
  Rakitin, 36
  Smerdyakov, 45, 84, 109
  Zosima: and artistic realism, 132–33; and
    church-state relations, 196; and conscience,
    88; and freedom, 85–86; and love and
    faith, 18–19, 33, 44, 240; and mystery,
    15–16, 42, 46, 151; and universal responsi-
    bility, 106–10
Browning, Elizabeth Barrett, 113

Carlson, Maria, 55
Carr, E. H., 39, 113
Carter, Stephen K., 158
Casuistry, 103–4
Catholicism, 182, 187, 223, 228. *See also* Church,
  Roman Catholic
Cervantes, Miguel de, 215
Chaadayev, Peter, 199
Châteaubriand, François René de, 33
Chauvinism. *See* Nationalism
Chernyshevsky, Nikolay, 11, 57–67, 77–78, 231
  on art, 118–23, 132, 138, 147, 153, 157
Christ, 35, 55, 190–91, 206, 210, 219
  and beauty, 11–12, 152–54
  Dostoevsky's faith in, 7, 18, 53, 76
  and the Grand Inquisitor, 73, 112, 116–17
  and morality, 11, 21, 75, 82–83, 91, 94,
    98–99, 116–17
Christianity, 53, 55, 101–2, 170, 183, 192, 194
Church, Roman Catholic, 41, 56. *See also*
  Catholicism
Church, Russian Orthodox, 13, 16, 39, 92, 195.
  See also Orthodoxy
Civilization, 192, 239
Classes, social, 88, 205
Common consent argument, 43–44, 50, 89, 97,
  235
Commune. *See* Obshchina
Communism, 12, 177, 182, 185. *See also* Social-
  ism
Communist Manifesto, The, 182
Communist Party, 13
Congress of the League of Peace and Freedom
  (1867), 179, 182
Conscience, 114, 195, 237
  and the aesthetic sense, 154–56
  and the moral law, 63, 86–99, 103, 191–92,
    208, 212, 232, 242
  relativistic conception of, 95–99, 236
Consciousness, 31–32, 102, 113, 239
Constantinople, 159, 222–23
Contemporary, The. See Sovremennik
Corday, Charlotte, 96
Creativity, 127–37, 232–33

Crime, 103, 195
Crime and Punishment, 103, 105, 133, 231
  Marmeladov, 111
  Raskolnikov, 81, 90, 92, 99, 111, 115–16, 150
  Sonya Marmeladova, 81, 115–16, 150
  Svidrigaylov, 81, 93, 103, 150
Crimean War, 200, 206, 212, 221
Crusades, 226
Crystal palace, 62, 186–88
Czechs, 220, 222

Danilevsky, Nikolay, 222
Decembrists, 7, 200
Democracy, 172–74
Demons, 24–25, 36, 39, 90, 133, 148, 175–77,
  231
  Kirillov, 38, 48–49, 85, 176–77
  Maria Lebyadkina, 178
  Shatov, 155, 176, 178, 194, 237
  Stavrogin, 85, 93, 101, 155, 178
  Tikhon, Father, 81, 85, 101, 178
  Verkhovensky, P. S., 176–77, 179
  Verkhovensky, S. T., 24–25, 27, 38, 128
Deontology, 89–90, 97, 176
Descartes, René, 20
Design, argument from. *See* Teleological argu-
  ment
Determinism, 65–67, 69–73, 100, 103, 218, 234
Devils, The. See Demons
Dialectical method, 4, 231
  Hegelian, 165, 192
Diana (goddess), 128
Diary, A Writer's. See Writer's Diary, A
Dobrolyubov, Nikolay, 119, 123–26, 141–43,
  145–46, 231
Don Quixote (Cervantes), 153
Dostoevskaya, Maria Dmitrievna (Dostoevsky's
  first wife), 21, 24, 164
Dostoevsky, Fyodor Mikhailovich
  arrest and imprisonment of, 17–18, 158, 200
  his interest in philosophy, 1–2, 42
  in Siberia, 7, 74, 92, 114, 169, 171–72, 212
  See also individual works
Dostoevsky, Mikhail A. (Dostoevsky's father),
  16, 168
Dostoevsky, Mikhail M. (Dostoevsky's brother),
  9, 14, 16, 41, 62, 75–76, 200
Double, The, 84, 90, 145
Dowler, Wayne, 119, 129, 152, 159–60, 171,
  213
Dualism, ontological, 14–15, 53, 79, 89. *See also*
  Metaphysics

Education, moral, 91
Egoism, 25, 60, 64, 110–11, 115–17, 162–65, 208

and altruism, 11, 154, 193–95, 242
ethical, 66, 70–73, 79
and the moral law, 83
and personal will, 21, 177, 233–34
psychological, 65, 67–70, 79
and socialism, 181, 183
See also Personality: law of; Rational Egoism
Elssler, Fanny, 123
Emancipation of the serfs (1861), 168–69, 171, 206–7
Emerson, Caryl, 3, 60
Enlightenment, the, 5, 36, 159–61, 235
Enthymeme, 28, 34
Environment, influence of, 73–74, 100–102, 113–14, 234. See also Determinism; Pochvennichestvo; Writer's Diary, A
Epilepsy, 46–49, 129, 150, 238
Epistemology, 5–8, 15, 19, 37, 39–40, 54, 235–41
Epokha (Epoch), 62
Equality, 173, 229
"Eternal Husband, The," 84
Eternity, 44, 48
Ethics, 11, 81–117. See also Morality
Evil, 77, 84, 99
    in human nature, 93–94, 241–43
    problem of, 42, 51–53
Evlampiev, I. I., 38
Existentialism, 5, 69, 233

Faith, 17, 26, 29, 51–53, 75–76
    epistemology of, 19, 37, 238–41
    and love, 18–19, 240–41
    and morality, 87, 94–99, 103
    and reason, 5–8, 39, 50, 53–56, 238–41
Fantasy, 133, 142
Fedotov, G. P., 110
Fet, Afanasy, 128
Feuerbach, Ludwig, 216
Florovsky, George, 2
Fonvizina, Natalya, 7, 17–18, 239
Fourier, François, 180, 204
Frank, Joseph, 5, 10, 22, 115, 142, 206, 227
    on Dostoevsky's conception of God, 48–49
    on Dostoevsky's opposition to serfdom, 169, 172
    on Notes from Underground, 58–59, 64
Franks, 204–5
Fraternity, 203–12, 218–19. See also Altruism
Freedom, 85–86, 111–12, 162–63, 174, 178, 185–89, 234
Free will, 58, 65, 67, 70–76, 101, 232–33. See also Determinism
Future, uncertainty of, 89–90, 135–36, 233
Fyodorov, Nikolay, 190

Gambler, The, 111
Games. See Art: play theory of
Garibaldi, Giuseppe, 179
Gauls, 204–5
Ge, Nikolay, 143
Geneva Congress (1867), 179, 182
God
    arguments for the existence of, 41–53, 235
    Dostoevsky's persistent belief in, 16–19
    philosophical and religious conceptions of, 43, 45, 50–52, 54, 238, 240
Gogol, Nikolay, 122
Golosovker, I. E., 22
Gradovsky, A. D., 95, 170, 232
Gradualism, 179–80
Grand Inquisitor. See Brothers Karamazov, The
Great Reforms of the 1860s, 206
Greeks, 221
Grigoryev, Apollon, 119, 152, 159, 200, 214
Groos, Karl, 131–32
Guilt. See Responsibility, moral
Gulyga, Arseny, 6, 101, 209, 226

Harmony
    aesthetic, 128–29, 133–36, 138, 157
    ethical, 151–52, 156
    metaphysical, 48–49, 129–30, 157
    See also Beauty
Hegel, Georg Wilhelm Friedrich, 29–30, 165, 192
Hell, 116
Herder, Johann Gottfried von, 159, 203, 225
Herzen, Alexander, 60, 199, 204
Hirsch, E. D., Jr., 10
History, 9
    Dostoevsky's theory of, 12, 21, 146, 182, 189–96, 199
    Russian, 194–96, 204–7
Hobbes, Thomas, 166–67
House of the Dead. See Notes from the House of the Dead
Hubben, William, 38
Hugo, Victor, 145, 148
Humanity, normal condition of, 26–29, 39–40
Husserl, Edmund, 32

Idiot, The, 31, 84, 118, 141, 152
Ippolit, 19–20, 147
Keller, 94
Prince Myshkin, 46–48, 81, 88, 92, 129, 147, 150–53, 237
Nastasya Filippovna, 84
Iliad, The, 128, 136
Immoralism, 37, 45

Immorality. *See* Egoism; Personality: law of
Immortality, 78, 85, 89, 164, 232
    arguments for, 19–40, 235
    Dostoevsky's persistent belief in, 16–17
    and the existence of God, 44–45, 50
    importance of, for Dostoevsky, 16, 19–20, 26
Imperialism, Russian, 159. *See also* Messianism
Incarnation, the, 55, 153
Infinity, 42–45, 48–51, 235
Insanity, temporary, 100–102
Insulted and Injured, The, 84, 110–11, 115, 150
Intentionality, 32
Intuition, 20, 47, 237
Investigating Commission of 1849, 171, 181, 204
Irrationalism, 4–8, 37, 57–60, 235, 239
Isaev, Pavel (Dostoevsky's stepson), 6
Ivanova, A. A., 8
Ivanova, Sofya (Dostoevsky's niece), 113, 152

Jackson, Robert Louis, 2–3, 18, 20, 35, 37, 57, 74
    on Dostoevsky's aesthetics, 118, 129, 144, 146–47, 150
Jesus Christ. *See* Christ
Jews, 169, 182, 185, 198, 209–11, 219, 222
John, Saint, Gospel of, 153
John Paul II, Pope, 56
Judicial Reform of 1864, 113

Kant, Immanuel, 10, 21–23, 37, 132, 170, 237
Kapital, Das (Marx), 182
Karamzin, Nikolay, 22, 171, 199, 213
Kashina, Nadezhda, 118, 138, 141, 157
Kaufmann, Walter, 5
Kavelin, Konstantin, 95–98, 232, 236, 241
Kelly, Aileen, 3, 37, 88, 158, 181
Kepler, Johannes, 170
Khomyakov, Aleksey, 199
Kierkegaard, Soren, 5–6, 37
Kireevsky, Ivan, 199
Kline, George L., 29–30
Kornblatt, Judith Deutsch, 15
Kornilova, Ekaterina, 102–4, 110
Kostalevsky, Marina, 194
Kovalevskaya, Sofya, 49–50
Kutaisi (Georgia), 211

"Landlady, The," 84, 111
Lange, Konrad, 131–32
Lapshin, Ivan, 118
Laqueur, Walter, 227
Lauth, Reinhard, 39, 48, 54
"Legend of the Grand Inquisitor." *See Brothers Karamazov, The*
Leibniz, Gottfried Wilhelm, 51

Leontyev, Konstantin, 190
Lermontov, Mikhail, 125
Levin (*Anna Karenina*), 87, 89, 98, 236
Liberty. *See* Freedom
Life of a Great Sinner, The, 41
Literature, 122–26, 132–34, 138, 150
"Little Hero, A," 60
Locke, John, 166–67
Logic, 4–8, 37, 58
Love, 75, 177
    and faith, 18–19, 240–41
    and immortality, 18–19, 34–37, 240–41
    law of: and conscience, 93, 236–37, 242; and freedom, 234; and the law of personality, 82, 86, 191, 232; and moral beauty, 151; and Orthodoxy, 220; and the Russian character, 207–8; and society, 160, 167
    See also Altruism
Lyubimov, N. A., 53

Mark, Saint, Gospel of, 18
Markovich, Maria Aleksandrovna (pseud. Marko Vovchok), 123–25, 148
Marriage, 165, 191–92
Marx, Karl, 67, 182
Masochism, 59, 110–12
Materialism, 49, 55, 77, 85, 127, 184. *See also* Dualism, ontological
Matter. *See* Dualism, ontological
Matthew, Saint, Gospel of, 165
Maykov, Apollon, 139, 152, 168, 198, 213, 217, 221
McDaniel, Tim, 198, 230
Meritocracy, 227, 229
Messianism, 12, 198, 212–13, 217–26, 229
Metaphysics, 14–56, 100, 108–9, 150–51, 156. *See also* Dualism, ontological
Mickiewicz, Adam, 98
Miracle, 55, 153, 188–89
Mochulsky, Konstantin, 7, 153, 175
Morality, 9, 11, 81–117
    and art, 147–57
    epistemological ground of, 86–99, 154–55
    need for, as argument for immortality, 33–37, 40
    See also Deontology; Utilitarianism
Moral perfection
    demand for, as argument for immortality, 21–24, 82
    question of the possibility of attaining, 21–24, 189–96
Moral sense. *See* Conscience
Morson, Gary Saul, 91, 101, 103, 167, 179, 233
Moskvitianin (The Muscovite), 199
"Most Unfortunate Incident, A," 84

Mozart, Wolfgang Amadeus, 123
"Mr. ——bov and the Question of Art," 119,
    126–37, 141, 148, 156–57
"Mr. Prokharchin," 104
"Mr. Shchedrin, or a Schism among the Ni-
    hilists," 76–80, 131
Mystery, 42, 50, 55, 151, 188
    of man, 9, 197, 231, 243
Mysticism, 55, 100, 108–9, 116, 150–51, 237–38.
    See also Religious experience

Napoleon I, 200
Napoleon III, 96
Nationalism, 12–13, 197–230, 243
    chauvinistic, 198, 218–19, 226–27
Nationality, 197–230, 232, 240
Native Soil movement. See Pochvennichestvo
Nature
    Dostoevsky's philosophy of, 35–36, 53–54
    state of, 166–67
Needs, human, 71, 76–80, 119–37, 162
    aesthetic, 11, 127–37
    artificial, 119–20
    material, 78, 80, 183–84, 232
    spiritual, 88–89, 127–37
Nicholas I, 168–69, 200
Niebuhr, Reinhold, 227
Nihilists, Russian, 11–12, 57, 66, 78, 100, 177,
    231–32, 235–39
Nikitin, I. S., 123–25
Normans, 204
Notes from the House of the Dead, 74, 84–85, 93,
    97, 101, 111, 114, 139
    A-v (Aristov, Pavel), 84, 93
Notes from Underground, 56–76, 78–79, 186–89,
    231
    Liza, 62–63
    Underground Man, the, 57–76, 81, 83, 86,
        100, 110–13, 130–31
Novel, 126

Obolenskaya, Varvara, 133
Obshchina, 160, 185, 206
Odoevsky, V. F., 213
Ontology. See Dualism, ontological; Metaphysics
Orsini, Felice, 96, 98
Orthodoxy, 16, 41, 55, 94, 101, 110, 112
    and "the Russian idea," 200, 206, 219–21, 223
    See also Church, Russian Orthodox
Ottoman Empire, 190
Ownership. See Property
Ozmidov, Nikolay, 29, 34, 39–40, 45

Pain. See Suffering
Painting, 132, 140–41, 143–44

Panhumanism, 201–2, 216. See also Universality,
    Russian
Pan-Slavism, 220–23
Paperno, Irina, 27, 38
Paris Commune, 155
Pascal, Blaise, 16, 27
Patriarchalism, 171–72, 175, 205–6
Paul, Saint, 29, 170
Personality (lichnost'), 115–16
    law of, 82–86, 191–92, 194, 196, 207, 232–34,
        241
    See also Egoism; Love: law of
Peter I (the Great), 180, 206, 213–14
Peterson, N. P., 6
Petrashevsky circle, 60, 158, 168, 180
Pevear, Richard, 63
Pickwick, Mr. (Dickens), 153
Pisarev, Dmitry, 11, 231
    and aesthetics, 119–23
    and Rational Egoism, 57, 65, 67, 69, 71, 73
Pisemsky, Aleksey, 62, 139
Plato, 2, 92
Play theory. See Art: play theory of
Pleasure, 111
Pobedonostsev, Konstantin, 13
Pochvennichestvo, 158–59, 171, 184–85, 200–211,
    228–29, 234, 240
Pogodin, Mikhail, 199, 204–5
Poles, 198, 220, 222
Polish revolutions, 221
Polyglotism, Russian, 215–16
Polyphony, 2–4, 231
Poor Folk, 60, 116
Populists, 185
Pragmatism, 38–40, 54
Preservation of organisms, law of the, 29–31,
    40
Property, 166, 182, 184–85
Prophecy, 144–46, 236
Psychology, 27, 31, 39–40
Punishment, theory of, 113–15
Pushkin, Alexander, 122, 125, 133, 215,
    217
Pushkin memorial speech (1880), 95, 170,
    214–15, 219–20, 228, 243

Rassudok. See Reason
Rational Egoism, 11, 57–80, 126. See also Ego-
    ism
Rationalism. See Reason
Razum. See Reason
Realism
    in art, 122, 126, 132–33, 137–47, 149, 232
    in metaphysics, 53–54
    Socialist, 145–46

Reason, 55–56, 87, 155
  Dostoevsky's use of, 8, 19, 101, 234–41
  and faith, 5–6, 55–56
  rassudok and *razum*, 6–8, 19, 46–47, 71, 237
Reductio ad absurdum, 8, 30, 40, 43, 70, 76, 96, 231
  casual and strict, 23, 30
Religion, 9, 43–44, 94, 166. *See also* Catholicism; Orthodoxy
Religious experience, 45–50, 54, 235. *See also* Mysticism
Responsibility, moral, 99–110, 232
  and free will, 58, 73–74, 233
  for one's own actions, 99–104
  universal, 104–10
Responsiveness, universal, 214–17, 225, 234
Resurrection, 24, 165, 190
Revelation, 50
Revolution, 90, 175–80
Rice, James L., 49
Ridiculous Man. *See Writer's Diary, A*
Riemann, Georg, 42
Rights, 183, 191, 202, 210, 228
Roman Catholicism. *See* Catholicism; Church, Roman Catholic
Romanov, Alexander. *See* Alexander III
Romanticism, 141, 159, 197, 213
Rosenshield, Gary, 15
Rousseau, Jean-Jacques, 35, 155, 166–67
Rozanov, Vasily, 31, 58
Rubini, Giovanni, 123
Russian idea, the, 12–13, 197–230, 243
Russkii vestnik (Russian Messenger), 173–74
Russo-Turkish War, 86, 159, 221, 223

Sade, Marquis de, 35, 97
Saltykov-Shchedrin, M. E., 77–80
Sand, George, 16, 181
Sandoz, Ellis, 55, 227
Satire (in *Notes from Underground*), 58
Schelling, Friedrich, 119, 129
Schiller, Johann Christoph Friedrich von, 51, 132, 215
Science, 44, 54, 89, 123, 146, 155, 181
Scottish moralists, 35
Seddon, J. H., 60
Self-sacrifice, 61, 115–17, 152, 178, 180, 224
  See also Love: law of
Serfdom, 124–25, 158, 168–72, 175
Shakespeare, William, 170–71, 184, 215, 229
Shestov, Lev, 37
Skepticism, 16, 54, 238
Slavophiles, 13, 158–59, 185, 199, 201, 204, 206
Slavs, 86, 205, 213, 219–24
Social contract, 161–63

Socialism, 111, 152, 158, 161, 180–89, 223, 231–32
  Russian, 181–82
Socialist Realism, 145–46
Sociobiology, 35
Solovyov, Vladimir, 24, 55, 194, 198, 238
  on Dostoevsky, 4–5, 149–51, 190, 226, 228
Soul, 10, 14, 232. *See also* Immortality; Dualism, ontological; Metaphysics
Soviet Union of Writers, 145
Sovremennik (The Contemporary), 77–78, 123, 199
Spanish Inquisitor, 97
Spirit. *See* Dualism, ontological; Metaphysics
Spiritualism, 43, 55, 238–39
Spite (in Dostoevsky's characters), 73, 84
Stammler, Heinrich, 6, 119, 129
State of nature, 166–67
Strakhov, Nikolay, 2, 4, 33, 48, 119, 142, 155
Strel'tsova, G. Ia., 16
Suffering, 99, 110–17, 232
  as instrumental good, 113–15, 117
  as morally neutral, 110–12
  as terminal good, 115–17
Suicide, 26–27, 31, 128
Sutherland, Stewart R., 52
"Swallows, The" (Saltykov-Shchedrin), 78

Talma, François, 123
Tatars, 222
Teleological argument, 41–42, 151
Tendentiousness in art, 148–49
Tennyson, Alfred Lord, 35
Terras, Victor, 1, 4, 51–52, 93, 103, 134, 137, 150
Theism, 48, 50
Theocracy, 194–95
Theology, 16, 41, 51–53, 55
Thierry, Augustin, 204–5
Thomas Aquinas, Saint, 41–42, 56
Thompson, Diane, 96
Time. See Vremya
Titian, 143
Tolstoy, Leo, 2, 60, 82, 88, 99, 175, 233. *See also Anna Karenina*
Torop, P., 198
Truth, 7, 38–40
Tsarism. *See* Autocracy
Turgenev, Ivan, 60, 204
Turks, 221–22
"Two Camps of Theoreticians," 201–3, 214
Tyutchev, F. I., 15

"Uncle's Dream," 60, 84
Underground Man. *See Notes from Underground*
Universality, Russian, 204, 212–19, 227, 234

Universal responsiveness, 214–17, 225, 228
Uspensky, Nikolay, 140
Utilitarianism, 40, 54, 178, 224, 232
    in aesthetics, 118–27, 134–37, 145–46, 157
    in ethics, 11, 89–91, 111, 115–16
Utopia, Dostoevsky's conceptions of, 161–67

Valjean, Jean (Hugo), 153
Volokhonsky, Larissa, 63
Vovchok, Marko. See Markovich, Maria Alek-
    sandrovna
Vremya (Time), 123, 159, 200–202, 213, 217
Vucinich, Alexander, 110

Wallenrod, Konrad, 98
War, 99, 189, 223–24. See also Crimean War;
    Russo-Turkish War
Ward, Bruce K., 117, 224, 226
What Is to Be Done? (Chernyshevsky), 61–62, 66,
    78

Whitehead, Alfred North, 2
"White Nights," 116
Winter Notes on Summer Impressions, 61–62,
    115–16, 152, 183, 202, 207
Writer's Diary, A, 3, 86–91, 95, 102–3, 108, 168,
    179–80
    "Apropos of the Exhibition," 140–41,
        143–44
    "Dream of a Ridiculous Man," 84, 105, 153,
        155–56, 165–67, 170, 193
    "Environment," 73–74, 100–102, 113–14,
        234
    "Unsubstantiated Assertions," 25–29

Xenophobia, 198–99, 226

Zakharov, V. N., 96
Zasulich, Vera, 97
Zemstvo, 173
Zenkovsky, V. V., 35, 81